C# Essentials

ISBN 0-13-093285-X

9 790130 932852

90000

PRENTICE HALL PTR MICROSOFT® TECHNOLOGIES SERIES

.NET FRAMEWORK

- The Microsoft .NET Platform and Technologies
  Simmons, Rofail

NETWORKING

- Designing Windows 2000 Networks
  Wilson
- An Administrator's Guide to Windows 2000 TCP/IP Networks
  Wilson
- IP Solutions for Windows 2000
  Ammann
- Microsoft Technology: Networking, Concepts, Tools
  Woodard, Gattuccio, Brain
- NT Network Programming Toolkit
  Murphy
- Building COM Applications with Internet Explorer
  Loveman
- Understanding DCOM
  Rubin, Brain
- Web Database Development for Windows Platforms
  Gutierrez

PROGRAMMING

- C# for Windows Programming
  Pappas, Murray
- C# Essentials
  Pappas, Murray
- C# for Web Programming
  Pappas, Murray
- Pocket PC, Handheld PC Developer's Guide
  Grattan
- Office XP Development with VBA
  Aitken
- Windows 2000 Kernel Debugging
  McDowell
- Windows Script Host
  Aitken
- The Windows 2000 Device Driver Book, Second Edition
  Baker, Lozano
- Win32 System Services: The Heart of Windows 98 and Windows 2000, Third Edition
  Brain, Reeves
- Programming the WIN32 API and UNIX System Services
  Merusi
- Windows CE 3.0: Application Programming
  Grattan, Brain

- The Visual Basic Style Guide
  Patrick
- Windows Shell Programming
  Seely
- Windows Installer Complete
  Easter
- Windows 2000 Web Applications Developer's Guide
  Yager
- Developing Windows Solutions with Office 2000 Components and VBA
  Aitken
- Multithreaded Programming with Win32
  Pham, Garg
- Developing Professional Applications for Windows 98 and NT Using MFC, Third Edition
  Brain, Lovette
- Introduction to Windows 98 Programming
  Murray, Pappas
- The COM and COM+ Programming Primer
  Gordon
- Understanding and Programming COM+: A Practical Guide to Windows 2000 DNA
  Oberg
- Distributed COM Application Development Using Visual C++ 6.0
  Maloney
- The Essence of COM, Third Edition
  Platt
- COM-CORBA Interoperability
  Geraghty, Joyce, Moriarty, Noone
- MFC Programming in C++ with the Standard Template Libraries
  Murray, Pappas
- Introduction to MFC Programming with Visual C++
  Jones
- Visual C++ Templates
  Murray, Pappas
- Visual Basic Object and Component Handbook
  Vogel
- Visual Basic 6: Error Coding and Layering
  Gill
- ADO Programming in Visual Basic 6
  Holzner
- Visual Basic 6: Design, Specification, and Objects
  Hollis
- ASP/MTS/ADSI Web Security
  Harrison

C# Essentials

Chris H. Pappas
William H. Murray

PH
PTR

Prentice Hall PTR
Upper Saddle River, New Jersey 07458
www.phptr.com

A CIP catalog record for this book can be obtained from the Library of Congress

Editorial/Production Supervision: *MetroVoice Publishing Services*
Acquisitions Editor: *Jill Harry*
Marketing Manager: *Dan DePasquale*
Editorial Assistant: *Sarah Hand*
Cover Design: *Talar Agasyan-Boorujy*
Cover Design *Direction: Jerry Votta*
Art Director: *Gail Cocker-Bogusz*
Project Coordinator: *Anne R. Garcia*

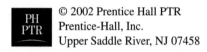

© 2002 Prentice Hall PTR
Prentice-Hall, Inc.
Upper Saddle River, NJ 07458

The publisher offers discounts on this book when ordered in bulk quantities.
For more information, contact: Corporate Sales Department, Phone: 800-382-3419;
FAX: 201-236-7141; Email: corpsales@prenhall.com; or write: Prentice Hall PTR,
Corp. Sales Dept., One Lake Street, Upper Saddle River, NJ 07458.

All rights reserved. No part of this book may be reproduced, in any form
or by any means, without permission in writing from the publisher.
Printed in the United States of America.

10   9   8   7   6   5   4   3   2   1

ISBN 0-13-093285-X

Pearson Education LTD.
Pearson Education Australia PTY, Limited
Pearson Education Singapore, Pte. Ltd.
Pearson Education North Asia Ltd.
Pearson Education Canada, Ltd.
Pearson Educación de Mexico, S.A. de C.V.
Pearson Education—Japan
Pearson Education Malaysia, Pte. Ltd.

Contents

Chapter 2

Unique C#   19

Chapter 3

Visual Studio.NET and C#   39

Chapter 4

· ·

Important Data, Identifiers, and Keywords   75

Chapter 5

· ·

Program Control   115

Chapter 6

Arrays   151

Chapter 7

Saying Goodbye to Pointers   181

Chapter 8

- -

Last Stop before Objects   213

Chapter 9

Objects   245

Chapter 10

- -

I/O in C#   287

Chapter 11

- -

Advanced C# Programming Considerations   315

Chapter 12

· ·

C# and Windows—Project Design Fundamentals   341

To our friends,
Frank and Liz Sabia

Preface

This is a book designed for the C or C++ programmer with beginning skills in these languages. The book's purpose is to introduce C and C++ programmers to the essential elements of C#. The book carefully examines key features of C#, in the context of C and C++. You will learn how to quickly develop code and discuss programming strategies.

C# Essentials is designed to take programmers quickly, but skillfully, into this new strain of C. You will discover all of the important features of C# explained along with ample sample code. Key concepts, along with complete working code examples, will quickly teach the features programmers, such as yourself, will want to master.

Welcome to a whole new world of programming!

The Journey to C#

On your mark, get set, GO! That pretty much describes how quickly and easily you are about to begin understanding and writing C# (pronounced C-sharp) code. Whether you are new to programming, or an old-salt at it, Microsoft's new, refreshing, powerful, and fun programming language, C#, will make a believer out of you!

Fun? Yes! C# provides the ease of GUI (Graphical User Interface) design and layout that has been available to Visual Basic programmers for years. This component of C# allows you to visually create an application or applet user interface by simply clicking on a control toolbar, dragging a control onto a design page, and setting the control's properties from intuitive drop-down lists.

With more of today's programs demanding a financially profitable and educationally informative Web presence, C# stands poised as the pinnacle of development languages. Incorporating the best of Java or J++, CGI, PERL, C/C++, and Visual Basic with the architecture independence of Java's *bytecode*, or native code format, code solutions have the potential to endure and evolve without total rewrites.

No longer will a Web-enabled solution require a Visual Basic programmer for interface design, a C++ programmer for pure, raw, data-crunching horsepower, and a Java, CGI, or PERL expert to make an entire package available worldwide.

To see just how familiar C# syntax is to today's state-of-the-art programming languages take a quick tour of Chapter 2, "Unique C+," then come right back to this chapter. What follows is a very brief but interesting history of programming languages leading up to the development of C#.

It All Began with Algol

Algol, CPL, BCPL, B, Basic, PL/I, Assembly Language, COBOL, Fortran, PL/I, Pascal, Modula-2, Ada, SmallTalk, Lisp, Java, J++, CGI, PERL, Visual Basic, C, C++, and now C#—the list is quite impressive. Why are there so many languages? Why can't someone invent one language to do it all? Which programming language or languages should I learn? Where will this all end?

C# is an easy-to-learn, easy-to-use, all encompassing problem solver. Before delving into this new language, let's take an historical look at how C# evolved. This journey will answer all of the questions posed in the previous paragraph.

As we look back, you will discover the roots and building blocks of many of today's languages. This information allows us to properly use these new development tools by explaining where each fits into the big picture. You will explore many individual language features that are included in C#. Reading between the lines of the travelogue you will also uncover secrets to predicting how programming languages will advance in future evolutions and/or revolutions!

Why I See C in C#!

A study of C's history is worthwhile because it reveals the language's successful design philosophy and helps you understand why C# may be the language of choice for years to come. Our archaeological dig for the origins of the C# language begins with Algol 60.

Algol 60 appeared in 1960 only a few years after FORTRAN was introduced. This European-based language was more sophisticated and had a strong influence on the design of future programming languages. Its authors paid a great deal of attention to the regularity of syntax, modular structure, and other features usually associated with high-level structured languages. Unfortunately, Algol 60 never really caught on in the United States. Many say this was due to the language's abstractness and generality.

The inventors of CPL (Combined Programming Language) set out to bring Algol 60's lofty intent down to the realities of an actual computer. However, just as Algol 60 was hard to learn and difficult to implement, so was CPL, which led to its eventual downfall. Still clinging to the best of what CPL had to offer, the creators of BCPL (Basic Combined Programming Language) wanted to boil CPL down to its basic good features.

When Ken Thompson, of Bell Labs, designed the B language for an early implementation of UNIX, he was trying to further simplify CPL. He succeeded in creating a very sparse language that was well suited for use on the hardware available to him (namely the DEC PDP-7, with an impressive 8-bit register size [small grin]!). However, both BCPL and B may have carried their streamlining attempts a bit too far; they became limited languages, useful only for dealing with certain kinds of problems.

As an example, no sooner had Ken Thompson implemented the B language on the Dec PDP-7 than a new machine, called the PDP-11 (a 16-bit word-size), was introduced. While the PDP-11 was a larger machine than its PDP-7 predecessor, it was still quite small by today's standards. It had only 24 K of memory, of which the system used 16 K, and one 512 K fixed disk. Some thought it was given to rewriting UNIX in B, but the B language was slow because of its interpretive design. There was another problem as well: B was byte-oriented, but the PDP-11 was word-oriented. For these reasons, work began in 1971 on a successor to B (just the *B*asics), appropriately named C (the *C*ombined best of its predecessors).

At this point we need to discuss the UNIX operating system, since both the system and most of the programs that run on it are written in C. The UNIX OS was originally developed at Bell Laboratories in Murray Hill, New Jersey. By design, this operating system was intended to be "programmer friendly," providing useful development tools, lean commands, and a relatively open environment. However, this does not mean that C is tied to UNIX or any other operating system or machine. The UNIX/C co-development environment has given C a reputation for being a *system programming language* because it is useful for writing compilers and operating systems. C is also very useful for writing major programs in many different domains.

Dennis Ritchie is credited with creating C, which restored some of the generality lost in BCPL and B. He accomplished this through a shrewd use of data types, while maintaining the simplicity and direct access to the hardware that were the original design goals of CPL.

Many languages developed by a single individual (C, Pascal, Lisp, and APL) contain a cohesiveness that is missing from those created by large programming teams (Ada, PL/I, and Algol 60). It is also typical for a language written by one person to reflect the author's field of expertise. Dennis Ritchie was noted for his work in systems software—computer languages, operating systems, and program generators.

Given Ritchie's areas of expertise, it is easy to understand why C is a language of choice for systems software design. C is a relatively low-level language that allows you to specify every detail in an algorithm's logic to achieve maximum computer efficiency. But C is also a high-level language that can hide the details of the computer's architecture, thereby increasing programming efficiency.

C versus Older High-Level Languages

At this point you may be asking, "How does C compare to other programming languages?" A possible continuum is shown in Figure 1–1. If you start at the bottom of the continuum and move upward, you go from the tangible and empirical to the elusive and theoretical. The dots represent major advancements, with many steps left out.

Early ancestors of the computer, like the Jacquard loom (1805) and Charles Babbage's "analytical engine" (1834), were programmed in hardware. The day may well come when we will program a machine by plugging a neural path communicator into a socket implanted into the temporal lobe (language memory) or Broca's area (language motor area) of the brain's cortex.

Cyborg Neural Path Symbiosis

.

.

.

Internet-Enabled Languages
Artificial Intelligence
Multitasking GUI Operating System Combinations
Object-Oriented Languages
Operating System Command Languages
Problem-Oriented Languages
Machine-Oriented Languages
Assembly Language

.

.

.

Actual Hardware

Figure 1–1   Theoretical evolution of programming languages.

The first assembly languages, which go back to the original introduction of electronic computers, provided a way of working directly with a computer's built-in instruction set, and were fairly easy to learn. Because assembly languages force you to think in terms of hardware, you had to specify every operation in the machine's terms. Therefore, you were always moving bits into or out of registers—adding them, shifting register contents from one register to another, and finally storing the results in memory. This was a tedious and error-prone endeavor.

The first high-level languages, including FORTRAN, were created as alternatives to assembly languages. High-level languages were much more general and abstract, and they allowed you to think in terms of the problem at hand rather than in terms of the computer's hardware.

Unfortunately, the creators of high-level languages made the fallacious assumption that everyone who had been driving a standard, so to speak, would prefer driving an automatic. Excited about providing ease in programming, they left out some necessary options. FORTRAN and Algol 60 were too abstract for systems-level work; they were *problem-oriented languages,* the kind used for solving problems in engineering, science, or business. Programmers who wanted to write systems software still had to rely on their machine's assembler.

In reaction to this situation, a few systems software developers took a step back-ward—or lower, in terms of the continuum—and created the category of *machine-oriented languages.* As you saw in C's geneology, BCPL and B fit into this class of very low-level software tools. These languages were excellent for a specific machine but not much use for anything else; they were too closely related to a particular architecture. The C language is one step above machine-oriented languages but still a step below most problem-solving lan-guages. C is close enough to the computer to give you great control over the details of an application's implementation, yet far enough away to ignore the details of the hardware. This is why the C language is considered at once a high- and low-level language.

Advantages of C

Every computer language you use has a definite look to its source code: APL has its hiero-glyphic appearance, assembly language its columns of mnemonics, and Pascal its easily read syntax. And then there's C. Many programmers encountering C for the first time will find its syntax cryptic and perhaps intimidating. C contains very few of the friendly English-like syntax structures found in many other programming languages. Instead, C presents the software engineer with unusual-looking operators and a plethora of pointers. New C pro-grammers will soon discover a variety of language characteristics whose roots go back to C's original hardware/software progenitor.

If you are already familiar with C/C++'s set of operators, you will be happy to know that C# uses the same definitions. Or, if you are learning C# for the first time, you will sum-marily learn C/C++'s operator set. And, since there will still be ample opportunity for your C# application/applet to interface with C or C++ code, you'll reap a double benefit.

At this point it is helpful to review the origins and history behind Ken Thompson's B language, a direct predecessor to C. Following is a comprehensive C lineage:

Language	Origins/Inventor
Algol 60	Designed by an international committee in early 1960
CPL	Combined Programming Language; developed at both Cambridge and the University of London in 1963
BCPL	Basic Combined Programming Language; developed at Cambridge by Martin Richards in 1967
B	Developed by Ken Thompson, Bell Labs, in 1970
C	Developed by Dennis Ritchie, Bell Labs, in 1972

Then, in 1983, the American National Standards Institute (ANSI) committee was formed for the purpose of creating ANSI C—a standardization of the C language.

From C to C++ and Object-Oriented Programming

Simply stated, C++ is a superset of the C language. C++ retains all of C's strengths, including its power and flexibility in dealing with the hardware/software interface; its low-level system programming; and its efficiency, economy, and powerful expressions. However, C++ brings the C language into the dynamic world of object-oriented programming and makes it a platform for high-level problem abstraction, going beyond even Ada in this respect. C++ accomplishes all of this with a simplicity and support for modularity similar to Modula-2, while maintaining the compactness and execution efficiency of C.

This new hybrid language combines the standard procedural language constructs familiar to so many programmers and the object-oriented model, which you can exploit fully to produce a purely object-oriented solution to a problem. In practice, a C++ application can reflect this duality by incorporating both the procedural programming model and the newer object-oriented model. This biformity in C++ presents a special challenge to the beginning C++ programmer; not only is there a new language to learn, but also a new way of thinking and problem solving.

Not surprisingly, C++ has an origin similar to C's. While C++ is somewhat like BCPL and Algol 60, it also contains components of Simula 67. C++'s ability to overload operators and its flexibility to include declarations close to their first point of application are features found in Algol 60. The concept of subclasses (or derived classes) and virtual functions is taken from Simula 67. Like many other popular programming languages, C++ represents an evolution and refinement of some of the best features of previous languages. Of course, it is closest to C.

Bjarne Stroustrup, of Bell Labs, is credited with developing the C++ language in the early 1980s. (Dr. Stroustrup credits Rick Mascitti with the naming of this new language.) C++ was originally developed to solve some very rigorous event-driven simulations for which considerations of efficiency precluded the use of other languages. C++ was first used outside Dr. Stroustrup's language group in 1983, and by the summer of 1987, the language was still going through a natural refinement and evolution.

One key design goal of C++ was to maintain compatibility with C. The idea was to preserve the integrity of millions of lines of previously written and debugged C code, the integrity of many existing C libraries, and the usefulness of previously developed C tools. Because of the high degree of success in achieving this goal, many programmers find the transition to C++ much simpler than when they first went from some other language, such as FORTRAN to C.

C++ supports large-scale software development. Because it includes increased type checking, many of the side effects experienced when writing loosely typed C applications are no longer possible.

The most significant enhancement of the C++ language is its support for object-oriented programming (OOP). You will have to modify your approach to problem solving to derive all of the benefits of C++. For example, objects and their associated operations must be identified and all necessary classes and subclasses must be constructed.

Once again, C#, the ancestor to C and C++, absorbs the best of C++'s object-oriented problem solving capabilities. However, C#'s approach is a little less intimidating by eliminating multiple-inheritance between a parent/base/or root object and its descendants.

Fun with Visual Basic

With the success of Windows 95/98/Me/2000, greater demand is being placed on the programmer to quickly and easily design applications for these graphics environments. Microsoft designed Visual Basic to specifically address these issues. Instead of the steep learning curve encountered by C or C++ programmers, Visual Basic offers the programmer a toolkit that allows quick construction of very advanced applications.

Applications design has changed drastically over the last few years as a result of user demand and dramatic hardware improvements. The advantage of Microsoft Windows is that it presents both the user and programmers with a common interface. The user has access to a graphical point-and-click environment that is the same across all applications. Visual Basic, from its inception, was designed to make developing a graphical Windows application as easy as possible. Visual Basic automatically takes care of the more tedious tasks of creating an application's graphical look. The programmer is freed to concentrate more on an application's features than on how to style it for Windows. Microsoft's C# extends the best features of Visual Basic into the raw horsepower provided by C and C++. C# adopts the ease of Visual Basic's interface design features with a look and feel that will immediately make any Visual Basic programmer feel right at home!

Onto the Internet

From IBM to grandmothers, everybody is getting into *WWW* (*World Wide Web*—A *hypertext*-based system of presenting information over the Internet) page development—the visually exciting way to say to the world, "I've arrived!" Undoubtedly the most exciting aspect of Web page construction is the easy-to-learn protocol of HTML. But let's not put the cart before the horse. HTML has a very interesting history.

NOTE

Hypertext—is an online document that has words or graphics containing links to other documents. Usually, selecting the link area onscreen (with a mouse or keyboard command) activates these links.

HTML Ancestry

It all began at the high-energy physics laboratory in Geneva, Switzerland, named CERN. The simple problem encountered by the scientists involved the time delay in disseminating research papers and other documents. And this time delay wasn't restricted to the nucleus of buildings on the CERN campus; their vital statistics were shared throughout the world. It is Tim Berners-Lee, who is credited with designing the system that would allow scientists to easily share fairly complex materials using a simple set of protocols over the Internet (the term used to describe all the worldwide interconnected TCP/IP networks).

NOTE

TCP/IP—is an abbreviation for Transmission Control Protocol/Internet Protocol. A set of protocols that applications use for communicating across networks or over the Internet. These protocols specify how packets of data should be constructed, addressed, checked for errors, and so on.

Tim broke his solution down into two parts: HTTP, the *Hyper Text Transfer Protocol* definition—which provided a simple way for users to request and receive files over the Internet—and the more familiar HTML or *Hyper Text Mark-up Language*. Unlike HTTP which defines how information is sent or received, HTML defines the visual presentation of the material on the receiving end.

Needless to say, as originally designed, HTML was never intended for the variety of display potentials presented by today's multitasking object-oriented operating systems like UNIX and Microsoft Windows. Nor was it ever designed to create wild multimedia sites that incorporated graphics and animation. The fledgling Internet was seen more as a library than as a virtual reality mall. As such, the original definition of HTML included as much output display control as would be needed by the typical scientific journal article.

Because HTML's protocols were succinct and complete, they were immediately accepted by the scientific community, which adopted it as their electronic typesetter. Scientists were particularly excited about HTML's ability to create links to other pages of information, making the documents much more alive than a static piece of paper. Unfortunately, this forward-only hot-link capability left something to be desired.

CGI

One of the earliest scripting languages was CGI or *Common Gateway Interface*. Its most common application is in forms processing. CGI allows you to create pages for users as individual requests come in, and you can customize pages to match that information.

The user usually fills out a form and clicks on a submit button. Then the user's browser sends a request to the server that includes information the user entered into the form. The server then sends this information on to another program for actual processing and responds with the appropriate output at the client or user end. Actually, depending on the kind of server your site resides on, you can write CGI programs in C++, PERL, and even *AppleScript*.

PERL

PERL is undoubtedly the most common language used for scripting CGI in UNIX environments with its combination of C syntax and the power of UNIX regular expressions. It is possible to write simple programs in PERL with a minimum of effort.

JavaScript and JScript

Netscape Version 2.0 is credited with the introduction of JavaScript. Immediately, Microsoft Internet Explorer 3.0 countered with its own flavor called JScript and VBScript based on the easy-to-learn Visual Basic. The good news is that JavaScript and JScript are evolving towards one another; however, various browsers still respond in non-uniform fashion.

These languages provide HTML developers with additional programming horsepower that enables them to make browsers do new and different things. Not everything has to take place on the server end; now the client can take on more of the responsibility of processing.

VBScript

Offering Visual Basic programmers the programming enhancements of a scripting language, VBScript came bundled with Microsoft's Internet Explorer 3.0. While JavaScript and JScript have a very C- or Java-based aroma, VBScript offers Visual Basic programmers the familiarity of their popular language. VBScript also easily integrates Microsoft's ActiveX controls in a Web environment.

Plug-Ins and ActiveX

Netscape is originally credited with developing the first plug-ins; Microsoft with developing *ActiveX* controls. The idea behind both is that the controlling software is loaded onto the user's computer (client), and then the Web page contains another file that contains the specific instructions or content.

While there are significant structural differences between plug-ins and ActiveX controls, their basic purpose on the page is basically the same. Like a Java applet, they add additional features and functionality to a Web page without directly affecting the host page. They also create a bidirectional communication between the end-user and the plug-in.

NOTE

Java Applet versus Java Application—Java applets are programs that will only run when hosted by a Web browser, while Java applications are stand-alone programs that are designed to run on any system and need no Web browser or Internet connection.

The downside to both technologies is that they add to the download time of the Web page. In addition to the time it takes to download and install the actual plug-in or control, there's also the extra time to download the content files. In addition, neither technology really provides interaction with other elements on the page. There are some ActiveX controls that provide features like tool tips or pop-up menus, but, like plug-ins, these items are operated directly by the control with no ability to go beyond the feature itself.

It Allows Every Type of Computer World Access!

The Web is, most importantly, platform independent. This means that you can access the World Wide Web regardless of whether you're running on a low-end PC, an Apple Mac, an expensive Silicon Graphics workstation, a VAX cluster, or a multi-million dollar Cray super computer!

Web Browsers—The Electronic SEARS Catalog

A Web browser, as mentioned earlier, is a program that you use to view pages on the World Wide Web, sometimes called web clients. A vast diversity of Web browsers are available for just about every type of architecture you can imagine, most importantly graphical-user-interface-based systems or GUI systems such as X11, Windows, and Mac platforms. There are even text-only browsers available for simple dial-up UNIX connections.

Full Color Shopping at Your Fingertips

One of the key features of Web browsers is their ability to display both text and graphics in full color on the same page, and all of this with a simple URL address, followed very often by nothing more than consecutive mouse clicks. If you are just jumping onto your Internet surfboard for the first time, you may not be aware that in its fledgling state the Internet was accessed by non-standard, confusing, command-line, text-only protocols. Of course, today's state-of-the-art rendition reacts to simple mouse clicks and is much more interesting with its new sound and streaming video capabilities. Even 3D virtual-reality simulations are possible with VRML (Virtual Reality Modeling Language).

NOTE

VRML—You can find a very interesting World Wide Web Virtual Library at www.w3.org, *supported by individuals interested in promoting/sharing information on this extremely exciting outgrowth of HTML.*

Info Info Everywhere

Of course, the very name, World Wide Web, indicates that the information you are downloading is potentially distributed throughout the entire globe. Since the information you are accessing occupies vast amounts of disk storage particularly when you include images, multimedia, and streaming video, there hasn't been a computer built to date that could house this bit explosion in one physical location.

Actually, this distributed diversity of data storage repositories is to your advantage. Were this information stored in a single location, imagine the chaos generated by a downed mainframe! The Web is so successful in providing so much information because that information is distributed globally across thousands of Web sites. And the best part about the interconnection is that if one leg of the information route is interrupted, for any reason, an alternate Web link takes over.

Provides Full Bidirectional Communication

An exciting aspect to Web interaction is its provisions for you to "talk back." Take, for example, a radio or television broadcast. This is one directional output.

The exciting news is that with today's evolution of HTML your document's display instructions are not limited to text only, but can now include graphical and auditory elements and can communicate back to the server.

C#—Another Pyramid Scheme?

At this point you may be asking yourself, is C# really capable of combining the best features of today's popular languages? Will C# really prove itself to be *the* one solution for Windows application development, or is C# just another approach by Microsoft to woo you deeper into the Microsoft empire? The answer is this: no matter how you feel about Bill Gates, or Microsoft's marketing strategies, C# is an exciting new programming language that will sell itself.

ANSI C#?

The single reason for C's and C++'s widespread adoption is the ANSI (American National Standards Institute) standardization. Dennis Ritchie and Bjarne Stroustrup left enough gray areas in their original language descriptions that were it not for some committee uniformly filling in the gaps, both languages would have died a slow, incompatible death. When Microsoft disclosed the C# language reference, they simultaneously announced the language's proposed standardization. The proposal was formally submitted to the ECMA Technical Committee (TC) 39. This is the same committee that is standardizing ECMA-Script or JScript.

Assuming the committee members accept the submission and agree to standardize C#, vendors beyond Microsoft can eventually implement the language freely. This will allow vendors to implement both "Standard C#" and their own proprietary C# extensions, just as they implement Standard C and C++ along with their own extensions today. In this sense, the eventual C# standard should mimic the C and C++ standards' balance between portable behavior and vendor invention.

What is MSIL?

Somewhat similar to Java's or J++'s architecture independent byte code, the C# compiler outputs MSIL which stands for *Microsoft Intermediate Language*. Contrary to popular belief, a virtual machine (VM) or similar technology does not interpret this IL (*Intermediate Language*). Instead, the IL is converted to native code, either when its application loads, or on demand by one of several just-in-time compilers. Once this translation occurs, the executed code is native. C# is not the only language using IL. All .NET compilers can emit IL. In fact, Microsoft researched about 20 languages during IL design and development. And you should not be surprised to see IL changes in response to the needs of these, or other, language vendors.

Microsoft and the .NET

Microsoft's decade long-term goal has always been the vision of a world with "Information at Your Fingertips." In the past, accessing information was anything but easy: modems were connected at 4800 baud, most messages were sent by fax rather than email, and few people had even heard of the Internet. Although Microsoft envisioned a world in which people could connect with the information they wanted, when they wanted it, from whatever device they wanted, there was no idea what technologies would help make that a reality. The Microsoft .NET solution will revolutionize computing and communications by being the first platform that makes "Information at Your Fingertips" a reality.

With Microsoft .NET technology you will have access to a new generation of advanced software joining the best of computing and communications in a revolutionary new way. The effect will be to totally transform the Web and every other aspect of the computing experience. .NET enables developers, businesses, and consumers to harness technology on their terms. .NET will allow the creation of truly distributed Web services that will integrate and collaborate with a range of complementary services to help customers in ways that today's dotcoms can only dream of.

The fundamental idea behind .NET is that the focus is shifting from individual Web sites or devices connected to the Internet to constellations of computers, devices, and services that work together to deliver broader, richer solutions. People will have control over how, when, and what information is delivered to them. Computers, devices, and services will be able to collaborate with each other to provide rich services, instead of being isolated islands where the user provides the only integration. Businesses will be able to offer their products and services in a way that lets customers seamlessly embed them in their own electronic fabric.

Microsoft .NET will make computing and communicating simpler and easier than ever. It will spawn a new generation of Internet services, and enable tens of thousands of software developers to create revolutionary online services and businesses. It will put you back in control, and enable greater control of your privacy, digital identity, and data. And software is what makes it all possible. However, Microsoft's .NET technology will only succeed if others adopt this new standard.

C# and the .NET

C# is one of four languages Microsoft will initially bring to .NET, along with C++, Visual Basic, and JScript. Other vendors are developing languages for this platform including: APL, COBOL, Eiffel, Perl, Python, and Scheme. What allows such interoperability is the .NET Common Language Runtime, or CLR. Within this runtime, all languages share the following set of resources:

- Object-oriented programming model (inheritance, polymorphism, exception handling, garbage collection)
- Security model
- Type system
- All .NET base classes
- Many .NET framework classes
- Development, debugging, and profiling tools
- Execution and code management
- IL-to-native translators and optimizers

Remember, all of these resources are available to every .NET language, not just C#.

Common Language Specification (CLS)

For some programming languages the common type system is too large. For this reason, Microsoft is creating a subset of that system. The subset is codified as a set of rules in the *Common Language Specification* (*CLS*). Languages conforming to these rules allow you to easily create a base class in COBOL, derive an APL class from the base, create a container of derived objects in C#, and manipulate the container with a Visual Basic method.

CLS Extensions to Visual C++

While C++ programmers can target .NET and use all C++ features in their code, the C++ code cannot be verified safe by the .NET runtime. Currently, C++ does not use the CLS rules, and programs written in it face certain restrictions. To get around these restrictions, Microsoft is adding non-standard "managed extensions" to Visual C++. Code written with these extensions can be CLS-compliant.

The Importance of Interoperability

Many of today's top programmers believe interoperability will fundamentally change how we all choose languages and implement designs. The advantages of interoperability may spur the creation and design of other new languages. Finally, the Microsoft .NET solution may be *the* answer to those who want out from under the C/C++ language domination.

C# Introduction and Overview

Currently, C and C++ are the most widely used languages for developing commercial and business software. While both languages provide the programmer with a tremendous amount of fine-grained control, this flexibility comes at a cost to productivity. Compared with a language such as Microsoft Visual Basic, equivalent C and C++ applications often take longer to develop. Due to the complexity and long cycle times associated with these languages, many C and C++ programmers have been searching for a language offering better balance between power and productivity.

C and C++ programmers have dreamt of a world where rapid code development and raw horsepower would provide access to all the functionality of any underlying platform. This ideal environment would also provide an environment that is completely in sync with emerging Web standards and one that provides easy integration with existing applications. Additionally, C and C++ developers would like the ability to code at a low level when and if the need arises. The Microsoft solution to this problem is a language called C#.

C#—The Broad Spectrum

C# is a modern, object-oriented language that enables programmers to quickly build a wide range of applications for the new Microsoft .NET platform, which provides tools and services that fully exploit both computing and communications. C# is a great choice for developing a wide range of components—from high-level business objects to system-level applications. Using simple C# language constructs, these components can be converted into Web services, allowing them to be invoked across the Internet from any language running on any operating system.

More than anything else, C# is designed to bring rapid development to the C++ programmer without sacrificing the power and control traditionally reserved for C and C++. Because of this heritage, C# has a high degree of fidelity with C and C++. Developers familiar with these languages can quickly become productive in C#.

C# Efficiency

In today's burgeoning and profitable Web economy, where competitors are just one click away, businesses are being forced to respond to competitive threats faster than ever before. Developers are called upon to shorten cycle times and produce more incremental revisions of a program, rather than a single monumental version. C# is designed with these considerations in mind. The language is designed to help developers do more with fewer lines of code and fewer opportunities for error.

C# and New Web Standards

Today's Web-based solutions require the use of new emerging Web standards like Hypertext Markup Language (HTML), Extensible Markup Language (XML), and Simple Object Access Protocol (SOAP). Existing development tools were developed before the Internet or when the Web as we know it today was in its infancy. As a result, they don't always provide the best fit for working with new Web technologies. C# programmers can leverage an extensive framework for building applications on the Microsoft .NET platform.

C# includes built-in support to turn any component into a Web service that can be invoked over the Internet—from any application running on any platform. Even better, the Web services framework can make existing Web services look just like native C# objects to the programmer, thus allowing developers to leverage existing Web services with the object-oriented programming skills they already have.

If current trends continue, XML will be the standard used to pass structured data across the Internet. Such data sets are typically very small. In this environment C# really shines; for example, to improve performance, C# allows XML data to be mapped directly into a struct data type instead of a class. This is a more efficient way to handle small amounts of data.

C# Makes You a Better Programmer!

Ask yourself this question, "How many times have you used an uninitialized variable in your code?" Even expert C++ programmers can make this simple mistake which can lead to unpredictable problems that can remain undiscovered for long periods of time. Once a program is in production use, it can be very costly to fix even the simplest programming errors. The modern design of C# eliminates the most common C++ programming errors. C# empowers the traditional C/C++ programmer by providing:

- Automated garbage collection that relieves the programmer of the burden of manual memory management
- Automatically initialized variables
- Type-safe variables

C# is a language that makes it far easier for developers to create and maintain applications that solve complex business problems.

C# Enhances an Application's Longevity

Adding software components to an existing product has always been an error-prone task. Code modifications can unintentionally change the semantics of an existing program. C# solves this problem by including versioning support. For example, method overriding must be explicit and cannot happen inadvertently as in C++ or Java. This helps prevent coding errors and preserve versioning flexibility. A related feature is the native support for interfaces and interface inheritance. These features enable complex frameworks to be developed and evolved over time. When combined, these features make the process of developing later versions of a project more robust and thus reduce overall development costs for the successive versions.

Accurate Transitions from Design to Implementation

For rapid and accurate code development it is necessary to have a close connection between an abstract business process and the actual software implementation. Unfortunately, most language tools don't have an easy way to link business logic with code. The C# language aids this transition by allowing typed, extensible metadata that can be applied to any object.

A project architect can define domain-specific attributes and apply them to any language element classes, interfaces, and so on. The developer can then programmatically examine the attributes on each element. This makes it easy, for example, to write an automated tool that will ensure that each class or interface is correctly identified as part of a particular abstract business object, or simply to create reports based on the domain-specific attributes of an object.

Extensive Interoperability

Many programmers are forced to use C++ even when they would prefer to use a more productive development environment because real-world experience has shown how some applications demand the use of "native" code to manage a type-safe environment for performance reasons or to interoperate with existing application programming interfaces. C# solves these problems by:

- Supporting native support for the Component Object Model (COM) and Windows®-based APIs.
- Supporting restricted use of native pointers.
- Implementing every object as a COM object.

No longer will developers have to explicitly implement COM interfaces. Instead, those features are built in. C# programs can use existing COM objects, no matter what language was used to author them. C# includes a special feature that enables a program to call out to any native API.

Inside a specially marked code block, developers are allowed to use pointers and traditional C/C++ features such as manually managed memory and pointer arithmetic. This is a huge advantage over other environments. It means that C# programmers can build on their existing C and C++ code base rather than discard it. In both cases—COM support and native API access—the goal is to provide the developer with essential power and control without having to leave the C# environment.

Summary

C# is a modern, object-oriented language that enables programmers to quickly and easily build solutions for the Microsoft .NET platform. The framework provided allows C# components to become Web services that are available across the Internet, from any application running on any platform. The language enhances developer productivity while serving to eliminate programming errors that can lead to increased development costs. C# brings rapid Web development to the C and C++ programmer while maintaining the power and flexibility that those developers call for.

CHAPTER 2

Unique C#

In programming, you often encounter catch phrases like, "Definition of recursion—see recursion," or "C is not for Children." The latest one is going to be—"Microsoft has developed one sharp new language."

There is no question that C# is as easy to learn and use as Visual Basic with the raw horsepower of an object-oriented C++! For years developers have been begging for a language that was easy to write, read, and maintain, but with the power and flexibility of C++. For those developers, the new C# language is here.

Microsoft has built C# with type safety, garbage collection, simplified type declarations, versioning and scalability support, and lots of other features that make developing solutions faster and easier, especially for COM+ and Web services. This chapter will give you a first look at C#, a language with the potential to revolutionize programming.

C# is a new programming language that makes it easier for C and C++ programmers to generate COM+-ready programs. In addition, C# has been built from the ground up to make it easier to write and maintain programs. It's a little like taking all the best of Visual Basic and adding it to C/C++ while streamlining the esoteric and rarely used advanced features of C++.

C#: A Quick Overview

Microsoft is promoting C# as the single best solution for developing COM+, Web, and Windows-based programs for enterprise computing. However, you won't have to migrate your existing C or C++ code. If you like the new features in C#, and you probably will, you can migrate your mindset to C#. Let's face it—C++ is a powerful language, but it isn't always programmer friendly. The main design goal of C# was simplicity rather than pure power. You do give up a little processing power, but you gain features such as type safety and automatic garbage collection in return. C# can make your code more stable and productive overall, meaning that you can more than make up that lost power in the long run. C# offers several key benefits for programmers, as shown in Table 2–1.

Table 2–1   C# Programmer Benefits

Ease-Of-Use	Consistency	Up-To-Date
Object-Oriented	Type-Safe	Scalability
Versioning	Portability	Flexibility

The following section gives you a hands-on understanding of these nine C# components.

Ease-of-Use

One of the most annoying syntax permutations found in an object-oriented C++ application is remembering when you should use the -> pointer operator, when you should use the : : scope-resolution operator for a class member, and when you should use the . period member operator. C# recognizes this annoying complexity of the C++ programming language and simplifies it. In C#, *all three* syntax categories are represented by a . period member operator. Whether you're looking at members, classes, namespaces, references, or what have you, you don't need to track which operator to use!

With today's international market resources, provided via the Internet, more and more applications must display their textual content in several human-language formats. This necessitates algorithms that can use ANSI ASCII text only, the new UNICODE standard, or switch-hits between the two code formats. This presents a significant design requirement for a typical C or C++ algorithm. C# eliminates the design bottleneck of C/C++'s char versus wchar_t data type, with a singular use of the data type char. No longer is there a char, unsigned char, signed char, and wchar_t to keep straight.

Finally, many C/C++ programmers use integers as Booleans values. This typically leads to assignment errors anytime the = assignment operator is accidentally inserted instead of the == logical equality operator. C# eliminates the confusion by separating the two types, providing a separate bool data type that solves this problem. A bool can be true or false and, *most importantly*, cannot be converted into other types (as in C/C++). Also, C# does not allow an integer or object reference to be tested against true or false (again as in C/C++). In C# the same comparison must be rewritten to test against the value zero, or null, in the case of an object reference. For example, a standard C/C++ if test could be written as:

```
int DataInList;
. . .
if (DataInList) . . .
```

C# would syntactically demand the following rewrite (Note: The familiar C/C++ != logical not equal operator):

```
int DataInList;
if (DataInList != 0) . . .
```

Sometimes C and C++ get a bad rap, simply because programmers are unaware of the languages' origins. From Chapter 1, you learned that, technically speaking, C is not a true high-level language. Instead, C is viewed as a middle-level language. By design, then, some features of C, carried over to C++ *do* appear to be arcane. Take, for example, the C/C++ switch statement syntax. In C/C++, you must knowledgeably insert or omit a `break;` statement, within the selected cases, in order to control the drop-through capabilities of the control structure. For example:

```
switch (Letter)
{
    case 'a':
    case 'e':
    case 'i':
    case 'o':
    case 'u':
        LowerCaseVowelCount++;
        break;
    case 'A':
    case 'E:
    case 'I':
    case 'O';
    case 'U':
        UpperCaseVowelCount++;
        break;
}
```

C# improves this situation by providing a more high-level language interpretation to a switch-case statement, similar to Pascal and Visual Basic. These languages *automatically* insert a break or go-to-type statement before each case statement. However, in C#, with a little reverse engineering, you can design a drop-through capability, as seen here:

```
switch (Letter)
{
    case 'a':
        goto case 'e';
    case 'e':
. . .
```

Consistency

C# unifies the type system by letting you view every type in the language as an object. Whether you're using a class, a struct, an array, or a primitive, you'll be able to treat it as an object. Objects are combined into namespaces, which allow you to access everything programmatically. This means that instead of putting `includes` in your file, as in:

```
#include <cstdio>
#include <iostream>
#include <string>
using namespace std;
```

you simply include a particular namespace in your program to gain access to the classes and objects contained within it:

```
using System;
```

In COM+, all classes exist within a single hierarchical namespace. In C#, the `using` statement lets you avoid having to specify the fully qualified name when you use a class. For example, the `System` namespace contains several classes, including `Console`. Console has a `WriteLine()` method that, as you might expect, writes a line to the system console. If you want to generate the output part of your typical, introductory, C# Hello World program you enter the following statement:

```
System.Console.WriteLine("Hello World");
```

Or, using namespace System, as in:

```
Using System;
Console.WriteLine("Hello World!");
```

That's almost everything you would need for a C# Hello World program.

Up-To-Date

As programmer needs evolve, so too must their tools. Applications written for a single-process DOS operating system needed to incorporate the concerns of an application coexisting with other concurrent tasks under a multitasking environment. The invention and inclusion of mouse-interfaces provided a convenient and graphical interaction for the end-user.

The dramatic increase in necessary resource management provided by these new environments demanded efficient code design. Add multimedia capabilities and communication (originally via modem) to global Internet connectivity, plus multi-human-language information presentation—and BOOM, Fortran, PL/I, COBOL, Pascal, or Modula-2 could no longer cut the mustard. Even today's C and C++ are beginning to oxidize!

C# went back to the think tank and emerged with several new features that help fortify C++. Garbage collection is one example—everything gets cleaned up when it's no longer referenced. However, garbage collection can have a price. It makes problems caused by certain risky behavior (for example, using unsafe casts and stray pointers) far harder to diagnose and potentially fatal.

Once again, from Chapter 1, remember that every C# change to C or C++ migrates the best of languages, written to design operating systems, over to application-development status. It's not that there was anything wrong with C or C++, but for today's programmer demands (typically *not* operating system development) C/C++ are less than ideal.

To protect against unsafe casts and stray pointers, C# implements type safety to ensure application stability. Of course, type safety also makes your code more readable, so others on your team can see what you've been up to! C# also has a richer intrinsic model for error handling than C++. C# improves on this situation by providing integral support for throw, try...catch, and try...finally as language elements. True, you could do this as a macro in C++, but now it's available right out of the box.

If you are familiar with several programming languages, you already know each language has its own strengths and weaknesses. However, the weaknesses are usually a result of operating system and hardware changes combined with more sophisticated end-user expectations. The main objective for any modern language is the ability to actually use it for something. It seems simple enough, but many languages completely ignore the needs for financial and time-based data types. Borrowing from languages like SQL, C# implements built-in support for data types like decimal and string, and lets you implement new primitive types that are as efficient as the existing ones.

Microsoft also addressed a programmer's need to efficiently debug an application. The traditional way to modify a program for debugging in C++ was to insert multiple #if defined(IDENTIFIER) ...#endif statement pairs, and indicate that large sections of code would only be executed during the debugging process. This gave a programmer access to two implementations—a debug build and a release build—with some of the calls in the release going to functions that do nothing. C# offers the conditional keyword to control program flow based on defined identifiers.

Object-Oriented

C# implements a streamlined version of C++ object-oriented programming capabilities by eliminating multiple-inheritance; instead, C# favors native support for the COM+ virtual object system. Encapsulation, polymorphism, and inheritance are preserved without all the pain. C# also eliminates the entire concept of global functions, variables, and constants. Instead, you can create static class members, making C# code easier to read and less prone to *identifier* (class, structure, member, constant, variable, etc.) name collisions.

By default, C# methods are nonvirtual. This requires a programmer to use an explicit *virtual* modifier and is one way to prevent the redefinition of a defined class member. Therefore, C# makes it much more difficult to accidentally override a method, making it much easier to provide correct versioning. Class members in C# can be defined as in C/C++ as *private, protected, public,* and the new C# *internal*, totally controlling member encapsulation.

C# provides method and operator overloading using a syntax that's a lot easier than the one used by C++. However, you can't overload global operator functions—the overloading is strictly local in scope. The COM+ component model is supported through the implementation of *delegates*—the object-oriented equivalent of function pointers in C++. Interfaces support multiple inheritances. Classes can privately implement *internal* interfaces through explicit member implementations without the end-user ever knowing about it.

Type Safe

Type safety has its good points and bad points. Take, for example, Pascal, where a character variable cannot hold an integer value (not directly), or vice versa. This language feature forces a matching between a variable's formal definition and type use throughout a program. Therefore, unlike C/C++, which are *loosely typed* languages, you could not assign the uppercase ASCII value of the letter "A" with the integer value 65.

Since Pascal was designed as a teaching language, designed-in stringent type checking forced a novice programmer to always scrutinize data manipulations. However, an experienced programmer could skillfully, knowledgably, and efficiently mix data representations within the same variable, one of C/C++'s strengths! Unfortunately, in today's programming environment with more and more applications (more appropriately, applets) running on multiple platforms, C/C++'s loose typing becomes an extra design burden.

There is no question that type safety promotes robust programs. Microsoft bundled C# with several Visual Basic features that promote proper code execution and more robust programs than Visual Basic. For example, all dynamically allocated objects and arrays are initialized to zero. Although C# doesn't automatically initialize local variables, the compiler will warn you if you use one before you initialize it. When you access an array, it is *automatically* range checked. Unlike C and C++, you can't overrun an array's bounds.

C# also prevents a programmer from creating an invalid reference. All casts are required to be safe, and you can't cast between integer and reference types. Garbage collection in C# ensures that you don't leave references dangling around your code. Hand in hand with this feature is overflow checking. Arithmetic operations and conversions are not allowed if they overflow the target variable or object. Of course, there are some valid reasons to want a variable to overflow. If you do, you can explicitly disable the checking.

Part of C#'s type safety comes from its newer data types. For example, the char type is always a UNICODE-compliant 2-byte (16 bit) value. Also, certain useful types, like decimal and string, are built in. Perhaps the biggest difference between C++ and C#, however, is the way C# handles arrays. C# arrays are *managed types*, meaning that they hold references, not values, and they are garbage collected. You can declare arrays in several ways, including multidimensional and as arrays of arrays.

Scalability

Many programmers are frustrated by C/C++'s inclusion of often-incompatible header files before they can compile all but the most trivial applications. C# gets rid of these frequently aggravating headers by combining the declaration and definition of types. It also directly imports and emits COM+ metadata, making incremental compiles much easier.

Source file management also changes in the new C# environment. C/C++ programmers are taught that when a project gets large enough, they should split the code solution into smaller source files. C# doesn't have any restrictions about where your source files reside or what they're called. When you compile a C# project, you can think of it as concatenating all the source files, then compiling them into one big file. You don't have to track which headers go where, or which routines belong in which source file. This also means that you can move, rename, split, or merge source files without generating fatal error compiler messages!

Versioning

Many programmers believe the file extension .dll stands for deadly lost library. Dynamic link libraries are a constant problem for users and programmers alike. So much so that Microsoft has an entire service dedicated specifically to users who need to track the different versions of system DLLs. There's nothing a programming language can do to keep a library author from messing around with a published API.

C# directly addresses this potential versioning nightmare by retaining binary compatibility with existing derived classes. When you introduce a new member in a base class as one that exists in a derived class, it doesn't cause an error. However, the designer of the class must indicate whether the method is meant as an override or as a new method that just hides the similar inherited method.

Syntactically, C# facilitates versioning with a modified use of C/C++'s namespace. In C#, classes and interfaces defined in class libraries must be defined in a hierarchical namespace instead of a standard flat model. Using this approach, applications can explicitly import a single member of a namespace so there won't be any collisions when multiple namespaces contain similarly named members. When you declare a namespace, subsequent declarations are considered to be part of the same declaration space.

Portability

C# supports the four common types of APIs used by all Windows platforms, while the old-style C APIs have integrated support in C#. To call C-style APIs applications use the N/

Direct features of COM+. C# provides transparent access to standard COM and OLE Automation APIs and supports all data types through the COM+ runtime. Most importantly, C# supports the COM+ Common Language Subset specification. If you've exported any entities that aren't accessible from another language, the compiler can optionally flag the code. For instance, a class can't have two members named `MyMethod()` and `mymethod()` because a case-insensitive language would flag the second identifier as an illegal attempt to redefine the same method.

Flexibility

C# does allow you to declare unsafe classes and methods that contain pointers, structs, and static arrays. Often times this is the only way a real-world application can get to the native code level—either for performance considerations or to use old-style APIs from other programs. These unsafe methods won't be type safe, but they will execute within the managed space so you don't have to marshal boundaries between safe and unsafe code. C# internally allows a developer to pin an object so that the garbage collector will pass over the object when it's doing its work. Unsafe code won't be executed outside a fully trusted environment. Programmers can even turn off garbage collection while an unsafe method is in progress.

Getting the "Big Picture"

If you are like most programmers, you can't wait to get started *using* C#! Now pay attention or you *could*:

1. end up not getting anything, other than a trivial C# program up-and-running!
2. clone some new C# syntax.
3. mix in a little Visual Basic familiarity.
4. spice up your algorithm with some C/C++ memorabilia.

These situations could all happen if you ignore the remainder of this chapter. Why? Similar to missing "the forest for the trees" concept, delving directly into C# syntax, like "shotgun" programming, will take you only so far.

Instead of having an instructor say, this is a brush, these are paints, this is a canvas, this is an easel, followed by a theoretical discussion of perspective, vanishing-point, and shading—only to have some student pose the question, "Just what are we doing?" The remainder of this chapter starts from the finished product, a framed painting: C# has cohesive design functionality that can only be understood properly in light of the final product.

Knowing how to dip a brush into paint doesn't make you a painter. Knowing where C# places semicolons doesn't make you a C# programmer. Not unless you know where you are going. For example, knowing C#'s syntax for variable declarations doesn't help you know where the variable is legally accessible.

Visibility

Declarations in a C# program define the structural elements of a program. C# programs organize these structural elements using namespaces which can contain type declarations and nested namespace declarations. Type declarations are used to define classes, structs, interfaces, enums, and delegates. The kinds of members permitted in a type declaration depend on the form of the type declaration. For instance, class declarations can contain declarations such as constructors, destructors, static constructors, constants, fields, methods, properties, events, indexers, operators, and nested types.

A declaration defines an identifier, or name, in the declaration space to which the declaration belongs. Except for overloaded constructor, method, indexer, and operator names, it is an error to have two or more declarations that introduce members with the same identifier in a declaration space. It is never possible for a declaration space to contain different kinds of members with the same identifier. For example, a declaration space can never contain a field and a method by the same identifier. There are several different types of declaration spaces, as described in the following text.

For all source files of a program, namespace member declarations with no enclosing namespace declaration are members of a single combined declaration space called the global declaration space. For all source files of a program, namespace member declarations within namespace declarations that have the same fully qualified namespace name are members of a single combined declaration space.

All class, struct, or interface declaration creates a new declaration space. Names are introduced into this declaration space through class member declarations, struct member declarations, or interface member declarations. Except for overloaded constructor declarations and static constructor declarations, a class or struct member declaration cannot introduce a member by the same name as the class or struct.

A class, struct, or interface permits the declaration of overloaded methods and indexers. A class or struct furthermore permits the declaration of overloaded constructors and operators. For instance, a class, struct, or interface may contain multiple method declarations with the same name, provided these method declarations differ in their signature.

Notice that base classes do not contribute to the declaration space of a class, and base interfaces do not contribute to the declaration space of an interface. Therefore, a derived class or interface is allowed to declare a member with the same name as an inherited member. Such a member is said to hide the inherited member.

All enumerated types create a new declaration space. Names are introduced into this declaration space through enum member declarations. All block or switch-blocks create a separate declaration space for local variables. Names are introduced into this declaration space through local variable declarations. If a block is the body of a constructor or method declaration, the parameters declared in the *formal parameter list* are members of the block's *local variable declaration space*. The local variable declaration space of a block includes any nested blocks. Therefore, within a nested block, it is not possible to declare a local variable with the same name as a local variable in an enclosing block.

Each block or switch-block creates a separate declaration space for labels. Names are introduced into this declaration space through labeled statements, and the names are referenced through `goto` statements. The label declaration space of a block includes any nested blocks. Therefore, within a nested block, it is not possible to declare a label with the same name as a label in an enclosing block.

The order of an algorithm's declarations is significant under the following circumstances:

- All local variables must be defined before they are used.

The order for enum member declarations is significant when constant expression values are omitted.

- The order for field declarations and local variable declarations determines the order in which their initializers (if any) are executed.

The declaration space of a namespace is "open ended," and two namespace declarations with the same fully qualified name are combined by the compiler into the same declaration space. For example,

```
namespace MyNamespace.Info
{    class MyClassA
    {
        . . .
    }
}
namespace MyNamespace.Info
{    class MyClassB
    {
        . . .
    }
}
```

In this example the compiler combines the two namespace declarations into the same declaration space, in this case declaring two classes with the fully qualified names `MyNamespace.Info.ClassA` and `MyNamespace.Info.ClassB`. Because the two declarations contribute to the same declaration space, it is illegal to have the same declaration of a class with the same name.

The scope of identifiers within a declaration space of a block includes any nested blocks. Therefore, in the following example, the `methodA()` and `methodB()` methods are in error because the name is declared in the outer block and cannot be redefined in the inner block.

```
class MyClass {
    void methodA() {
        int Value = 0;
        if (Start) { int Value = 1;    }
    }
    void methodB() {
        if (Start) { int Value = 0; }
        int Value = 1;
    }
    void methodC() {
        if (FlagA) { int Value = 0; }
        if (FlagB) { int Value = 1; }
    }
    void methodD() {
        for (int Value = 0; Value < 7; Value++)
            { ... }
        for (int Value = 0; Value < 7; Value++)
            { ... }
    }
}
```

Note, however, the `methodC()` and `methodD()` method is valid since the two `Value`'s are declared in separate non-nested blocks.

Members

Namespaces and types have *members*. All namespace or type members are available through the use of a qualified name that starts with a reference to the namespace or type, followed by a . *period member operator* and the name of the member. Members of a type are either declared in the type or *inherited* from the base class of the type.

When a type inherits its definition from a base class, all of the members of the base class, *except* constructors and destructors, become members of the derived type. The scope of a base class member does *not* control whether the member is inherited. Instead, inheritance extends to any member that isn't a constructor or destructor. However, an inherited member may not be accessible in a derived type, either because of its scope or because it is hidden by a declaration in the type.

Namespace Members

Whenever you declare a namespace or type that has no enclosing namespace, the declaration becomes a member of the *global namespace*. Namespaces and types declared within a namespace are members of that namespace. Namespaces have no access restrictions. It is not possible to declare *private*, *protected*, or *internal* namespaces, and namespace names are always publicly accessible.

Struct Members

Members of a structure are the members declared in the struct and the members inherited from class *object*. The members of a simple type correspond directly to the members of the struct type aliased by the simple type, as seen in Table 2–2.

Table 2–2   Standard C# Data Members

Type	Uses the member struct reference:
bool are the members of the	System.Boolean
byte are the members of the	System.Byte
char are the members of the	System.Char
decimal are the members of the	System.Decimal
double are the members of the	System.Double
float are the members of the	System.Single
int are the members of the	System.Int32
long are the members of the	System.Int64
sbyte are the members of the	System.Sbyte
short are the members of the	System.Int16
uint are the members of the	System.UInt32
ulong are the members of the	System.UInt64
ushort are the members of the	System.UInt16

Table 2–2 highlights this relationship between struct type and standard C# data members.

Enumerated Type Members

The members of an enumerated type are the constants declared in the enumeration and the members inherited from class object.

Class Members

A class definition may contain declarations for constants, fields, methods, properties, events, indexers, constructors, destructors, operators, static constructors, and types. The members of a class are those members declared within the class and those members inherited from the base class. Those members inherited from the base class include constants, fields, methods, properties, events, indexers, operators, and types of the base class, but not the constructors, destructors, and static constructors of the base class. Base class members are inherited without regard to their accessibility.

Interface Members

The members of an interface are the members declared in the interface and in all base interfaces of the interface, and the members inherited from class object.

Array Members

The members of an array are the members inherited from class System.Array.

Delegate Members

The members of a delegate are the members inherited from class System.Delegate.

Accessing Members

Where a C# programmer places an identifier's declaring statement determines the identifier's member access. C# programmers use the term *accessible* to refer to those members that are legally accessible, and *inaccessible* when access to a particular member is disallowed. Access to a member is permitted when the textual location in which the access takes place is included in the scope of the member. The accessibility of a member is established by the scope of the member combined with the accessibility of the immediately containing type, if any.

Public, Protected, Internal, Private Member Accessibility

C# provides five levels of *scope* for members: *public, protected, internal, protected internal,* and *private.*

- A *public* member is a member defined by including a public modifier in the member declaration. The compiler interprets the use of the public modifier as granting unlimited access.

- A *protected* member is a member defined by including a protected modifier in the member declaration. The compiler interprets the use of the protected modifier as granting limited access. This access is limited to the containing class or types derived from that class.

- An *internal* member is a member defined by including an internal modifier in the member declaration. The compiler interprets the use of the internal modifier as granting access just to this project.

- A *protected internal* member is a member defined by including both a protected and an internal modifier in the member declaration. The compiler interprets the use of the protected internal modifier as limiting access to the project or types derived directly from the class.

- Finally, a *private* member is a member defined by including a private modifier in the member declaration. The compiler interprets the use of the private modifier as granting access to just the containing type.

Depending on the context in which a member declaration takes place, only certain types of accessibility are allowed. Namespaces have an implied public scope and no access modifiers are allowed on namespace declarations.

- Class members can use any type of scope modifier but default to a private scope modifier. Likewise, any type declared as a member of a class can use any scope modifier. However, a type that is declared as a member of a namespace can use only the public or internal scope modifiers.

- Enumerated type members use an implied public modifier. Modifiers are not allowed with enumerated type members.

Interface members use an implied public accessibility. Modifiers are not allowed with interface members.

- Struct members can use public, internal, or private scope modifiers. They default to a private scope.

- Types declared in compilation units or namespaces can use a public or internal scope. They default to internal scope.

Furthermore, when a member declaration does not include any access modifiers, the context in which the declaration takes place determines the default scope.

Scope

The terms *accessibility domain* or scope of a member refer to the portions of a program where access to a member is granted. A member is referred to as *top-level* when it is not declared within a type. Members are *nested* when they are declared within another type. The *program text* of a project refers to all program text in all source code files attached to the project. Likewise, the program text of a type refers to program text falling between the opening and closing "{" and "}" French braces.

Predefined types, by definition, have unlimited scope. The scope of a top-level type is always, as a minimum, the program text of the project where the type is declared. The scope of a nested member is summarized in Table 2–3.

Table 2–3   Nested Member Scope Derivation

Nested Member	Scope
internal	NestedMember and TopLevelType and program text of the project.
private	NestedMember as program text of TopLevelType.
protected	TopLevelType (including derived types) and program text of TopLevelType.
protected internal	TopLevelType (including derived types) and program text of the project.
public	TopLevelType

From Table 2–3, you can see that the scope of a nested member is, as a minimum, the program text of the type where the member is declared.

Also, the scope of a member is never more inclusive than the scope of the type in which the member is declared. Consider the following portion of code:

```
public class publicClassOuter
{
    internal static int Able;
    private static int Baker;
    public static int Charlie;
}

internal class internalClass
{
    internal static int Able;
    private static int Baker;
    public static int Charlie;

    private class privateClass
    {
        internal static int Able;
        private static int Baker;
        public static int Charlie;
    }
    public class publicClassInner
```

```
        {
            internal static int Able;
            private static int Baker;
            public static int Charlie;
        }
    }
```

Here the classes and members have the following access privileges, as shown in Table 2–4.

Table 2–4   Sample Member Declarations and Accessibility Privileges

Member Reference	Visible In
publicClassOuter, publicClassOuter.Charlie	unlimited
publicClassOuter.Able, internalClass, internalClass.Charlie, internalClass.Able, internalClass.publicClassInner, internalClass.publicClassInner.Charlie, and internalClass.publicClassInner.Able	the program text of the containing project
publicClassOuter.Baker	the program text of publicClassOuter
InternalClass.Baker and internalClass.privateClass	the program text of internalClass, including the program text of internalClass.publicClassInner and internalClass.privateClass
InternalClass.publicClassInner.Baker	the program text of internalClass.publicClassInner
InternalClass.privateClass.Charlie, internalClass.privateClass.Able, and internalClass.privateClass.Baker	the program text of internalClass.privateClass

As the example illustrates, the scope of a member is never larger than that of its containing type.

All members of a base class are inherited by derived types including private members of a base class. The exception is constructors and destructors. The scope of a private member includes only the program text of the type in which the member is declared. Consider the following portion of code:

```
class ParentClass
{
    int parentsInt;
    static void methodA(ChildClass dummyArg) {
        dummyArg.parentsInt = 1; // Permitted
    }
}
class ChildClass: ParentClass
{
    static void methodA(ChildClass dummyArg) {
        dummyArg.parentsInt = 1; // Not Permitted
    }
}
```

In this case, the ChildClass class inherits the private member parentsInt from the ParentClass class. Since the member is private, it is only accessible within the *class-body* of ParentClass. As a result, access to dummyArg.parentsInt succeeds in the ParentClass.methodA() method, but fails in the ChildClass.methodA() method.

Protected Scope

To access a protected member outside the program text of the class in which it is declared, or when a protected internal member is accessed outside the program text of the project in which it is declared, the access is required to take place through the derived class type in which the access occurs.

For example, a derived class can access a protected constructor of a base class in a *constructor*:

```
public class parentClass
{
    protected int value;
    static void methodA(parentClass member1,
                        childClass member2) {
        member1.value = 1;
        member2.value = 1;
    }
}
public class childClass: parentClass
{
    static void methodA(parentClass member1,
                        childClass member2) {
        member1.value = 1; // Access through childClass instance
        member2.value = 1;
    }
}
```

Here the scope of `parentClass` members makes it possible to access `value` through instances of both `parentClass` and `childClass`. This is possible because the access takes place through an instance of `parentClass` or `member1` class derived from `parentClass`. However, within `childClass`, it is not possible to access value through an instance of `parentClass`. This is because the `parentClass` does not derive from `childClass`.

Scope Restrictions

Several constructs in the C# language require a type to be at least as accessible as a member or another type. For example, a type `TopLevelType` is considered to be at least as accessible as a member or type `NestedMember` when the scope of `TopLevelType` is a superset of the scope of `NestedMember`.

Mangling

In C# all methods, constructors, indexers, and operators are characterized by their *signatures*. *Mangling* is the term used in assigning an identifier's signature.

Method signatures are made up of the name of the method along with the number, modifiers, and types of its formal parameters. The signature does not include the return type.

Constructor signatures are made up of the number, modifiers, and types of its formal parameters.

Indexer signatures are made up of the number and types of its formal parameters. The signature does not include the element type.

Operator signatures are made up of the operator along with the number and types of its formal parameters. The signature does not include the result type.

Signatures allow *overloading* of members in classes, structs, and interfaces. For example, an overloaded class constructor will allow a class or struct to declare multiple constructors with unique signatures.

The following code segment shows an example of method overloading with associated signatures:

```
interface SampleInterface
{
    // OverloadedMethod()
    void OverloadedMethod(void);
    // OverloadedMethod(int)
    void OverloadedMethod(int i);

    // prototype is illegal - does not meet the
    // rules for uniqueness
    // OverloadedMethod(int)
    // int  OverloadedMethod(int i);
```

```
    // OverloadedMethod(out int)
    void OverloadedMethod(out int i);
    // OverloadedMethod(ref int)
    void OverloadedMethod(ref int i);
    // OverloadedMethod(float, int)
    void OverloadedMethod(float x, int y);
    // OverloadedMethod(out int,float)
    void OverloadedMethod(out int x,float y);
    // OverloadedMethod(string)
    int  OverloadedMethod(string st);
}
```

Note that formal argument modifiers, such as `ref` and `out` are part of the signature. Therefore, `OverloadedMethod(int)`, `OverloadedMethod(ref int)`, and `OverloadedMethod(out int)` are all unique signatures. Also, notice that the third attempt to overload the method would be illegal since the formal argument lists are *not* unique, even though the return types are!

Name Resolutions

The scope of an identifier is the portion of program text where it is permissible to refer to the entity, declared by the identifier, without qualification of the identifier. Scopes can be *nested*, and an inner scope may be assigned an identifier different from the outer scope. The identifier from the outer scope is considered *hidden* in the region of program text covered by the inner scope. Access to the outer identifier is then possible by qualifying the identifier. For example, the scope of a namespace member declared by a *namespace-member-declaration* with no enclosing *namespace declaration* is the entire program text of each compilation unit.

Name Hiding

The scope or visibility of identifiers usually encompasses program text greater than the declaration space of the identifier. For example, the scope of an identifier may include declarations that introduce new declaration spaces containing entities of the same identifier. This type of declaration causes the original identifier to become *hidden*.

Consider the following portion of code:

```
class SomeClass
{
    int offset = 0;
    void methodA() {
        int offset = 1;
    }
    void methodB() {
        offset = 1;
    }
}
```

Here, within the `methodA()` method, the instance variable `offset` is hidden by the local variable `offset`, but within the `methodB()` method, `offset` still refers to the instance variable.

Hiding Through Inheritance

Name hiding through inheritance takes place when a class or struct re-declares names that were inherited from parent classes.

A derived class cannot declare an operator with the same signature as an operator in a base class so operators can never hide one another.

Summary

In this chapter you examined those features new and unique to C#. The good news, if you already knew some C and/or C++, is that C# has many logical and syntax similarities. In the next chapter you will explore how to use Visual Studio.NET's integrated development environment to enter, edit, save, compile, debug, and execute a simple C# application.

CHAPTER 3

Visual Studio.NET and C#

Chapter 1 detailed how programmers have gotten to the point of needing a new programming language. Today's applications combine the best of multi-tasking operating systems, visually interactive GUI interfaces, and the commercial revenues garnered by Internet access. Chapter 2, at a high level, enticed you with the newer features of C# and also presented a comforting *learning curve* as you recognized C#'s Visual Basic, Java or J++, and C/C++ ancestry.

The "Big Picture" Gets Bigger

This chapter is broken down into two main subdivisions. The later part of the chapter demonstrates how to use the Microsoft MDE (Microsoft Development Environment) to develop your first C# application. However, before jumping right into C# application development, you still need a little more background or "Big Picture" details. The first half of the chapter explains Microsoft .NET, NGWS (Next Generation Windows Services), IL (Intermediate Language), JIT compilers (Just-In-Time), CLR (Common Language Reference), Metadata, more on CLS (Common Language Specification), and the VES (Virtual Execution System) with its EE (Execution Engine).

The last half of the chapter demonstrates how to start the MDE, choose a solution type, compile, and execute a C# application. The chapter ends with an overview of the MDE's Integrated Debugger, what it is, why you would want to use it, and hands-on examples of the most frequently used Integrated Debugger commands.

Microsoft .NET

Microsoft envisions a new era of personal empowerment and business opportunities for consumers, businesses, and software developers through the use of its next generation of software and services called the *Microsoft .NET* platform. With the tremendous profit potential of Internet-based computing and communications, Microsoft .NET (pronounced dot-net) provides easier control over smart devices and Web sites through new software, a new language, C#, and additional Internet protocols and formats.

Microsoft .NET replaces the previous working title of Next Generation Windows Services (NGWS) and includes software for developers to build next-generation Internet experiences as well as power a new breed of smart Internet devices. Microsoft also plans to expand on the .NET platform, with new generations of the Microsoft Windows operating system, Windows DNA servers, Microsoft Office, the MSN network of Internet services, and the Visual Studio development environment.

Technically speaking, Microsoft .NET, or the older acronym NGWS, provides a runtime environment that manages the execution of code bundled with services that make programming easier. It may surprise you to discover C# *isn't* the only language to support NGWS. Microsoft's Visual Basic and C/C++ are both capable of NGWS output. The code that these compilers generate for NGWS runtime support is called *managed code*. Managed code provides several advantages.

First, managed code is cross-language enabled, meaning it supports the *CLS*, or *Cross-Language Specification*, and bundles in CLS exception handling. Managed code also automates garbage collection (memory management), enhances security through type safety, eliminates *.DLL* (Dynamic Link Library) nightmares through versioning, and provides a simplified model for component interaction.

.NET capabilities are only possible if a compiler outputs *metadata* along with the managed code. Compilers use metadata to describe the types in your program. This additional information is inserted into the executable file. Of course, the impressive goal behind .NET's runtime, with its cross-language features, is tight integration across multiple different programming languages. The best news is that it works! For example, with a few prerequisites (discussed in later chapters) you can actually derive a C# class from a Visual Basic object or vice-versa.

.NET solutions really benefit when deploying a managed application or component. Because managed applications contain metadata, the .NET runtime can use this information to ensure that your application has the specified versions of everything it needs. Indirectly, this ensures that your code will not break due to some missing dependency. .NET solutions also streamline the Windows Registry by inserting metadata into the same file where the code resides.

Intermediate Language

.NET-enabled compilers do not directly output native code, instead, they generate what is called *Intermediate Language* code or *IL*. Turning this architecture-independent IL code into native code requires the machine executing the program to have a machine-specific compiler, similar in design to the Java or J++ applet requirement. The metadata provided by the compiler details more about the program, including a definition for each type, and the signatures of each type's members. This type of information is exactly what libraries, Windows Registry entries, and COM objects use.

Just-in-Time Compilers

C# takes advantage of IL, metadata, and the resulting *PE* (*portable-executable*) file by using just-in-time, or JIT, compiling. The advantage of JIT is efficiency. Why compile every line of code when it is likely the end-user will only use a small subset of an entire algorithm's definitions? It is much more efficient to compile as you go.

JIT functions by taking each type used in a program and attaching a stub to each method of the type. When a method is called for the first time, the stub passes control to the JIT. The JIT compiler then compiles the IL into native code and changes the stub to point to the cached native code. From this point forward, the JIT compiler sits idle until a new type is referenced.

Common Language Reference

Traditionally, as with Java, the standard model of a *virtual object system* or *CLR* continually interprets a sequence of *bytecodes* that describe the intent of a Java applet or application. Each time the CLR encounters a bytecode, even if it has interpreted it many times before, there is a lengthy translation process. Even though various approaches exist for speeding up the design, this interpretation process accounts for significantly slower execution performance compared to equivalent compiled native code.

To improve this performance, JIT compilers interact with the CLR and compile appropriate IL sequences into an equivalent piece of native machine code. This process occurs at runtime rather than at compile time, as is traditionally the case with compiled languages such as C and C++. Rather than interpret the same IL repeatedly, the hardware can now execute the native code. This can allow quite dramatic performance gains in the execution speed. There is, however, a tradeoff. The time that the JIT compiler takes to compile the IL is added to the overall execution time. For example, when a method executes only once and does not contain any loops, the overall performance might be reduced when JIT compilation occurs.

The performance hit generated by JIT compilers does not, however, override the potential advantages over traditional code compilation. JIT compilers can efficiently target a specific architecture on which the program is actually running instead of a more general, most-likely-used architecture, which is the best that traditional approaches (such as targeting a generic x86 platform) can achieve.

CLR is capable of supporting a wide range of programming languages. Indirectly, this means it must include support for procedural as well as object-oriented languages. CLR also simplifies the confusion between often similar yet dissimilar types. Take, for example, a 16-bit C integer data type used instead in a C++ program. A similar situation exists between Visual Basic's 16-bit versions versus C++.

The compatibility worsens as you extend into more complex structures such as data base types, dates, and time formats. These inconsistencies overly complicate the creation and maintenance of distributed applications built upon multiple programming languages. Types created and debugged in one programming language are left unusable in another. Even the syntax and meanings for events, properties, and persistence vary from one environment to the next.

CLR eliminates these inconsistencies by providing two entities called values and objects. For a *value*, the type describes the storage representation as well as its legal operations. For *objects*, the type is explicitly stored in its representation with each object having a unique identity. These identities include:

1. What the objects are.
2. The relationships that exist between objects.
3. Property values for each object or relationship.

Metadata

The .NET runtime uses metadata to locate and load classes, to lay out instances of these classes in memory, to resolve method calls, to translate IL into native code, and to enforce type safety. Metadata is an automatic by-product of the code-to-IL C# compiler. This binary metadata goes into the PE in a standardized format unlike the C and C++ compilers.

Most importantly, the .NET runtime is capable of distinguishing between library versions using the same context since the libraries themselves are no longer referenced through the Windows Registry, but through the metadata bundled internally within the executable file itself.

Common Language Specification

Nested within the CLR is a set of specifications known as the *Common Language Specification* or *CLS*. CLS details a set of types used by CLR along with guidelines for making an application CLS-compliant. Any programmer following these guidelines can now generate class libraries that are portable across CLS-compliant languages.

By structuring and codifying class methods, properties, and events it is now possible to design a CLS-compliant component in C++, derive a VB subclass with enhanced functionality, and use the same definitions in a C# component. Some of the most frequently used CLS rules govern the use of primitive type definitions, array syntax, abstract types, properties, exceptions, events, and delegates.

The Virtual Execution System and the Execution Engine

The CLS provides an *Execution Engine* (*EE*) that creates the Virtual Execution System (VES) needed to implement the .NET runtime. This EE actually executes your C# program. The important components of the VES include:

- Conversion of IL into native code, including when a method is first invoked (JIT compilation). IL conversion is really a compilation.

- Insertion and management of security tests based on code identity, type safety, and administrative (trust management) controls.

- IL that can be easily and effectively targeted by a wide range of compilers including C++, Visual Basic, and C# compilers.

- Loading managed code (i.e., code written in accordance to VES requirements) including resolving names, performing class layout, and creating stubs needed to transition between managed and unmanaged code.

- Management of threads, contexts, and remoting.

- Profiling and debugging services, including mapping native code instruction addresses back to IL addresses and lengthening the lifetime of local variables.

- Services based on stack format: garbage collection of memory containing managed data; and initiation, propagation, and intercepting exceptions.

- Verification of the type safety of methods written in IL, as well as the integrity of the metadata describing those methods.

Using MDE to Create C# Applications

Microsoft's Visual Studio.NET comes bundled with four languages (Enterprise Edition): Visual Basic, Visual C/C++, Visual FoxPro, and their newest language, C#, as seen in Figure 3–1's File Manager window. (Note: The "Microsoft Visual Studio.NET\vc7" subdirectory hosts all three C flavors: C/C++/C#.) The Microsoft Development Environment, or MDE, uniformly advances all of the necessary program development features—from code creation, editing, compiling, to integrated debugging—across all four languages.

The advantage for a programmer using any one of the four languages is an immediate carry-over in product familiarity when learning and using all other Microsoft supported languages. The time savings gained by not having to relearn menu options, editor commands, solution management tools, and debugging features, can be significant. Not to mention the potential confusion avoided by conflicting or missing development environment capabilities.

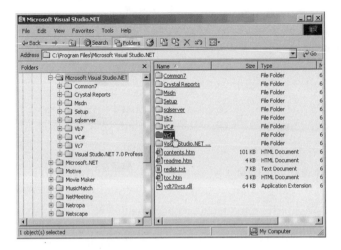

Figure 3–1   Microsoft Visual Studio.NET languages (Enterprise Edition).

If you have already used Microsoft Visual Studio 6.0 or 7.0 and are familiar with how to start, enter, edit, save, and compile a program, you can quickly scan the following sections of "Getting Started" for those minor initialization details necessary to create a C# program. However, if you are unfamiliar with the MDE, you need to read the following discussions carefully.

Getting Started

To launch the MDE, click on your Desktop's Programs ➤ Microsoft Visual Studio.NET 7.0 ➤ Microsoft Visual Studio.NET 7.0 menu option, seen in Figure 3–2.

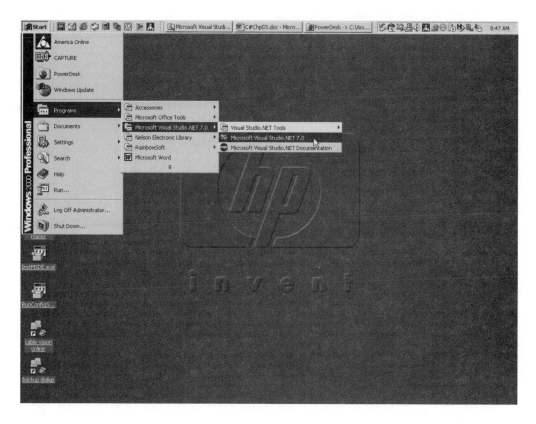

Figure 3–2   Launching Microsoft Visual Studio.NET 7.0 MDE.

If you are using Microsoft Visual Studio.NET 7.0 for the first time, allow the program additional time to initialize. Depending on the speed of your processor, this could take a few more seconds than you might expect; just be patient. When the program finally loads, you should see a window similar to Figure 3–3.

The initial, interactive "VS Home Page" provides instant access to the "Start" options. "What's New" discusses the new features to Visual Studio and all its components. The "Online Community" accesses a list of topic related Web-site hotlinks. "Headlines" targets specific developer-area interests. The live "Search Online" option may be, at times, your only recourse to solving cutting-edge technology queries. Finally, the "My Profile" section allows you to customize Visual Studio.

You should explore these tools as time and interest permit. For now, you are interested in the "Get started on a recent, exisiting, or new project" section; the default mode seen in Figure 3–3.

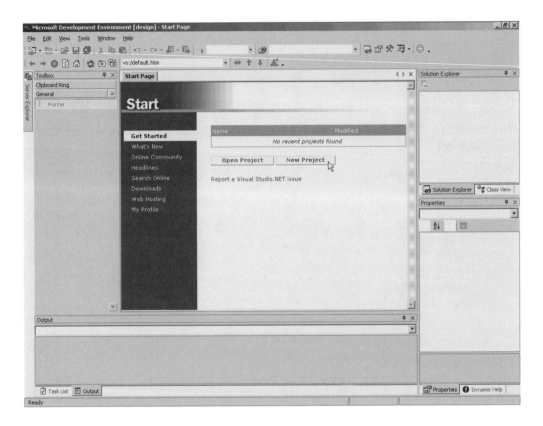

Figure 3–3   Initial Microsoft Development Environment window.

Create New Project

To begin developing a new C# program, click on the "New Project" link pointed to in Figure 3–3.

To open a previously saved program you have two options. You can click on the "Open Project" link, which launches a File Manager window for locating the program in question. The second method simply requires clicking on one of the listed previously saved programs, for example, the MyHelloWorld program used in this chapter.

Setting "New Project" Parameters

Figure 3–4 shows an example "New Project" dialog box. It is at this stage where you can easily, accidentally select the wrong type of project. Notice the default project type is Visual Basic! In fact, you will have to change all of the initial settings.

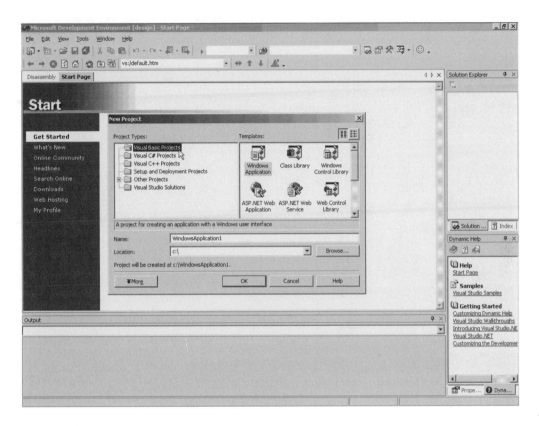

Figure 3–4   Setting "New Project" Parameters.

You begin fine-tuning your design by first selecting the "Visual C# Projects" folder in the "Project Types" pane (see Figure 3–5). Next, in order for you to stay focused on learning the core of the C# language, you will want to choose the "Win32 Project" from the "Templates" pane (pointed to in Figure 3–5).

If you are like most programmers, knowing which *default* folder any product uses for file storage can necessitate a frustrating search process. Take a moment to "Browse..." a location that is meaningful for your production environment and enter the path in the "Location" edit window. Finally, give the project a "Name." The program discussed in this chapter is titled "MyHelloWorld."

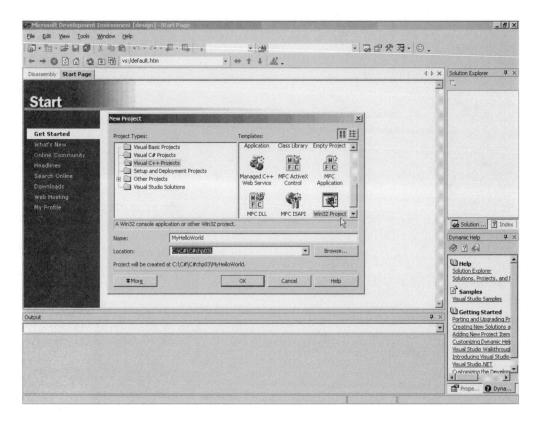

Figure 3–5   Updated: "Project Types," "Templates," "Location," and "Name."

When you have made all the necessary dialog box changes, click on the OK button.

`MyHelloWorld.cs` Application

Figure 3–6 shows the initial MDE configuration for a C# application. The `DebugVars.cs` (`cs` is the file extension for C# source files) is selected, by default, for Edit pane display.

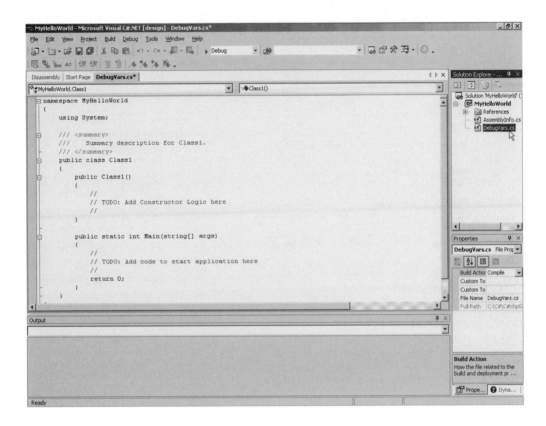

Figure 3–6   Initial MyHelloWorld window.

DebugVars.cs contains the *minimal code template* necessary to get a C# console application up and running. The minimal code template is reproduced below for easy viewing. Note that a few closing comments were added for clarity:

```
namespace MyHelloWorld
{
    using System;

    /// <summary>
    ///     Summary description for Class1.
    /// </summary>
    public class Class1
    {
        public Class1()
        {
```

```
        //
        // TODO: Add Constructor Logic here
        //
    }

    public static int Main(string[] args)
    {
        //
        // TODO: Add code to start application here
        //
        return 0;
    }
  } // END: public class Class1
} // END: namespace MyHelloWorld
```

From Chapter 2's discussion of namespaces you can see the application is defining namespace MyHelloWorld. This will encapsulate all of the identifiers declared within the French braces,

```
namespace MyHelloWorld
{
.
.
.
} // END: namespace MyHelloWorld
```

protecting them from any name collisions should you include MyHelloWorld in another application. The next statement within the minimal code template:

```
using System;
```

is similar to the C++ statement:

```
using namespace std;
```

Both statements pull in the minimal functionality necessary to get their respective programs up and running.

C++ programmers know that the using namespace std; provides access to the entire C++ standard set of library definitions. Selective C++ access is alternately accomplished with the scope resolution operator : : as in:

```
std::cout << "My Hello World!";
```

C# simplifies the syntax by treating the library routines more like class methods; for example, instead of using System; in a C# program, you could write:

```
System.Console.WriteLine("My Hello World!");
```

The C# minimal code template assumes you will be using more than one System object and defaults to the *using* statement form instead.

If you are already familiar with HTML (Hyper Text Markup Language) or XML (eXtensible Markup Language), the minimal code template's C# comment block will look quite familiar. Otherwise, the <summary> and </summary> components of the comment block need explaining.

```
/// <summary>
///     Summary description for Class1.
/// </summary>
```

Documentation is an extremely important part of software, especially with components that are to be used by other developers. However, if you are like most programmers, commenting code seems to fall under a category similar to flossing—You know you should do it, but somehow you never get around to it.

C# comes to your rescue with a built-in documentation feature automating the entire process (discussed in more detail in Chapter 11). C# uses XML tag pairs like <summary> and </summary> to automatically build your documentation right from within your code's comments!

The minimal code template continues with the following Class1 definition:

```
public class Class1
{
.
.
.
} // END: public class Class1
```

There are two methods nested within the formal Class1 definition. The first one:

```
    public Class1()
    {
        //
        // TODO: Add Constructor Logic here
        //
    }
```

is Class1's constructor. If you are new to object-oriented programming the term constructor needs some explanation.

The main difference between procedural programming languages and object-oriented languages is, well, objects. However, in the purest sense, objects do not give your program any more horsepower than an equivalent procedural solution. Instead, objects automate and/or encapsulate the same horsepower for the purposes of robustness.

In a procedural programming language you typically have two types of subroutines: functions and procedures. *Functions* differ from procedures in one sense: they *must* return *one* value, while *procedures* may return from none to many. Languages like C and C++ officially limit subroutine types to one—functions.

Now, a C++ program can have functions and *methods* (sometimes called *member functions* or *behaviors*). What's the difference, you ask? Simple. A C++ method is nothing more than a C++ function tied to a specific object—with some additional function header syntax!

And, what's an object? That's straightforward, too. Many programming languages have what is called a *record* (as in Pascal) or *structure* (as in Assembly Language, C, and C++). Structures are collections of mixed-data types (integer, float, string, etc.) all combined to logically represent some real-world scenario. Take, for example, all the mixed data types and individual variables needed to track an employee's payroll history. The variables within the structure are called *fields* (as in Pascal) or *members* (as in C and C++).

Procedural languages would individually define subroutines to input the employee's information, process any needed statistics, and output/store the calculated results. These external subroutines often reside in different source files other than their respective structure, data member declarations, making it difficult to physically (within source files) locate, share, and reuse the definitions.

Object-oriented languages solve this global chaos by simply moving the function definitions into the same scope as the structure's data members. C# and C++ use the same language keyword `class` to accomplish the packaging. When a stand-alone, external function physically moves its definition within the protective scope of a `class` definition the stand-alone subroutine's type-name of "function" changes to "*method*," sometimes referred to as *member function* or *behavior.*

Since the syntax for structures and the syntax for structure member references is so similar to the formal `class` construct, you can easily see why a class' data component is also called a *member* and the bundled horsepower (encapsulated function definitions) is called a *member function.* With "member function" being slightly verbose, most programmers use the shorter term—method.

Constructor

Object-oriented methods come in several flavors. The C# minimal code template defines one *Class1* method with the *same name* as the class itself, namely *Class1*. Most object-oriented languages use this syntax to flag a special category of class method called a *constructor.*

Going back to procedural language solutions, it is common for one of the subroutines in a procedural application to initialize variables and validate the quality of user input. That is the idea behind a constructor method. However, constructors go one step further in that they are automatically invoked.

Unlike constructors, class methods, like stand-alone procedural subroutines, must be called in the program's code. Even if a method were written to initialize the class, the user of your class definition would have to make certain to call the initialization routine. Here, a good design (remembering to write a code segment to initialize all variables) would fail from lack of proper use (forgetting to invoke it). Constructors, however, are automatically invoked whenever an instance of the formal class is created. Since the C# compiler has created a class by the name `Class1`, its matching constructor shares the same name.

The second method defined within `Class1` is `Main`:

```
public static int Main(string[] args)
{
    //
    // TODO: Add code to start application here
    //
    return 0;
}
```

C#, C, and C++ are all examples of programming languages that are case-sensitive. *Case-sensitivity* means that the two identifiers *Size* and *SIZE* are unique. If you are new to case-sensitive languages, they can be a pain-in-the-neck. You always have to marshal your every keystroke and the SHIFT key.

The first place a C/C++ programmer could run into trouble using C# is the case for the main method. C/C++ programmers spell the method `main()` unlike C# which cases the method as `Main()`.

`Main()` is where C# program execution begins and should end. `Main()` must be defined within a class. There can be only one class defined with this signature, unless you advise the compiler which `Main()` method it should use.

Understanding public, static, Instantiation, and Instances

The C# minimal code template makes multiple use of the keyword `public` and special use of the keyword `static` for the `Main()` method. Going back to the earlier analogy between procedural and object-oriented programming languages, procedural language subroutines were either *global* or *nested* (as in Pascal). C#, C, and C++ programmers would define the same scope as *external* or *internal*.

Object-oriented class methods have a similar capability. Class methods (and/or data members) marked `public` would be most closely related to a procedural language's global scope. Classes use two permutations on nested method definitions called `private` or `protected`. These translate most closely to a procedural language's nested subroutines. C# requires the `public` definition for the method `Main()` in order to make it accessible outside the formal class' members.

The use of the keyword `static` in front of `Main()`'s formal definition tells the compiler that the method is usable without instantiating an instance of the class itself. In a procedural language, when you syntactically allocate memory for a specific data type, you are said to be "declaring a variable." Object-oriented terminology names the equivalent process for object-memory allocation with the term *instantiation*.

Procedural programmers then go on to talk about the variable throughout the code while object-oriented programmers talk about the *instance*. Normally, a class's members (data and/or method) cannot be accessed until the formal class definition is instantiated, creating an accessible instance. The `static` keyword overrides this requirement for class members by allocating memory for the member before the program begins execution, thereby making it accessible *without* an instantiation.

The remaining syntax for `Main()`:

```
public static int Main(string[] args)
```

defines the method's integer return type, `int`, and one formal argument, `args`. `args` is very similar to C and C++'s `char * argv[]` or, alternately, `char** argv` argument to `main()` (C/C++'s counterpart). Both C#'s `args` and C/C++'s `argv` allow the operating system to pass command-line arguments directly to the application whenever it is launched. However, unlike the C/C++ counterpart, C#'s `args` does not contain the application's path in an array entry. Only the parameters are contained in this array.

Technically, `Main()` could return either an integer, `int`, or nothing, `void`. These two forms look like:

```
public static int Main(string[] args)
public static void Main(string[] args)
```

While the Visual Studio C# minimal code template opts for the more general `int` version, this can be misleading. Why? Because no one cares. For the default `int` return type to be meaningful, how the C# application terminates, as in successfully or with a fatal error, would have to be monitored by some supervisory task. This task would examine the returned integer and make some decision as to whether the C# application could or should be restarted, and if so, possibly what to do to prevent another failure. Your initial C# programs won't return a value monitored by any task. Properly written source code never misleads another programmer; `void` works better with the lie detector. It also does away with the required `return 0;` statement found at the end of `Main()`'s formal definition.

Of course, before the minimal code template can do anything, you need to insert executable C# code statements. Modify the template by going into the `Main()` method and add the statement:

```
Console.WriteLine("My Hello World");
```

`Main()` should now look like:

```
public static int Main(string[] args)
        {
            //
            // TODO: Add code to start application here
            //
            Console.WriteLine("My Hello World");
            return 0;
        }
```

The Interactive MDE

If you are new to the Microsoft Visual Studio Development Environment, you are in for a few pleasant surprises. Don't let the plethora of menu options, views, panes, and tabbed dialog boxes intimidate you.

As you begin entering the C# output statement to the minimal code template, you will see the interactive portion of the MDE activate. No sooner do you type the period member operator . after the object name `Console`. than a drop-down list magically appears (see Figure 3–7).

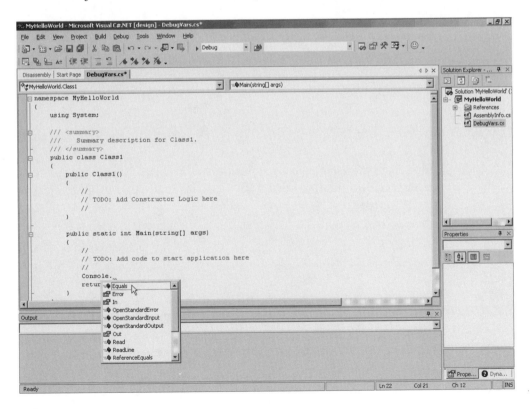

Figure 3–7   Automated MDE displaying the Console method's drop-down list.

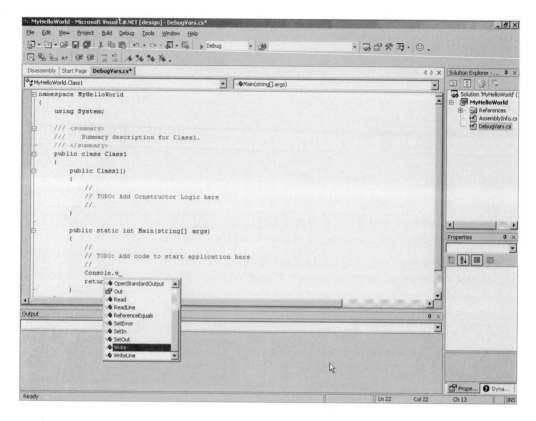

Figure 3–8   Drop-down list showing Console methods beginning with "W."

This list enumerates the valid methods for the `Console` object. Next, when you begin typing the `w` in `WriteLine`, the drop-down lists contents auto-cycle to those methods beginning with a "W" (see Figure 3–8).

To the right edge of the highlighted *Write* method, you'll notice a small text box (see Figure 3–9).

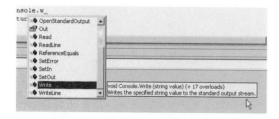

Figure 3–9   Expanded *Write* method description.

The expanded text box details the selected method's prototype. If the method is overloaded, there is a count for the number of permutations. This is followed by an English-like description of what the method actually does, along with any default assumptions.

Of course, for the `MyHelloWorld` program, you need the `WriteLine` method immediately below `Write`.

You can select the method one of two ways. First, you could hit the down-arrow and press Enter, or click on the *WriteLine* listing. However, if you just keep typing: `riteL`, the drop-down list's contents will automatically find the matching method (see Figure 3–10).

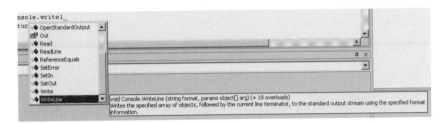

Figure 3–10   *WriteLine* method description.

Once again, the text box highlights the method's prototype, including the return type and any formal arguments. After enumerating the number of overloaded permutations, the English-like description summarizes the method's use and defaults.

You can have the MDE automatically complete `WriteL` by pressing the Enter key on the highlighted method. By the way, the expanded text box automatically disappears after a few seconds of viewing. At this point, you should have added,

```
Console.WriteLine
```

to the minimal code template. At this point, as you begin typing the opening parenthesis `(`, the MDE automatically responds with a text box displaying the syntax for the first of 18 overloaded `WriteLine` methods (see Figure 3–11).

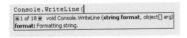

Figure 3–11   MDE displaying the first of 18 overloaded *WriteLine* methods.

You can easily cycle through any of the 18 prototypes with a simple click on either the up or down buttons in the text box window; for example, clicking on the down button once shows the second overloaded `WriteLine` method's syntax (see Figure 3–12).

Figure 3–12   Selecting alternate overloaded *WriteLine* method prototypes.

Having this type of information instantaneously and automatically available is price-less, especially when trying to master a new language. We can all thank Microsoft for making this new language development environment programmer-friendly.

The next automated MDE help feature reveals itself as you complete the string argument to WriteLine. As you place the closing quote mark on the string:

```
Console.WriteLine("My Hello World"
```

the MDE **bolds** the string to flag its completion (see Figure 3–13). As a programmer, have you ever had problems matching pairs of parentheses? Although it may be difficult to detect in a photo-reproduced screen shot image, Figure 3–14 shows how the MDE **bolds** matching parenthesis in an attempt to visually aid their pairing.

```
//
Console.WriteLine("My Hello World"
return 0;
```

Figure 3–13   The MDE auto-bolding a completed string definition.

```
//
Console.WriteLine("My Hello World")
return 0;
```

Figure 3–14   The MDE bolding paired parentheses.

As soon as you complete the code statement with the required semicolon, the bolding disappears. At this point you are ready to compile the program.

Compiling Your First C# Program

To compile a C# application you first click on the Build main menu item, seen in Figure 3–15.

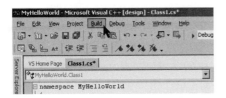

Figure 3–15   Choosing the Build main menu item.

After clicking on the Build main menu item, you need to click on the Build at the top of the drop-down list (see Figure 3–16). If you are wondering just what the difference is between the Build and Rebuild submenu items, well, it's subtle, yet potentially dangerous.

Build versus Rebuild

When any application contains multiple source files possibly containing multiple class definitions created by other team programmers on your large project, file synchronization becomes a serious focal point for code misuse. A Project, Workspace, or Solution File helps collect and organize these files. However, when it comes to compiling all the source files in a Project, Workspace, or Solution, the MDE makes an effort to optimize the entire process. It does this by compiling and relinking *updated* source files only.

Figure 3–16   Choosing the Build submenu item.

This optimization feature can't get you into trouble if you haven't compiled any of the source files, but can get you into serious trouble after you have created an executable version. With an existing executable file, future Builds will cause the MDE to compare the date on the existing executable file against the date stamp on all of the Project, Workspace, or Solution file listings. The MDE will then only import the source files with *newer* date stamps than the executable, compile them, then make any necessary link adjustments. So why is this a problem?

In a real-world corporate environment where system maintenance personnel are typically overstretched, or worse, eliminated due to budget cuts, a critical component of many-site PCs gets neglected, namely, each PC's system clock. Here's the nightmare scenario. Each team member begins their C# class solution descriptions on corporate machines with up-to-date system clocks. The first Build flies through with colors, even subsequent Builds on the same machines cause the resulting executable to reflect all code updates.

However, later that day, or the next, one of the programmers moves to another site location, taps into one of the C# source files over the company's Intranet, saves it and... you guessed it, using an improperly maintained PC with an out-of-date setting, unknowingly stamps the updated source code with an out-of-date stamp! The next day, everybody is informed of the updated code's characteristics and everyone incorporates the new design's philosophies, only to find that the executable behaves just like it did the day before.

Now the MDE provides a simple solution to the nightmare. Instead of choosing the Build submenu item, choose Rebuild. Unlike Build which checks the dates between source and executable files, Rebuild ignores this optimization phase, brute-forcing a recompile and link and all listed Project, Workspace, or Solution files.

After choosing either Build or Rebuild, you should see a window similar to Figure 3–17. If not, cycle back, check your code, and execute a second Build or Rebuild.

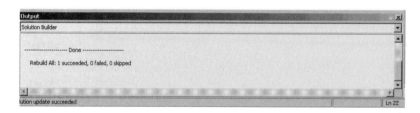

Figure 3–17   Successful MyHelloWorld Build.

Executing a C# Program

To execute a C# program, first click on the Debug main menu item, seen in Figure 3–18.

Figure 3–18   Selecting the Debug main menu item to begin program execution.

There are actually quite a few ways to execute a C# program, as seen in Figure 3–19. The easiest approach would be to click on *Start Without Debugging*. By the way, if you have forgotten to first execute a Build or Rebuild, attempting to execute your program will first automatically invoke a Build.

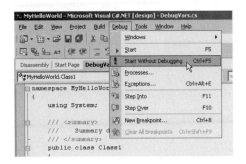

Figure 3–19   Debug main menu item drop-down list.

Two quick and easy hot-key combinations to remember are the Ctrl + F5 counterpart to *Start Without Debugging* and just F5 to begin program execution *with* debugging.

Output from `MyHelloWorld.cs`

Using whichever approach you prefer, mouse/menu or hot-key, execute the `MyHello-World.cs` program. You should see a window similar to Figure 3–20. When you execute a C# application, the MDE automatically switches screen focus to the Output window (the large black window superimposed on the MDE window).

The `MyHelloWorld.cs` program outputs the *My Hello World* statement seen in the Output window. The MDE, not anything in the C# source file, outputs the *Press any key to continue* prompt. This automatic feature prevents the Output window from snapping shut right before your eyes, leaving you dazed as to whether your program *did* or *did not* execute properly.

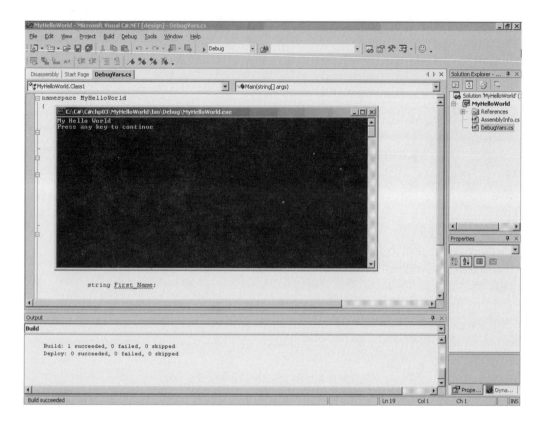

Figure 3–20   Execution of `MyHelloWorld.cs`.

Once you are satisfied with the output from your program, pressing any key will auto-matically terminate the execution of any C# application, close the Output window, and return you to the MDE.

Using the Integrated Debugger

If you have never used a stand-alone debugger, or better yet, an integrated debugger, you are in for quite a surprise. Debuggers provide a suite of tools enabling efficient code analysis. While entire books have been written on debuggers alone, the good news is that you do not need to know *all* the features of a debugger to debug an algorithm.

There are basically two major features to a debugger. First, they allow you to execute your program, line-by-line, at your pace, not full-speed. In addition to this slow execution pace, debuggers simultaneously display the contents of your variables. The idea being, as you execute each statement in your program you view the effect on all related variables, immediately detecting incorrect actions.

Other features of a debugger are advanced permutations on the two just mentioned. Some of these are immediately accessible from the Debug main menu drop-down list seen in Figure 3–19.

Starting the Integrated Debugger

You can start the MDE's integrated debugger by first clicking on the Debug main menu item, and then selecting one of three frequently used options:

- Start
- Step Into
- Step Over

The Step Over option is the easiest to understand. You will always know you are in the integrated debugger because a small (usually yellow) arrow shows up on the extreme left edge of your Edit pane (see Figure 3–21).

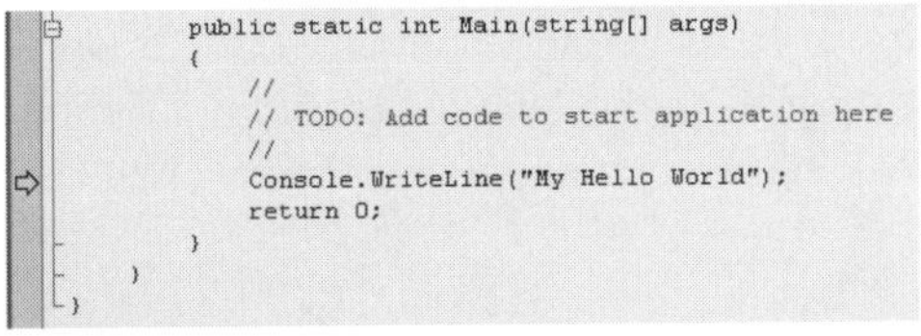

```
    public static int Main(string[] args)
    {
        //
        // TODO: Add code to start application here
        //
        Console.WriteLine("My Hello World");
        return 0;
    }
}
```

Figure 3–21   Viewing the integrated debugger's next-line-to-execute pointer.

The arrow actually points to the *next-line-to-execute* statement. Meaning, the arrow is *not* pointing to the line it *just* executed, but to the statement it will execute the *next* time you single-step the integrated debugger.

Using Step Over

The Step Over option executes the current statement being pointed to, stopping at whatever statement follows it. Actually, the Step Into option does the same thing. So why are there two options? The only place Step Over and Step Into differ in functionality is when the next-line-to-execute arrow is pointing to a statement containing a subroutine call (function or class method).

Using Step Into

Whenever you want to debug *into* a subroutine, you choose the logically named Step Into option. However, if you know the subroutine being invoked is OK, then why waste your time debugging it? So, whenever the integrated debugger is about to execute a subroutine you know is fine, choose the logically named Step Over option.

Using Start with Breakpoints

The Start option is actually not a single-step integrated debugger option. Start is really a full-speed-ahead run. Imagine that you have a 500-line source file, three quarters of which are from a previously debugged algorithm. Single-stepping through three to four hundred lines you know are clean is inefficient. Under these circumstances what you really want the debugger to do is full-speed execute the clean code, and stop at the recently added statements.

If you take a quick glance back to Figure 3–19, you'll notice that the Debug main menu drop-down list contains another option—*New Breakpoint...* The Start and New Breakpoint options have a symbiotic relationship. When you set a breakpoint in your source code, what you are telling the integrated debugger is that you want it to stop on that line. To get to the breakpoint *without* single-stepping (remember the idea was to avoid unnecessary single-steps for clean code), click on Start. While Start is a full-speed execution, it does recognize set breakpoints and stops execution at that point.

To set a breakpoint, first click on the Debug main menu item, then from the drop-down list (Figure 3–19), choose the *New Breakpoint...* option. This opens up a dialog box similar to Figure 3–21 (File tab selected).

Since the `MyHelloWorld` program contains only one code statement, there is only one line *22* available for use. Figure 3–22 shows this entry in the *Line:* edit window. To find out the line number for any statement, simply click on the statement and then look at the lower right edge of the MDE status window, seen in Figure 3–23.

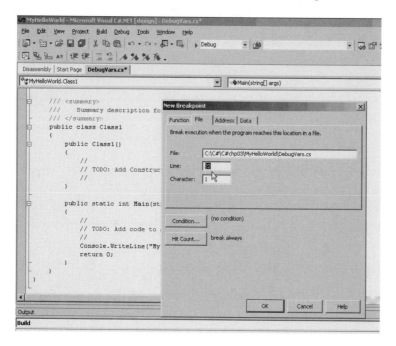

Figure 3–22   Setting the New Breakpoint Line number.

Figure 3–23   MDE Status window displaying selected statements line or Ln number.

After you type in the line number, simply click on the OK button. If you look closely at the left edge of the Edit window you'll see a (usually red) stop sign icon (see Figure 3–24) indicating the location of the breakpoint.

```
//
// TODO: Add code to start application here
//
Console.WriteLine("My Hello World");
return 0;
}
```

Figure 3–24   Integrated debugger flagging breakpoint with stop sign icon.

You are now ready to full speed execute the algorithm with Start, stopping on this statement.

Removing Set Breakpoints

Removing a breakpoint is as simple as setting one. Simply click on the Debug main menu item, and then from the drop-down list choose the now ungrayed, or active *Clear All Breakpoints* option (see Figure 3–25).

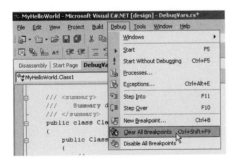

Figure 3–25   Using the Clear All Breakpoints option.

Integrated Debugger Option Shortcuts

Once you familiarize yourself with the most frequently used integrated debugger options, you would probably like to know that there are faster ways to activate them besides clicking on multiple menu/submenu options.

Using Hot-Key Combinations

The first approach involves hot-keys. The following list localizes these commands for easy reference.

Start	F5
Start Without Debugging	Ctrl + F5
Step Over	F10
Step Into	F11
New Breakpoint…	Ctrl + F10, then N
Clear All Breakpoints	Ctrl + Shift + F9
Restart the Debugger (from current location)	Ctrl + Shift + F5
Stop the Debugger	Shift + F5

Using Menus

Once you have launched the integrated debugger you'll notice that the Debug main menu item's drop-down list expands its set of options (see Figure 3–26).

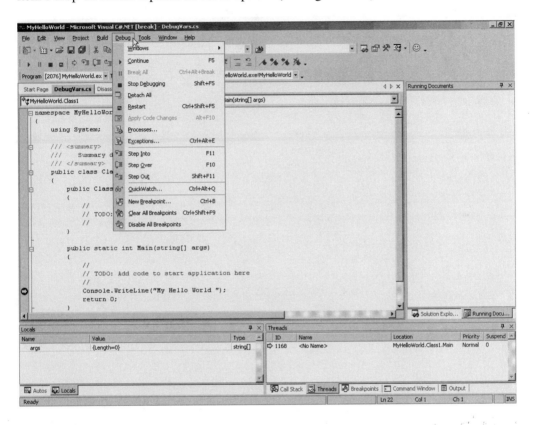

Figure 3–26   Debug drop-down list options available while debugging.

A similar options list appears automatically if you simply right-click your mouse, anywhere within the Edit window, as seen in Figure 3–27.

The contents displayed within the local menu are context-sensitive. Figure 3–27 displays the options available when right-clicking on a statement already set as a breakpoint. Notice the *Remove Breakpoint* option. With a little practice you will probably opt to efficiently interact with the integrated debugger via hot-key and local menu options.

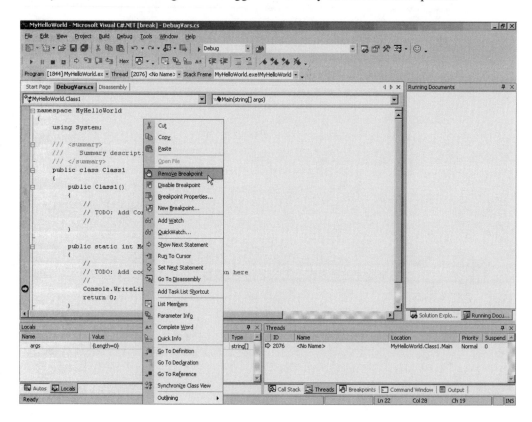

Figure 3–27   Integrated debugger's local menu (right-click accessible).

Viewing Variable's Contents

Single-stepping an algorithm would be meaningless if you could not inspect the results of the statement just executed. Since the `MyHelloWorld` program performed no internal calculations, there is little need to debug the application. To give you a quick overview of how you watch variables respond to the interactive single-step-mode, you will need to create (or modify) a new source file. Modify your `MyHelloWorld.cs Main()` with the **bolded** statements in the following listing:

```
namespace DebugVars
{
    using System;

    /// <summary>
    ///     Summary description for Class1.
    /// </summary>
    public class Class1
    {
        public Class1()
        {
            //
            // TODO: Add Constructor Logic here
            //
        }

        public static int Main(string[] args)
        {
            //
            // TODO: Add code to start application here
            //

string First_Name;

Console.Write("\nEnter a First Name: ");
First_Name = Console.ReadLine();

            return 0;
        }
    }
}
```

Save the application under `DebugVars.cs`. Start the integrated debugger—the quickest way is to press either F10 or F11. If you haven't executed a Build, pressing F10 or F11 will do that first. Once again, you'll see the debug arrow show up in your Edit window (see Figure 3–28).

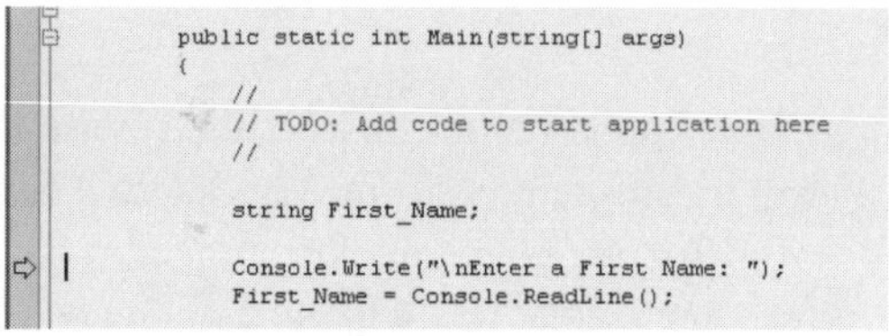

```
        public static int Main(string[] args)
        {
            //
            // TODO: Add code to start application here
            //

            string First_Name;

            Console.Write("\nEnter a First Name: ");
            First_Name = Console.ReadLine();
```

Figure 3–28   Debugging *First_Name.*

Notice the integrated debugger skips over all formal class definitions and stops on the first executable statement, `Console.Write(...)`;. You are now ready to Step Over, either with the Debug main menu option or by pressing F10. Whichever approach you used to Step Over, you should now see a screen similar to Figure 3–29.

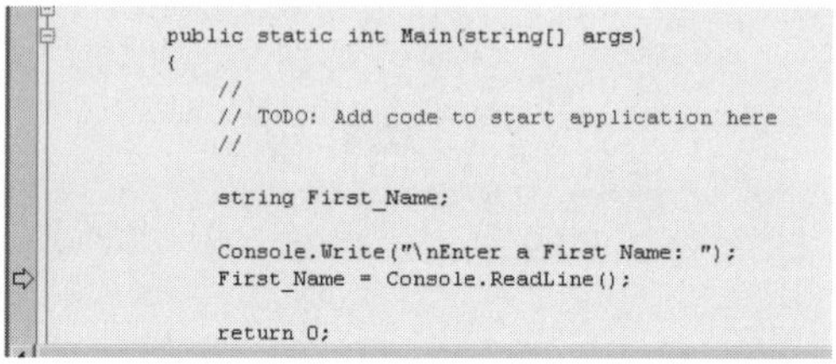

```
        public static int Main(string[] args)
        {
            //
            // TODO: Add code to start application here
            //

            string First_Name;

            Console.Write("\nEnter a First Name: ");
            First_Name = Console.ReadLine();

            return 0;
```

Figure 3–29   Single-stepping the *Console.Write(...);* statement.

From Figure 3–29 it looks like nothing happened except for the debugger's trace arrow moving down one line. The MDE's integrated debugger only auto-switches to the Output window to trace input statements (or when the program terminates, as in the case of the `MyHelloWorld.cs` program).

If you want to switch to the Output window manually, there's, well, you guessed it, a hot-key combination that does the job—Alt + Tab. Try it now. You should see a screen that looks similar to Figure 3–30.

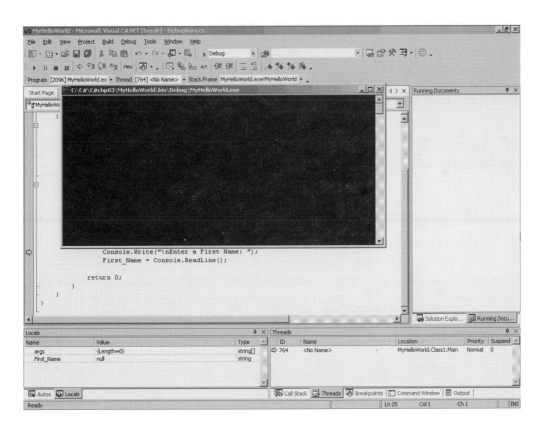

Figure 3–30   Using Alt + Tab to manually switch to Output window.

To switch back to the MDE manually, just press Alt + Tab a second time. You will need to do that now since the integrated debugger is not yet tracing an input statement.

You are now ready (assuming you switched back to the MDE with the second Alt + Tab) to Trace Over the `First_Name = Console.ReadLine();` statement pointed to by the Trace arrow in Figure 3–30. Once again, one quick press of F10 will accomplish the action. This time the MDE will once again automatically switch to the Output window and stop there while you respond to the prompt.

Figure 3–31 shows the name *Jean* being entered in the Output window. As soon as you press the Enter key, you will need to do a manual switch back to the MDE with another Alt + Tab key combination.

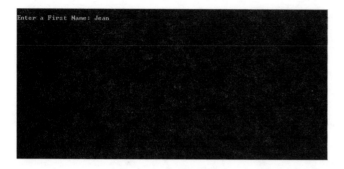

Figure 3–31   Entering a *First_Name* of Jean.

In the lower left corner of the MDE's main window, you'll notice that the *Autos* window displays the contents of `First_Name`, `"Jean"` just entered (see Figure 3–32). The *Autos* window also displays `First_Name`'s Type of `string`.

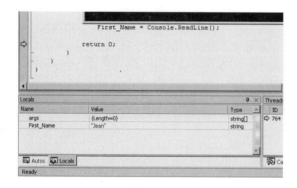

Figure 3–32   Viewing the Autos and Locals window contents.

The integrated debugger provides three ways to view your program's variables. The first, called *Autos,* is where the integrated debugger *auto*matically displays those variables "in scope." These context-sensitive variable lists are dynamic and continually update as you move in and out of code segments.

The *Locals* Tab, seen at the bottom of the MDE's main window (see Figure 3–32), is where you can view variables in local scope (internal to a subroutine).

Both Tab views list variables by name, their current internal contents, and their type. When used interactively with the single-step modes, this symbiotic relationship instantaneously reports any code statement producing unacceptable results. Now that you know how to enter, build, execute, and debug a C# application using the Microsoft Visual Studio Development Environment, you are ready to learn the C# language.

Summary

In this chapter you learned everything necessary to enter, edit, save, build, execute, and debug a C# console application. Chapter 4 delves into the details of C#'s keywords, data types, and identifiers. C# has enough similar to C and C++ to catch the unwary C# programmer, so make certain you read all of Chapter 4 to avoid bugs generated when rolling your understanding over from C/C++ to C#!

Important Data, Identifiers, and Keywords

As many recent earthquakes have proven, a building may look well constructed to the naked eye and yet, under severe tests, crumble to the ground. The same holds true for an algorithm; it too can be well constructed, logically clean, syntactically correct, and yet, under severe tests, instantly break apart. Why? Often times the answer lies in incorrect data type selection. Oh, sure, when numeric or text input falls within "reasonable" ranges, the algorithm performs flawlessly; however, push the code to calculate the spacecraft trajectory to Mars and, well, oops, you misfire a five billion dollar project!

C# Fundamentals

Though tedious to wade through, this chapter presents the nuts 'n bolts of C#'s data types. With C# being designed as a powerful programming language intended for enterprise application development and an evolution of C and C++, it uses many C++ features in the areas of statements, expressions, and operators. C# also introduces several major improvements and innovations in areas such as type safety, versioning, events, and garbage collection—all designed to prevent miscalculations and get the spacecraft to Mars, in time, and on budget.

In addition, C# provides access to the common API styles: .NET, COM, Automation, and C-style APIs. C#'s unsafe mode, when needed, allows you to use pointers to manipulate memory that is not under the control of the garbage collector. C# provides for durable system-level components by virtue of the following features:

- Code integrity via garbage collection and type safety
- COM/platform support for existing code integration

- Security through intrinsic code trust mechanisms
- Support for extensible metadata concepts

Add to this impressive list C#'s ability to easily integrate with other languages and multiple architectures, and legacy data through the use of:

- COM+ 1.0 and .NET services through library-based access
- Versionability to provide ease of administration and deployment
- XML support for Web-based component interaction

Keywords

A *keyword*, sometimes referred to as a *verb*, is a sequence of characters that is reserved, and cannot be used as an identifier except when prefaced by the @ character. Keywords, or verbs, have special meanings to the compiler. For example, @abstract is a legal identifier but abstract is not because it is a keyword. Table 4–1 lists all of C#'s keywords.

Table 4–1   C# Keywords

abstract	enum	long	stackalloc
as	event	namespace	static
base	explicit	new	string
bool	extern	null	struct
break	false	object	switch
byte	finally	operator	this
case	fixed	out	throw
catch	float	override	true
char	for	params	try
checked	foreach	private	typeof
class	goto	protected	uint
const	if	public	ulong
continue	implicit	readonly	unchecked
decimal	in	ref	unsafe
default	int	return	ushort

Table 4–1   C# Keywords *(Continued)*

delegate	interface	sbyte	using
do	internal	sealed	virtual
double	is	short	void
else	lock	sizeof	while

Looking closely at Table 4–1 you will notice many of C#'s keywords have direct C/C++ counterparts. These matching verbs not only have the same keyword names but perform the same function in all three flavors of C/#/++.

Preprocessor Directives

C and C++ have a category of statements known as preprocessor directives. So too does C#. All three languages use the same syntax which requires the use of a pound sign (#) placed immediately before the specific directive.

NOTE

Unlike C and C++ preprocessor directives, you cannot use C#'s preprocessor directives to create macros. All preprocessor directives must appear on their own instruction line.

In C/C++, which has a genuine two-pass compile sequence, preprocessor directives allow you to rewrite the source code, making it architecture- and application-specific *before* it is compiled at pass two. C# does *not* have a true two-pass compile phase, however, C# preprocessor directives *are* treated similarly in their capability to their C/C++ counterparts. This section discusses the C# language's preprocessor directives.

#if

You use the #if preprocessor for conditional testing of a symbol, sometimes called a label or identifier, to see if it has been previously defined. If the symbol exists, the compiler evaluates all the code between the #if and the next directive. #if evaluates to either true or false. The syntax takes this form:

```
#if symbol [operator symbol]...
```

symbol—represents the label you want to test. You can also use true and false. symbol can be prefaced with the negation operator. For example, !true will evaluate to false.

The *operator*—the following operators are legal prefixes to the specified `symbol` and evaluate multiple symbols:

```
==  (equality)
!=  (inequality)
&&  (and)
||  (or)
```

Groups of symbols and operators are possible with the addition of parentheses to control operator precedence levels and parsing sequencing. You typically combine #if with other preprocessor directives like #define, #undef, #else, #elif, and #endif, to include or exclude code segments based on the pre-existence of one or more symbols.

When used properly, this allows you to permanently insert debug code that switch hits. Here is a small portion of code:

```
#define DEBUGON
any statement(s) following:
#if DEBUGON
  .
  .
  .
#endif   // ALL conditional preprocessor
         // directives MUST end with #endif!
```

Here, a simple #define, is activated and included in the executable file. Commenting out the #define statement switches off all debug code, omitting the statements from the executable yet leaving the built-in capability available without any major code rewrites. This can be most useful when compiling code for a debug build or when compiling for a specific configuration.

NOTE

A conditional preprocessor statement, beginning with an #if *directive,* must be *explicitly terminated with a matching* #endif *directive!*

#else

The #else preprocessor directive is often a complementary component to the conditional #if, allowing you to create compound conditions, such that, if none of the expressions in the preceding #if or #elif directives evaluate to `true`, the compiler will evaluate all code between #else and the subsequent #endif. The straightforward syntax takes this form:

```
#else
```

NOTE

The #endif *must be the next preprocessor directive after* #else!

#elif

While #else logically operates as a drop-through for a failed #if, #elif lets you create a compound conditional directive. The #elif expression is evaluated if neither the proceeding #if or any proceeding #elif directives evaluate to true. If an #elif expression evaluates to true, the compiler evaluates all the code between the #elif and the next directive.

```
#elif symbol [operator symbol]...
```

symbol—the label you want to test. You can also use true and false or prefix the label with the negation operator. For example, !false will evaluate to true.

operator—the following operators are legal prefixes to the specified symbol and evaluate multiple symbols:

```
== (equality)
!= (inequality)
&& (and)
|| (or)
```

Groups of symbols and operators are possible with the addition of parentheses to control operator precedence levels and parsing sequencing. You typically combine #if with other preprocessor directives like #define, #undef, #else, #elif, and #endif to include or exclude code segments based on the preexistence of one or more symbols.

#elif is a more efficient alternative to:

```
#else
#if
```

This form does not require the matching #endif.

#endif

The #endif preprocessor directive is included to flag the end of a conditional directive, which began with the #if directive.

```
#endif
```

Each #if directive requires a corresponding #endif.

#define

Use the #define preprocessor directive to insert a label into the symbol table. The syntax takes this form:

```
          ʌ
#define symbol
```

Here, symbol is the label being defined.

Labels typically define conditions for compilation. You can test for the label with either #if or #elif or use the C# conditional attribute to perform conditional compilation.

Unlike C or C++, C#'s #define statement only allows you to insert a label into the symbol table, but you cannot assign a value to a symbol. Again, unlike C or C++, which allow #define preprocessor directives to appear where needed, the C# #define directive *must* appear in a file before you use any instructions that are not also directives.

A label you #define will not conflict with a variable of the same name. That is, a variable name should not be passed to a preprocessor directive and a symbol can only be evaluated by a preprocessor directive.

The scope of a label being inserted into the symbol table is the file in which it is defined. You can undefine a symbol with #undef.

#undef

The #undef preprocessor directive is the syntactical and logical inverse of #define, allowing you to undefine a label. The syntax takes the following form:

#undef symbol

Here, symbol is the name of the symbol you want to undefine.

The #undef directive must appear in the file before you use any statements, not preprocessor directives.

#warning

Use the #warning preprocessor directive to generate a level one warning from a specific location in your code. The syntax takes the following form:

#warning literal

Here, literal is the string representing the warning you want to appear in the compiler's output.

A common use of #warning is in a conditional directive. It is also possible to generate a user-defined error with #error.

Consider this portion of code:

```
#define DEBUGON
 .
 .
 .
#if DEBUGON
   #warning DEBUGON is defined
#endif
```

It is also possible to generate a user-defined error with `#error`.

#error

The `#error` preprocessor directive generates error messages from a specific location in your code. The syntax takes the following form:

#error *literal*

Here, `literal` is the string representing the error message you want to appear in the compiler's output. For example, in the following code segment:

```
#define DEBUGON
 .
 .
 .
#if DEBUGON
   #error DEBUGON is defined
#endif
```

the error message follows the `#error` directive.

#line

You can improve upon the quality of output `#warning` or `#error` message diagnostics with a simple use of the `#line` preprocessor directive. `#line` instructs the compiler to include line numbers and, optionally, the offending source file's name. The syntax takes the following form:

```
#line number "sourceFile"
```

Here, `number` is the number you want to specify for a line in a source code file and `"sourceFile"` is the owning code file's name. Consider the following portion of code:

```
#line 31 "myClass.sc"
```

By default, the actual `sourceFile` name is the source code file used.

NOTE

The file name must be in double quotes.

#region

The `#region` preprocessor directive is used in conjunction with the outlining feature of Visual Studio's Code editor. `#region` allows you to define a code segment you can expand or collapse. The syntax looks like:

```
#region regionName
```

Here, `regionName` is the label you want to see output in the Visual Studio Code Editor.

NOTE

A `#region` block must be terminated with a `#endregion` directive. A `#region` block cannot overlap an `#if` block.

```
#region someClass definition
public class someClass {
   public static void Main() {
   }
}
#endregion
```

The `#region` preprocessor directive may appear within an `#if` block, and an `#if` block may be nested within a `#region` block.

#endregion

Similar to all conditional preprocessor directives needing a matching `#endif` statement, all `#region` preprocessor directives must have a closing `#endregion` to signal the end of a `#region` block. The syntax takes the following form:

```
#endregion
```

While the compiler does not have a separate preprocessor, the directives described in this section are processed as if there was one; these directives are used to aid in conditional compilation.

Operators

Arithmetic expressions are made up of *operands* and *operators*. Examples of operators include +, -, *, /, and sizeof(). Operators fall into three broad catagories:

- Binary—takes two operands (in the form x + y).
- Ternary—C# has only one ternary operator, the conditional operator (? :). The ternary operator takes three operands and uses infix notation (in the form expression ? x : y).
- Unary—takes one operand and uses either prefix notation (in the form −x) or postfix notation (in the form x++).

The order of evaluation of operators in an expression is determined by the precedence and associativity of the operators. Operator operands can be expressions, literals, local variables, and member data. Operator overloading, permissible with some operators, permits user-defined operator implementations. These implementations are written for cases where the operand(s) are of a user-defined class or struct type.

C# Operator Categories

Table 4–2 lists C# operators by category. As mentioned, some of these operators can be overloaded.

Table 4–2   C# Operators

Operator Category	Operators
Arithmetic	+ - * /
Assignment, compound assignment	= += -= *= /= %= &= |= ^= <<= >>=
Cast	( )
Conditional	? :
Delegate concatenation and removal	+ -
Increment, decrement	++ —
Indexing	[]
Indirection and address	* -> [] &
Logical (bitwise and boolean)	true false & | ^ ! ~ && ||
Member access	.

Table 4–2   C# Operators *(Continued)*

Operator Category	Operators
Object creation	`new`
Overflow exception control	Can be `checked` or `unchecked`
Relational	`== != < > <= >=`
Shift-left or right	`<< >>`
String concatenation	`+`
Type information	`is sizeof() typeof`

This large group of operators provides significant programming flexibility.

Operator Precedence Levels

When combining operators you must take into consideration *operator precedence levels*. The precedence of the operator controls the order in which the expression is evaluated. Table 4–3 ranks all C# operator precedence levels.

Table 4–3   C# Operator Presidence Levels

Category	Level	Operators
Additive	4	`+ -`
Assignment	14	`= *= /= %= += -= <<= >>= &= ^= |=`
Conditional	13	`? :`
Conditional AND	11	`&&`
Conditional OR	12	`||`
Equality, non-equality	7	`== !=`
Logical AND	8	`&`
Logical OR	10	`|`
Logical XOR	9	`^`
Multiplicative	3	`* / %`

Table 4–3   C# Operator Presidence Levels *(Continued)*

Category	Level	Operators
Primary	1	`(x) x.y f(x) a[x] x++ x-- new` `typeof sizeof() checked unchecked`
Relational	6	`< > <= >= is`
Shift-left/right	5	`<< >>`
Unary	2	`+ - ! ~ ++x --x (T)x`

Note that the highest priority level is 1 and the lowest is 14.

The expression x - y / z, for example, is evaluated as x - (y / z) because the divide operator (/) has a higher precedence level than the subtraction operator (-).

Operator Associativity

When two operators have the *same* precedence level, the rules of *associativity* are applied to control the order in which the operators are parsed. All binary operators are *left-associative* except for the assignment operators. For this case, operations are performed from left to right. For example, w - x - y - z is evaluated as ((w - x) - y) - z.

The assignment operators and the trinary conditional operator (? :) are *right-associative*. This means that the operations are performed from right to left. For example, w = x = y = z is evaluated as w = (x = (y = z)).

Normal operator precedence and associativity can be modified with parentheses. For example, x + y / z first divides by z and then adds the result to x, but (x + y) / z first adds x and y and then divides the result by z.

Overflow and Underflow

You can avoid overflow and underflow calculation errors by watching the following four categories of calculations:

When an arithmetic expression generates an overflow, the compiler will either throw an `OverflowException` or discard the most significant bits of the result. For example, integer division by zero always throws a `DivideByZeroException`.

When a decimal expression performs a miscalculation, an `OverflowException` will be thrown. For example, decimal division by zero throws a `DivideByZeroException`.

Floating-point overflows or divide by zero operations do not throw exceptions. Instead, they return NaN (not a number) based upon the results of the IEEE floating point standard.

When integer overflow occurs an `OverflowException` can be thrown. Whether it is thrown or not thrown is dependent upon its checked/unchecked context.

Assignment and Compound Assignment Operators

The assignment operator is = and the compound assignment operators are +=, -=, *=, /=, %=, &=, |=, ^=, <<, =>, >=.

The assignment operators are right-associative. This means that operations are grouped from right to left. For example, w = x = y = z is evaluated as w = (x = (y = z)).

Relational Operators

C#'s relational operators include ==, !=, <, >, <=, >=. Operands using the relational operators are permuted to the parameter types of the selected operator. The type for the returned result is the type associated with the operator.

The predefined relational operators are listed and described in Table 4–4.

Table 4–4   C# Boolean Operators

Operation	Result
x != y	true is x is not equal to y
x < y	true is x is less than y
x <= y	true is x is less than or equal to y
x == y	true is x is equal to y
x > y	true is x is greater than y
x >= y	true is x is greater than or equal to y

All predefined relational operators return a result of type `bool`.

Logical Operators

C#'s *logical operators* are identical to those used by C and C++, and include AND, Exclusive-OR, and OR:

    &, ^, and |

Expressions using the logical operators permute the operands to the parameter types of the selected operator, and the type of the result is the return type of the operator.

Increment and Decrement Operators

The increment (++) and decrement (–) operators both come in two forms: prefix and postfix. If the operand of a prefix increment or decrement operation is a property or indexer access, the property or indexer must have both a get and a set accessor. If this is not the case, a compile-time error occurs.

Predefined increment (++) and decrement (--) operators exist for the following types: `sbyte`, `byte`, `short`, `ushort`, `int`, `uint`, `long`, `ulong`, `char`, `float`, `double`, `decimal`, and any `enum` type. The predefined ++ operators return the value produced by adding 1 to the operand, and the predefined – operators return the value produced by subtracting 1 from the operand.

The use of both postfix increment and postfix decrement are easiest to understand. Take, for example, the following expression:

```
y = x++;
```

To properly evaluate the statement, view it as two separate statements:

```
y = x;
x = x + 1;
```

In other words, postfix increment or decrement are *not* applied until the original value of the operand is used.

This is not the case for prefix increment and decrement. Take for example:

```
y = --x;
```

The equivalent longhand version would resemble:

```
x = x -1;
y = x;
```

Obviously, the order of evaluation changes with prefix, where the prefix operation is evaluated *prior* to the assignment operator.

Shift Operators

The C# bitwise left-shift (<<) and right-shift (>>) operators are used to perform bit manipulations.

The << operator shifts x left by a number of bits computed as described below. The most-significant bits of x are discarded, the remaining bits are shifted left, and the low-order empty bit positions are set to zero. Shift-rights are performed in the same manner.

When the left operand of the >> operator is a signed integral type, the operator performs an *arithmetic* shift right. The value of the most-significant bit (the sign bit) of the operand is retained. When the left operand of the >> operator is of an unsigned integral type, the operator performs a *logical* shift right. The most-significant bit is set to zero.

Floating-Point Comparison Operators

The following list represents the available floating-point comparison operators:

```
bool operator !=(double x, double y);
bool operator !=(float x, float y);
bool operator <(double x, double y);
bool operator <(float x, float y);
bool operator <=(double x, double y);
bool operator <=(float x, float y);
bool operator ==(double x, double y);
bool operator ==(float x, float y);
bool operator >(double x, double y);
bool operator >(float x, float y);
bool operator >=(double x, double y);
bool operator >=(float x, float y);
```

The operators compare the operands using the IEEE floating point standard. NaN results in false evaluations except for the != operator.

Operator Overloading

Several operators can be overloaded. For unary operators the following operators can be overloaded:

```
+    -    !    ~    ++    --    true    false
```

For binary operators, the following can be overloaded:

```
+    -    *    /    %    &    |    ^    <<    >>    ==    !=    >    <    >=    <=
```

User-defined overload operators cannot change the associativity, precedence, or syntax of an operator.

Operators Compared by Language

Many seasoned programmers learn best by coded example or when a new language's features are compared with a language they are already familiar with. Table 4–5 compares C#'s operators with several popular languages.

Table 4–5   C# Operators Compared with C++, Visual Basic, Java, and Jscript

Operator	Microsoft C#	C++	Microsoft Visual Basic	Java	Microsoft JScript
Addition (+) or (+=)	Yes	Yes	Yes	Yes	Yes
Address of (&)	Yes, in unsafe mode only	Yes	Use AddressOf	No	No
Array element [ ]	Yes	Yes	Use ()	Yes	Yes
Assignment (=)	Yes	Yes	Yes	Yes	Yes
Bitwise-AND (&) or (&=)	Yes	Yes	Use BitAnd	Yes	Yes
Bitwise-exclusive-OR (^) or (^=)	Yes	Yes	Use BitXor	Yes	Yes
Bitwise-inclusive-OR (|) or (|=)	Yes	Yes	Use BitOr	Yes	Yes
Boolean AND (&&)	Yes	Yes	Use AND	Yes	Yes
Boolean OR (||)	Yes	Yes	Use OR	Yes	Yes
Comma (,)	No	Yes	No	Yes	Yes
Compare strings (==)	Yes	Yes	Use =	Use String.equals	Yes
Compare two object reference variables (==)	Yes	No	Use Is	Yes	No
Concatenate (+) or (+=)	Yes	No	& or &=	Yes	Yes
Conditional (? :)	Yes	Yes	Use IIf()	Yes	Yes
Division (/) or (/=)	Yes	Yes	Yes	Yes	Yes
Equal (==)	Yes	Yes	Use =	Yes	Yes
Exponentiation (^)	No	No	Yes	No	No
Function call ( )	Yes	Yes	Yes	Yes	Yes

Table 4–5   C# Operators Compared with C++, Visual Basic, Java, and Jscript *(Continued)*

Operator	Microsoft C#	C++	Microsoft Visual Basic	Java	Microsoft JScript
Greater than (>) or Greater than or equal to (>=)	Yes	Yes	Yes	Yes	Yes
Indirection (*)	Yes, in unsafe mode only	Yes	No	No	No
Integer division (\) or (\-)	No	No	Yes	No	No
Left shift (<<) or (<<=)	Yes	Yes	No	Yes	Yes
Less than (<) or Less than or equal to (<=)	Yes	Yes	Yes	Yes	Yes
Logical-AND (&&)	Use &	Yes	And	Yes	Yes
Logical-NOT (!)	Yes	Yes	Use Not	Yes	Yes
Logical-OR (||)	Use |	Yes	Use Or	Yes	Yes
Member selection (.)	Yes	Yes and also ->	Yes	Yes	Yes
Modulus (%) or (%=)	Yes	Yes	Use Mod for (%). No (%=)	Yes	Yes
Multiplication (*) or (*=)	Yes	Yes	Yes	Yes	Yes
Not equal (!=)	Yes	Yes	Use <>	Yes	Yes
One's complement (~)	Yes	Yes	Use BitNot	Yes	Yes
Pointer to member (->)	Yes, in Unsafe mode only	Yes	No	No	No

Table 4–5   C# Operators Compared with C++, Visual Basic, Java, and Jscript *(Continued)*

Operator	Microsoft C#	C++	Microsoft Visual Basic	Java	Microsoft JScript
Postfix and Prefix decrement (--) and increment (++)	Yes	Yes	No	Yes	Yes
Reference (&)	No	Yes	No	No	No
Right shift (>>) or (>>=)	Yes	Yes	No	Yes	Yes
Scope resolution (::)	No	Yes	Use .	No	No
Size of type (sizeof())	Yes	Yes	No	No	No
Subtraction (-) or (-=)	Yes	Yes	Yes	Yes	Yes
Type cast (cast type)	Yes	Yes	Use Cint, CDbl, ..., or CType	Yes	No

This table will provide a quick reference if you intend to port an application from one of the listed languages to C#.

Predefined Types

C# provides a set of predefined types similar to those seen in C/C++. The predefined reference types are object and string. The type `object` is the ultimate base type of all other types, and the type `string` is used to represent UNICODE string values.

The predefined value types include signed and unsigned integral types, floating point, `bool`, `char`, and `decimal`. The signed integral types are `sbyte`, `short`, `int`, and `long`; the unsigned integral types are `byte`, `ushort`, `uint`, and `ulong` with the floating point types including `float` and `double`.

The C# type `bool` can totally eliminate one of the most common, unintentional C/C++ syntax error—that being the use of the assignment operator (=) instead of the logical test for equality (==). Take, for example, the following `if...else` statement:

```
int i = 0;
if (i = 0)   // should read (i == 10)
…..;
else…..;
```

C/C++ would assign i the value of 0 and since 0 is viewed as a logical false, C/C++ would *always* execute the else statement(s). Under the newer C#, the same typo would be flagged as illegal since the expression requires the type bool!

The char type is used to represent Unicode characters. A variable of type char represents a single 16-bit UNICODE character, unlike C/C++, which have both an 8-bit char and 16-bit wchar. Windows even confuses the issue with tchar, which is a defined type that can, at one location in a program, represent the 8-bit char, and seconds later switch to the 16-bit UNICODE counterpart. The final C/C++/Windows hit comes from 8-bit evolutions of EOF to 16-bit WEOF and whether or not the application developer *knows* these family-tree expansions exist!

C# uses a decimal type in order to provide accurate financial calculations. This new data type is ideal for calculations where rounding errors are unacceptable. Now your mortgage calculations can match those of your bank! Other examples include tax computations and currency conversions. The decimal type provides 28 significant digits of precision. Table 4–6 lists C#'s predefined types with a brief example to illustrate proper syntax.

Table 4–6   C# Predefined Types

Data Type	Explanation	Sample Code
bool	Boolean, where bool evaluates to true or false	bool val1 = true; bool val2 = false;
byte	8-bit unsigned integer	byte val1 = 12; byte val2 = 12U;
char	Character, where char value is a Unicode character	char val = 'D'; char val = 't';
decimal	decimal (28 significant digits of precision)	decimal val = 1.23M;
double	Double-precision floating point	double val1 = 12.34; double val2 = 67.89D;
float	Single-precision float point	float val = 12.34F;
Int	32-bit signed integer	Int val = 123;
long	64-bit signed integer	long val1 = 123; long val2 = 123L;
sbyte	8-bit signed integer	sbyte val = 12;
short	16-bit signed integer	short val = 12;
string	String type	string s = "Literal";

Table 4–6   C# Predefined Types *(Continued)*

Data Type	Explanation	Sample Code
uint	32-bit unsigned integer	`uint val1 = 12;` `uint val2 = 12U;`

ulong	64-bit unsigned integer	`ulong val1 = 12;`
		`ulong val2 = 12U;`
		`ulong val3 = 12L;`
		`ulong val4 = 12UL;`

ushort	16-bit unsigned integer	`ushort val1 = 12;` `ushort val2 = 12U;`

Since C#'s predefined types use operator overloading, the comparison operators `==` and `!=`, have different semantics for different predefined types:

- Two expressions of type `int` are considered equal if they represent the same integer value.
- Two expressions of type `object` are considered equal if both refer to the same object, or if both are null.
- Two expressions of type `string` are considered equal if the string instances have identical lengths and identical characters in each character position, or if both are null.

Look at the following example and see if you can predict the output:

```
string st1 = "Example";
string st2 = string.Copy(st1);
Console.WriteLine((object)st1 == (object)st2);
Console.WriteLine(st1 == st2);
```

The program displays:

```
False
True
```

The first comparison uses two expressions of type `object`, where the pointers to each instance are *not* the same. The second comparison uses two expressions of type `string`.

Built-In Types Table

Table 4–7 provides a list of built-in C# types. These types are aliases of predefined types found in the System namespace.

Table 4–7   C# Built-In Types

C# Type	.NET Type
bool	System.Boolean
byte	System.Byte
char	System.Char
decimal	System.Decimal
double	System.Double
float	System.Single
int	System.Int32
long	System.Int64
object	System.Object
sbyte	System.SByte
short	System.Int16
string	System.String
uint	System.Uint32
ulong	System.Uint64
ushort	System.Uint16

The C# type and their aliases can be interchanged. Consider the following portion of code:

```
int y = 2468;
System.Int32 y = 2468;
```

The GetType() method can be used to display the C# type. For example, the following statement displays the system alias that represents the type of *someVariable*:

```
Console.WriteLine(y.GetType());
```

C# also provides the typeof() method for returning the same information.

Integer Types Table

For quick numeric data type selections, Table 4–8 lists the nine integer types and ranges.

Table 4–8   Sizes and Ranges of C# Integer Types

Type	Range	Size
byte	0 to 255	Unsigned 8-bit integer
int	–2,147,483,648 to 2,147,483,647	Signed 32-bit integer
long	–9,223,372,036,854,775,808 to 9,223,372,036,854,775,807	Signed 64-bit integer
sbyte	–128 to 127	Signed 8-bit integer
short	–32,768 to 32,767	Signed 16-bit integer
uint	0 to 4,294,967,295	Unsigned 32-bit integer
ulong	0 to 18,446,744,073,709,551,615	Unsigned 64-bit integer
ushort	0 to 65,535	Unsigned 16-bit integer

NOTE

When the value represented by an integer literal exceeds the range of ulong, *a compilation error will occur.*

Floating Point Types

C# supports the two floating point types float and double. The float and double types are represented using the 32-bit single-precision and 64-bit double-precision IEEE 754 formats.

The float type can represent values ranging from approximately 1.5×10^{-45} to 3.4×10^{38} with a precision of 7 digits. The double type can represent values ranging from approximately 5.0×10^{-324} to 1.7×10^{308} with a precision of 15–16 digits.

bool

The bool keyword is an alias for System.Boolean and is used to declare variables that implement the Boolean values true and false. You can assign a Boolean value to a bool variable in several ways. First, a direct Boolean literal assignment of true or false, as in:

```
bool booleanVariable = false;
```

or via an expression that evaluates to bool as in:

```
bool isUppercaseChar = (c > 64 && c < 123);
```

In C++, a value of type bool can be converted to a value of type int; in other words, false is equivalent to zero and true is equivalent to nonzero values. In C#, there is no conversion between the bool type and other types. For example, the following if statement is legal in C/C++, while it is illegal in C#:

```
int flagON = 1;
if(flagON)    // not allowed in C#
...
```

The required C++ to C# syntax rewrite would take this form:

```
int flagON = 1;
if (flagON == 1)    // The C# equivalent
...
```

decimal

The C# decimal data type represents a 128-bit data type. Compared to floating-point types, the decimal type has a greater precision and a smaller range, which makes it suitable for financial and monetary calculations. The approximate range and precision for the decimal type are shown in Table 4–9.

Table 4–9   Range and Precisions for C# Decimal Type

Type	Approximate Range	Precision	.NET Type
Decimal	1.0×10^{-28} to 7.9×10^{28}	28–29 significant digits	System.Decimal

If you want a numeric real literal to be treated as a decimal, use the suffix m or M, for example:

```
decimal dollarValue = 250.75m;
```

Without the suffix m or M, the number is treated as a double and generates a compiler error. All integral types are implicitly converted to decimal and the result evaluates to decimal. Therefore, you can initialize a decimal variable using an integer literal without the suffix as in:

```
decimal decimalValue = 250;
```

However, there are no implicit conversions between floating-point types and the `dec-imal` type. As a result, you must use an implicit cast to convert from a floating-point type to `decimal` as in:

```
decimal dollarValue = 250.75m;
double doubleValue = (double) dollarValue;
dollarValue = (decimal) doubleValue;
```

C# allows you to mix `decimal` and numeric integral types in the same expression. However, mixing `decimal` and floating-point types without a cast results in a compilation error.

NOTE

The additive operator + cannot be applied to operands of type `double` *and* `decimal`. *To format* `decimal` *results you use the* `Format` *method in the C# runtime library of the .NET Framework.*

enum

User-defined or enumerated data types perform only one function: they make your source code self-documenting. Like C/C++, C# uses the `enum` keyword to declare an enumeration, consisting of a set of named constants called the enumerator list. Every enumeration type has an underlying type, which can be any integral type except `char`. The declaration of an `enum` variable takes the form:

[*attributes*] [*modifiers*] **enum** *identifier* [*:base-type*]
{*named constants*};

`attributes` (Optional)—Additional declarative information.

`modifiers` (Optional)—new, along with the four *access modifiers*.

`Identifier`—The user-defined name for the enumeration set.

`base-type` (Optional)—Any of the integral types except `char`. The default is `int`.

`named_constants`—The named constants, separated by commas, may include an explicit value assignment.

By default, C#'s enumeration elements are of type `int` with the first named constant having the value 0, and the value of each successive enumerator is increased by one. For example:

```
enum Weekdays {MON, TUE, WED, THUR, FRI, SAT, SUN};
```

In this enumeration, MON is 0, TUE is 1, WED is 2, and so forth. Enumerators can have initializers to override the default values. For example:

```
enum Weekdays {MON = 1, TUE, WED, THUR, FRI, SAT, SUN};
```

In this enumeration the sequence of elements is forced to start from 1 instead of 0.

Default Values Table

Table 4–10 lists the default return values for the value types shown.

Table 4–10   Default Values Returned by Dynamic Memory Allocation with new

Value Type	Default Value
bool	False
byte	0
char	'\0'
decimal	0.0M
double	0.0D
enum	Returns (E)0, when E is the enum name.
float	0.0F
int	0
long	0L
sbyte	0
short	0
struct	Member values are generated by setting all value-type fields to their default values and all reference-type fields to null.
uint	0
ulong	0
ushort	0

These results occur when the default constructors are invoked with a call to the new operator.

Numeric Conversions

Not to pick on NASA's missing the planet Mars, which was not so much a numeric miscalculation as it was an English vs. metric mishap, incorrect calculations are usually a result of behind-the-scenes numeric conversions. This section is designed to prevent these nefarious pitfalls by detailing just how C# deals with mixed-mode operations.

C#, just like C/C++, performs automatic numeric promotions with the predefined unary and binary numeric operators. Numeric promotion is not a distinct mechanism, but rather an effect of applying overload resolution to the predefined operators. However, this automatic promotion is not applied to user-defined operators. For example, consider the predefined implementations of the binary multiplication (*) operator:

```
decimal operator *(decimal x, decimal y);
double operator *(double x, double y);
float operator *(float x, float y);
int operator *(int x, int y);
long operator *(long x, long y);
uint operator *(uint x, uint y);
ulong operator *(ulong x, ulong y);
```

When using these overloaded operators, C# selects the first overloaded operator, for which an implicit conversion exists, from the operand types. For example, for the operation x * y, where x is a byte and y is a short, overload resolution selects operator *(int, int) as the closest match. As a result, x and y are converted to int, and the type of the result is int. Likewise, for the operation a * b, where a is an int and b is a double, overload resolution selects operator *(double, double) as the closest match.

Implied Numeric Promotions

Table 4–11 displays the predefined implied numeric promotions.

Table 4–11   Implied Numeric Conversions

From	To
byte	short, ushort, int, uint, long, ulong, float, double, or decimal
char	ushort, int, uint, long, ulong, float, double, or decimal
float	Double
int	long, float, double, or decimal
long	float, double, or decimal
sbyte	short, int, long, float, double, or decimal

Table 4–11   Implied Numeric Conversions   *(Continued)*

From	To
short	int, long, float, double, or decimal
uint	long, ulong, float, double, or decimal
ulong	float, double, or decimal
ushort	int, uint, long, ulong, float, double, or decimal

There is potential for a loss of precision when converting from int, uint, or long to float or from long to double.

Explicit Numeric Promotions

C#'s explicit numeric promotions convert any numeric type to any other numeric type, for which there is no implicit conversion, by using a cast expression as listed in Table 4–12.

Table 4–12   Explicit Numeric Conversions

From	Can Be Cast To
byte	sbyte or char
char	sbyte, byte, or short
decimal	sbyte, byte, short, ushort, int, uint, long, ulong, char, float, or double
double	sbyte, byte, short, ushort, int, uint, long, ulong, char, float, or decimal
float	sbyte, byte, short, ushort, int, uint, long, ulong, char, or decimal
int	sbyte, byte, short, ushort, uint, ulong, or char
long	sbyte, byte, short, ushort, int, uint, ulong, or char
sbyte	byte, ushort, uint, ulong, or char
short	sbyte, byte, ushort, uint, ulong, or char
uint	sbyte, byte, short, ushort, int, or char
ulong	sbyte, byte, short, ushort, int, uint, long, or char
ushort	sbyte, byte, short, or char

Table 4–13 lists several possible conversion situations.

Table 4–13   Explicit Floating-Point Promotions

Converting From	To Type	Result Promotion
a `float`, `double`, or `decimal`	`integer`	`value` is rounded to the nearest integer. When outside the range an `InvalidCastException` is thrown.
`decimal`	`float` or `double`	Rounded to the nearest `double` or `float` value.
`double`	`float`	Rounded to the nearest `float` value. If the result is too small or too large the result will be zero or infinity.
`float` or `double`	`decimal`	Converted to `decimal` representation. Rounded to the nearest number after the 28th decimal place if necessary.

The explicit numeric conversion may cause loss of precision or result in throwing exceptions.

C# Programming Elements

In the following sections we'll examine key elements of the C# language. These are elements that we will use throughout the book. From time to time, additional C# information will be introduced, but the material in the following sections will be used repeatedly.

Arrays

C# supports the same variety of arrays as C and C++, including both single and multidimensional arrays. This type of array is often referred to as a rectangular array, as opposed to a jagged array.

To declare a single dimension integer array named `myarray`, the following C# syntax could be used:

```
int[] myarray = new int[12];
```

The array could then be initialized with 12 values using a `for` loop in the following manner:

```
for (int i = 0; i < myarray.Length; i++)
    myarray[i] = 2 * i;
```

The contents of the array could be written to the screen with a `for` loop and `Write-Line()` statement.

```
for (int i = 0; i < myarray.Length; i++)
    Console.WriteLine("myarray[{0}] = {1}", i, myarray[i]);
```

Note that i values will be substituted for the `{0}` and `myarray[i]` values for `{1}` in the argument list provided with the `WriteLine()` statement.

Other array dimensions can follow the same pattern. For example, the syntax used for creating a two-dimensional array would take on the following form:

```
int[,] my2array = new int[12, 2];
```

The array could then be initialized with values using two `for` loops in the following manner:

```
for (int i = 0; i < 12; i++)
    for (int j = 0; j < 2; j++)
        my2array[i, j] = 2 * i;
```

The contents of the array could then be displayed on the console with the following syntax:

```
for (int i = 0; i < 12; i++)
    for (int j = 0; j < 2; j++)
        Console.WriteLine("my2array[{0}, {1}] = {2}",
                          i, j, my2array[i, j]);
```

Three dimensional arrays can be handled with similar syntax using the form:

```
int[,,] my3array = new int[3, 6, 9];
```

In addition to handling multidimensional rectangular arrays, C# handles jagged arrays. A jagged array can be declared using the following syntax:

```
int[][] jagarray1;
int[][][] jagarray2;
```

For example, suppose a jagged array is declared as:

```
int[][] jagarray1 = new int[2][];

jagarray1[0] = new int[] {2, 4};
jagarray1[1] = new int[] {2, 4, 6, 8};
```

Here, `jagarray1` represents an array of an array of `int`. The jagged appearance of the structure gives rise to the array's type name. The following line of code would print the value 6 to the screen:

```
Console.WriteLine(jagarray1[1][2]);
```

For a little practice, try to write the code necessary to print each array element to the screen.

Attributes, Events, Indexers, Properties, and Versioning

Many of the terms in this section are employed when developing applications for Windows. If you have worked with Visual Basic or the MFC and C++, you are familiar with the terms attributes, events, and properties as they apply to controls. In the following sections, we'll generalize those definitions even more.

Attributes

C# attributes allow programmers to identify and program new kinds of declarative information. For example, public, private, and protected are attributes that identify the accessibility of a method.

An element's attribute information can be returned at runtime using the MGWS runtime's reflection support.

Events

Events are used to allow classes to provide notifications as to which clients can provide executable code. This code is in the form of event handlers. Again, if you have developed MFC C++ Windows code, you are already familiar with event handlers.

Here is code for a button click event handler, extracted from a project developed later in this book.

```
protected void button1_Click(object sender, System.EventArgs e)
{
    radius = Convert.ToDouble(TextBox1.Text);
    TextBox2.Text = (radius * radius * 22 / 7).ToString();
    TextBox3.Text = (radius * 2.0 * 22 / 7).ToString();
}
```

The event handler contains code that will be executed when a button click event occurs. The button is a pushbutton that resides on a form in a C# Windows application.

Indexers

Indexers are used by C# to expose array-like data structures, such as an array of strings. This data structure might be used by a C# Windows control, such as a CheckedListBox control.

```
public class CheckedListBox: Control
{
    private string[] items;
    public string this[int index] {
        get {
            return items[index];
        }
        set {
            items[index] = value;
            Repaint();
        }
    }
}
```

The CheckedListBox class can then be altered with the following code:

```
CheckedListBox MyListBox;
MyListBox[0] = "List box title";
Console.Write(MyListBox[0]);
```

The array-like access provided by indexers is similar to the field-like access provided by properties.

Properties

A property is an attribute that is associated with a class or object. Windows controls offer a wide variety of changeable properties, including caption name, ID value, color, font, location, size, text, and so on.

Here is a small portion of a C# Windows program that modifies the properties of a button control.

```
Button1.Width = 128px;
Button1.Height = 35px;
Button1.TabIndex = 6;
Button1.Text = "Push to Calculate";
Button1.Visible = True;
```

Properties can be read or written to, as the need arises.

Versioning

C# supports versioning by addressing two levels of compatibility. The first is source compatibility. Source compatibility occurs when code developed on an early version can be simply recompiled to work on a later version.

The second type of compatibility is binary compatibility. Binary compatibility occurs when code developed under an earlier version works under a newer version without recompiling.

Boxing, Unboxing, and the Unified Type System

All types in C# can be treated as objects. For example, the following line of code is acceptable in C#:

```
Console.WriteLine(12345.ToString());
```

In this case the `ToString()` method is used on the integer `12345` by treating it as an object.

An object box can be used when a value is to be converted to a reference type. This is called *boxing*. *Unboxing* is used to convert a reference type back to a value. For example,

```
int num1 = 12345;

object myobject = num1;        // boxed

int num2 = (int) myobject;     // unboxed
```

Here, the integer number, `12345`, is first converted to a reference type with the use of boxing, then converted from an object back to an integer value by casting the object (unboxing).

Classes, Structures, and enum

C# provides simple, but unique, implementations to these common object-oriented features.

Classes

C# classes allow only single inheritance. Members of a class can include constants, constructors, destructors, events, indexers, methods, properties, and operators. Each member can, in turn, have a public, protected, internal, protected internal, or private access.

The makeup of a class is similar to that used in C and C++. For example:

```
public class Form1 : System.WinForms.Form
{
    // variable declaration
    public double radius = 7.5;

    /// <summary>
    ///     Required designer variable
    /// </summary>
    private System.ComponentModel.Container components;
    private System.WinForms.Label label1;
    private System.WinForms.Button button1;
    private System.WinForms.TextBox textBox1;
      .
      .
      .
```

In this example, the class itself is public and contains a variable with public access. The designer variables, however, use a private qualifier to limit access. Classes use a pass by reference scheme as compared to a structures pass by value. For this reason, they tend to be faster than the equivalent structure.

Structures

Structures, as in C and C++, are very similar to classes. As a matter of fact, they can be created with members similar to those described for classes. Structures differ from classes in that they are value types with values being stored on the stack. This tends to make them slower than an equivalent class because passing by value is slower than passing by reference.

`Point` is typically used and implemented in C, C++, and C# as a structure.

```
struct Point
{
    public int x, y;
    public Point(int x, int y) {
        this.x = x;
        this.y = y;
    }
}
```

This example illustrates the typical syntax for creating a structure.

enum

The `enum` type declaration is used to provide a type name for a group of symbolic constants. These constants are usually related to one another. For example:

```
enum vehicle {
    Chrysler,
    Ford,
    GM
}
```

Use vehicle GM to access the GM element, and so on.

Namespaces

C# uses namespaces as an organization system applied both internally and externally. As a convention, developers usually name namespaces after the company they are developing code for.

The Visual C# AppWizard uses the following convention when creating a C# console code template.

```
namespace tester
{
using System;

public class Class1
{
    public Class1()
    {
    }

    public static int Main(string[] args)
    {
        int[] myint = new int[] {1,2,3,4,5};

        foreach (object o in myint) {
            Console.Write("the value of myint is: ");
            Console.WriteLine(o);
        }

        return 0;
    }
}
}
```

We can modify that code to take on the following appearance:

```
namespace Nineveh_National_Research.CSharp.Tester
{
using System;

public class ForEachDemo
{
    public ForEachDemo()
    {
    }

    public static int Main(string[] args)
    {
        int[] myint = new int[] {1,2,3,4,5};

        foreach (object o in myint) {
            Console.Write("the value of myint is: ");
            Console.WriteLine(o);
        }

        return 0;
    }
}
}
```

The namespace `Nineveh_National_Research.Csharp.Tester` is hierarchical. It really means that there is a namespace `Nineveh_National_Research` that contains a namespace named `CSharp` that itself contains a namespace named `Tester`.

The `using` directive can be employed as shorthand notation instead of writing out the entire namespace name. In the previous listing, the `using` directive allows all of the types in `System` to be used without qualification.

Statements

Statement syntax in C# is basically the same as that for C and C++. In the following sections you'll see several familiar coding examples.

Blocks

C# allows blocking code so that one or more statements can be written in sequence. The following portion of code shows several blocks.

```
// block 1
Console.WriteLine("This is the first block");
{
    // block 2
    Console.WriteLine("This is the second block");
    {
        // block 3
        Console.WriteLine("This is the third block");
    }
}
```

Any number of blocks can be created using this format.

The do Statement

A do statement continues to execute a statement until the Boolean test is false. The following is a small portion of code:

```
int num1 = 0;

do {
    Console.WriteLine(num1);
    num1 += 2;
}
while (num1 != 20);
```

The output from this code will be the numbers 0 to 18. Every do statement will be executed at least one time with the Boolean test being made after the statement.

The Expression Statement

An expression statement evaluates a given expression and discards any value calculated in the process. Expressions such as `(x + s)`, `(y * 3)`, `(t == 2)`, and so on are not allowed as statements. The following is an example of an expression statement.

```
static int HereWeGo() {
    Console.WriteLine("We made it to HereWeGo");
    return 0;
}

public static int Main(string[] args)
{
    //
    // TODO: Add code to start application here
    //

    HereWeGo();
    return 0;
}
```

Once again, the value returned by `HereWeGo()` is discarded.

The `for` Statement

The `for` statement, like its C and C++ counterparts, initializes the expression then executes an expression while the Boolean test is true. For example:

```
for (int i  = 0; i < 10; i++) {
    Console.Write("the value of i is: ");
    Console.WriteLine(i);
}
```

This portion of code will report the value of `i` to the screen. The value of `i` increments from 0 to 9 before the Boolean condition is false.

The `foreach` Statement

The `foreach` statement is used to enumerate the contents of a collection. For example:

```
int[] myint = new int[] {1,2,3,4,5};

foreach (object o in myint) {
    Console.Write("the value of myint is: ");
    Console.WriteLine(o);
}
```

In this collection, each integer element will be reported to the screen. The collection, in general, can be any type.

The `if` and `if-else` Statements

The `if` statement executes based on a Boolean decision. If the statement is true, the expression will execute. If false, the statement will not execute. When used in conjunction with `else`, the `if-else` combination will pass operation to the `else` when the `if` statement is false.

For example:

```
int i = 2 * 23 / 12;

if ( i >= 5)
    Console.WriteLine("This is a big number");
else
    Console.WriteLine("This is a reasonable number");
```

This portion writes one message or another based upon the calculated value of the integer result.

The Label and `goto` Statements

The `goto` statement is used in conjunction with a label to transfer program control. For example:

```
goto C;

A: Console.WriteLine("This should be printed last");
return 0;

B: Console.WriteLine("This should be printed second");
goto A;

C: Console.WriteLine("This should be printed first");
goto B;
```

This concept is fairly straightforward. We recommend, however, a limited use of `goto` statements.

The `switch` (case-break) Statement

C# `switch` statements, like those of C and C++ execute statements that are associated with the value of a particular expression. When no match occurs a default condition is executed.

```
string str = "Top";

switch (str.Length) {
    case 0:
        Console.WriteLine("No characters in the string.");
        break;
    case 1:
        Console.WriteLine("One character in the string.");
        break;
    case 2:
        Console.WriteLine("Two characters in the string.");
        break;
    case 3:
        Console.WriteLine("Three characters in the string.");
        break;
    default:
        Console.WriteLine("A lot of characters in the string.");
        break;
}
```

A default option should always be provided in switch statements.

The while *Statement*

A while statement continues to execute while the Boolean result is true. For example:

```
int i = 5;

while (i <= 300) {
    i += 5;
    Console.WriteLine("Not there yet!");
}
```

The value of i is initialized to 5. When the final increment is made, the value in i will be 305, and thus the loop will stop executing. The while statement continues to execute until the value of i is equal to or exceeds 300.

Value and Reference Types

C# lends support to main categories of types. These are value and reference types. You are already familiar with value types.

Value types include char, enum, float, int, struct, and so on. The key feature of the value type is that the variable actually contains the data.

Reference types, on the other hand, include class, array, delegate, and interface types. It is possible that an assignment to a reference type can affect other reference types derived from that reference type.

C# Compiler Options Listed by Category

No doubt you will continually refer back to this chapter for proper selection of C# data types and their related overloaded operators. Table 4–14 adds compiler options, sorted by category, to your reference materials.

Table 4–14   C# Compiler Options Listed by Category

Category	Option	Purpose
Optimization	/optimize	Enable/disable optimizations.
Output Files	/doc	Process documentation comments to an XML file.
	/nooutput	Compile but do not create an output file.
	/out	Give output file.
	/target	Give the format of the output file using one of four options: /target:exe, /target:library, /target:module, or /target:winexe.
.NET Assemblies	/addmodule	Give module(s) to be part of this assembly.
	/nostdlib	Do not import mscorlib.dll.
	/reference	Import metadata from a file containing an assembly.
Debugging/ Error Checking	/bugreport	Create a file for reporting a bug.
	/checked	Specify whether integer arithmetic that overflows the bounds of the data type will cause an exception at runtime.
	/debug	Emit debugging information.
	/fullpaths	Specify the absolute path to the file in compiler output.
	/nowarn	Suppress ability of compiler to generate specified warnings.
	/warn	Set warning level.
	/warnaserror	Warnings to errors.
Preprocessor	/define	Define preprocessor symbols.

Table 4–14   C# Compiler Options Listed by Category *(Continued)*

Category	Option	Purpose
Resources	/linkresource	Link a .NET resource to an assembly.
	/resource	Embed a .NET resource into output file.
	/win32icon	Insert a .ico file into output file.
	/win32res	Insert a Win32 resource into output file.
Miscellaneous	/?	List compiler options to stdout.
	/baseaddress	Give the preferred base address for a DLL load.
	/codepage	Give the code page for source code files in compilation.
	/help	List compiler options to stdout.
	/incremental	Enable incremental compilation of source code files.
	/main	Give location of the Main method.
	/nologo	Suppress compiler banner information.
	/recurse	Find subdirectories for source files to compile.
	/unsafe	Compile code that uses the unsafe keyword.
	@	Give a response file.

Summary

This chapter has reviewed the important identifiers, keywords, operators, and logic flow control statements as they relate to the C# language. You also saw that while many C# features mimic their C/C++ counterparts, there are catchy, subtle differences; for example, the switch...case syntax. As most readers will already be comfortable with C/C++, caution is the keyword when dashing off to code your first C# algorithm! In the next chapter we'll examine various C# program control statements and see how they relate to robust C# code development.

CHAPTER 5

Program Control

T his chapter discusses C#'s control statements. Many of these control statements are similar to other high-level language controls, such as `if`, `if-else`, and `switch` statements and `for`, `while`, and `do-while` loops. However, there are several new control statements unique to C#/C/C++, such as the `? :` (conditional), `break`, and `continue` statements.

The *new* controls, introduced here, typically have no equivalent in the traditional older high-level languages such as FORTRAN, COBOL, and Pascal. Therefore, beginner C#/C/C++ programmers leave them out of their problem solutions. That is unfortunate for two reasons. First, it means you are not taking advantage of the coding efficiencies provided by these new controls. Second, it immediately flags you as a beginner.

NOTE

In the code listings, if a statement is in **bold**, *that statement contains a logic or syntax which could easily trip-up an experienced C/C++ programmer!*

Language Equivalents

The first section in the chapter is designed to quickly highlight the similarities and differences between C#'s control statements and those found in Visual Basic, Java, C++, JScript, or Visual FoxPro. If you know one of these languages you can save yourself some time by only scanning those sections, for example C++, to see how C# uses the same construct. The later part of the chapter goes into greater detail highlighting any particular areas of concern when learning C#'s logic flow control statements.

NOTE

Whether or not you have previous knowledge of any programming language, reviewing the following multi-language syntax comparisons will help you discover C#'s adoption of their tried and true constructs!

Commenting Code

All software engineers know the advantages and disadvantages of comments. The disadvantage is that they take time to embed. However, anyone, whether the author of a code segment, or a software engineer getting "onboard" someone else's code, knows how a meaningful comment can spell the difference between immediately understanding an algorithm, and hours of traces, desk checks, or code walkthroughs!

The following section contrasts comment block syntax in today's most popular programming languages.

Visual Basic

```
' Visual Basic comment syntax using single quote mark
someVar = 1    ' end-of-line comment
Rem using keyword to flag single-line comment
```

Java

```
/* Java marquee comment block
   spanning several code lines */

/*
   SomeClass marquee comment block
*/
```

C++

```
// C++ single-line comment terminated by carriage return

/* C++ marquee comment block
   spanning several code lines */

/*
   SomeClass marquee comment block
*/
```

C#

```
// C++ single-line comment terminated by carriage return

/* C++ marquee comment block
   spanning several code lines */

/*
   SomeClass marquee comment block
*/
```

JScript

```
// JScript single-line comment terminated by carriage return

/* JScript marquee comment block
   spanning several code lines */
```

Visual FoxPro

```
* Visual FoxPro single-line comment

DO WHILE gnIterator <= 10   && end-of-line comment starts with &&

NOTE using keyword to flag single/marquee comment;
     preceding statements terminated with semi-colon;
     flag marquee comment block;
     statement not ending with semi-colon terminates marquee block
```

Variable Declarations

If you are already familiar with the rules for legal identifiers (your names for variables, constants, functions, and methods) the following section quickly translates your understanding of how to declare variables into C# syntax.

Visual Basic

```
Dim someVar As Integer
Public someVar As Integer = 99
```

Java

```
int someVar;
int someVar = 99;
```

C++

```
int someVar;
int someVar = 99;
```

C#

```
int someVar;
int someVar = 99;
```

JScript

```
var someVar : int;
var someVar : int = 10;
```

Visual FoxPro

```
LOCAL someVar
someVar = 99
```

Assignment Statements

All assignment operators make copies of the rValue and store the clone in a legal lValue. However, with a quick glance at the following segment, you'll notice that this simple operation has some interesting language syntax variations.

Visual Basic

```
lValue = 10
```

Java

```
lValue = 10;
```

C++

```
lValue = 10;
```

C#

```
lValue = 10;
```

JScript

```
lValue = 10;
```

Visual FoxPro

```
lValueA = 10
STORE 10 to lValueB
```

If...Else Statements

French braces! Except for Visual Basic and Visual FoxPro if...else syntax translations, most other languages use a similar if...else syntax. The issue then becomes proper placement of French braces {} to guarantee proper if...else logic flow.

Visual Basic

```
If LoopControl <= MAX_ELEMENTS Then
    Accumulator += LoopControl
    LoopControl += 1
Else
    Accumulator += LoopControl
    LoopControl -= 1
End If
```

Java

```
if (LoopControl <= MAX_ELEMENTS){
    Accumulator += LoopControl;
    LoopControl++;
}
```

C++

```
if(LoopControl <= MAX_ELEMENTS) {
 Accumulator += LoopControl;
 LoopControl++;
 }
else {
    Accumulator += LoopControl;
    LoopControl --;
 };
```

C#

```
if (LoopControl <= MAX_ELEMENTS)
{
    Accumulator += LoopControl;
    LoopControl++;
}
```

JScript

```
if(LoopControl < MAX_ELEMENTS) {
   Accumulator += LoopControl;
   LoopControl ++;
 }
else {
   Accumulator += LoopControl;
   LoopControl --;
 };
```

Visual FoxPro

```
IF LoopControl < MAX_ELEMENTS
   Accumulator = Accumulator + LoopControl
   LoopControl = LoopControl + 1
ENDIF
```

Switch Statements

Selection statements can vary greatly in capabilities and/or syntax as you roll over from a familiar programming language to Microsoft's new C#.

Visual Basic

```
Select Case intValue
   Case 0
      MsgBox ("Case 0 entered.")
'     Visual Basic exits the Select at the end of a Case.
   Case 1
      MsgBox ("Case 1 entered.")
   Case 2
      MsgBox ("Case 2 entered.")
   Case Else
      MsgBox ("Default case entered.")
End Select
```

Java

```
switch(intValue) {
  case 0:
    System.out.println("Case 0 entered.\n");
    break;
  case 1:
    System.out.println("Case 1 entered\n");
    break;
  default:
    System.out.println("Default case entered.\n");
}
```

C++

```
switch(n) {
 case 0:
  printf("Case 0 entered.\n");
  break;
 case 1:
  printf("Case 1 entered.\n");
  break;
 case 2:
  printf("Case 2 entered.\n");
  break;
 default:
  printf("Default case entered.\n");}
```

C#

```
switch(intValue) {
case 0:
    Console.WriteLine("Case 0 entered.");
    break;
case 1:
    Console.WriteLine("Case 1 entered.");
    break;
case 2:
    Console.WriteLine("Case 2 entered");
    break;
default:
    Console.WriteLine("Default case entered.");
}
```

JScript

```
switch(intValue) {
    case 0 :
       Response.Write("Case 0 entered.");
       break;
    case 1 :
       Response.Write("Case 1 entered.");
       break;
    case 2 :
       Response.Write("Case 2 entered.");
    default :
       Response.Write("Default case entered.");
}
```

Visual FoxPro

```
DO CASE
  CASE intValue = 0
    ? 'Case 0 entered.'
  CASE intValue > 0
    ? 'Value greater than 0'
  OTHERWISE
    ? 'Value less than 0'
ENDCASE
```

For Loops

Unlike switch syntax, for loop syntax retains a degree of consistency between programming languages.

Visual Basic

```
For i = 1 To 5
    MessageBox.Show("i = " & i)
Next
```

or

```
For Each prop In obj
    prop = 4
Next prop
```

Java

```
for(i = 1; i < 6;n++)
  System.out.println("i = " + i);
```

C++

```
for(int i = 1; i < 6; i++)
  printf("%d\n",i);
```

C#

```
for (int i = 1; i <= 5; i++)
    Console.WriteLine("i =  {0}", i);
```

JScript

```
for (var i = 0; i < 5; i++) {
   Response.Write("i = " + i);
}
```

or

```
for (prop in obj){
obj[prop] = 4;
}
```

Visual FoxPro

```
FOR i = 1 TO 5
 ? i
ENDFOR
```

While Loops

Rolling over your understanding of while loop syntax and logic to C#'s way of doing things is a straightforward process as long as you remember which language's keywords are uppercased, lowercased, or mixed case.

Visual Basic

```
While i < 50 ' Test at start of loop
   i += 1
```

Java

```
while (i < 50)
 i++;
```

C++

```
while(int i < 50)
   i++;
```

C#

```
while (i < 50)
   i++;
```

JScript

```
while (i < 50) {
i++; }
```

Visual FoxPro

```
DO WHILE i < 50
 i = i + i
ENDDO
```

Passing Arguments by Value

Though sometimes inefficient, call-by-value passes duplicate copies of actual arguments to their symbiotic dummy arguments. Changes to a called subroutine's dummy arguments have no translation to the calling routine's actual arguments.

Visual Basic

```
Public Sub someFunc(ByVal dummyArg As Long) 'dummyArg passed by
value.
'changes to dummyArg do not affect actualArg.
End Sub
```

`someFunc()` function call:

```
someFunc(actualArg) ' Call the procedure
```

Visual Basic allows you to coerce any parameters to be passed by value by simply enclosing the parameters in extra parentheses.

```
someFunc((actualArg))
```

Java

In Java, objects are all passed by reference to save the unnecessary duplication of the object's contents while simple data types are always passed by value.

C++

C++ passes all simple data types call-by-value. Objects, on the other hand, may be passed by value or reference, and all array types are passed call-by-reference.

```
void someFunction(int dummyA, int dummyB)
{
...
}
```

`someFunc()` function call:

```
someFunc(actualA,actualB);
```

C#

```
void someMethod(int actualArg)
{
    ...
}
```

`someMethod()` method call:

```
someMethod(actualArg);
```

JScript

```
someFunc(actualA,actualB);
```

Visual FoxPro

```
= someFunc(actualA)
```

Passing Arguments by Reference

Passing an actual argument by reference allows a called subroutine (function or method) to change *both* the dummy argument and the actual argument since both share the *same* memory location address.

Visual Basic

```
Public Sub someFunc(ByRef dummyArg As Long) ' dummyArg is by
reference:
'changes to dummyArg, are reflected in actualArg.
End Sub
```

`someFunc()` call statement:

```
someFunc(actualArg) ' Call the procedure
```

Java

Objects are always passed by reference, and primitive data types are always passed by value.

C++

```
// Prototype of someFunc that takes a pointer to integer
int someFunc(int *iptr);
someFunc(&iVariable);
//Prototype of someFunc that takes a reference to integer
int someFunc(int &idummyArg);
someFunc(iVariable);
```

C#

```
// someMethod
void someMethod(ref int actualArg)
{
    ...
}
// someMethod call statement
someMethod(ref i);
```

JScript

In JScript, all objects, including arrays, are passed call-by-reference. However, unlike other language's call-by-reference, in JScript the dummy object to which the variable refers *cannot* be changed in the called subroutine even though its properties and methods *can be* changed in the called subroutine.

```
/* Reference parameters are supported for external objects,
   but not internal JScript functions */
comPlusObject.SomeMethod(&actualObj);
```

Visual FoxPro

```
= someFunc(@actualArg)
```

or

```
DO someFunc WITH actualARg
```

Exception Handling

If you are unfamiliar with "exception handling," the idea is very simple. You are probably already well aware that an attempt to divide by zero can produce fatal runtime crashes. Many older high-level languages were unequipped to deal with such scenarios, requiring the software engineer to cleverly design and incorporate bulletproof algorithms.

Exception handling is a programming language's built-in capability to trap or capture these error conditions and then graciously deal with them. Dealing with near-fatal error conditions often involves nothing more than a call to a specialized subroutine, written by the software engineer, to handle the specific error. This next section contrasts how the various languages deal with exception handling.

Visual Basic

```
Try
    If someVal = 0 Then
        Throw New Exception("attempt to divide by zero")
    Else
        Throw New Exception("division may proceed")
    End If
Catch
    MessageBox.Show("Divide by Zero " & Err.Description)
Finally
    MessageBox.Show("Finally block entered.")
End Try
```

Java

```
try{
    if (someVal == 0)
        throw new Exception ("attempt to divide by zero");
    else
        throw new Exception ("division may proceed");
}
catch (Exception err){
    if (err.getMessage() == "attempt to divide by zero")
        System.out.println(err.getMessage());
        //Handle Error Here
}
```

C++

```
        __try{
        if (someVal == 0)
            throw new Exception ("attempt to divide by zero");
        else
            throw new Exception ("division may proceed");
            }
        __catch(Exception e)
    {
            Console.WriteLine("Error - divide by zero");
    }
        __finally
    {
            Console.WriteLine("Finally block entered.");
    }
```

C#

```
try
{
    if (someVal == 0)
        throw new System.Exception ("attempt to divide by zero");
    else
        throw new System.Exception ("division may proceed");
}
catch (System.Exception err)
{
    System.Console.WriteLine(err.Message);
}
finally
{
    System.Console.WriteLine("Finally block entered.");
}
```

JScript

```
try {
    if (someVal == 0) {
        throw new Error(513, "attempt to divide by zero");
    }
    else {
        throw new Error(514, "division may proceed");
    }
}
catch(e) {
    Response.Write("The error number was: " + e.number + "<BR>");
    Response.Write("The reason for the error: " + e.message +
"<BR>");
}
finally {
    Response.Write("Finally block entered.");
}
```

Initializing Object References

This next section highlights the differences in setting pointers to null. Since it is extremely difficult to tell when a pointer has a *valid address*, algorithms testing pointer contents find it easier to decide if the pointer officially points nowhere, in other words, the constant, null. This section is *not* demonstrating how to initialize primitive data types, just pointer variables.

Visual Basic

```
objectPtr = Nothing
```

Java

```
stringVarInstance = null;
```

C++ and C#

```
objectPtr = null;
```

JScript

```
objectPtr = null;
```

Visual FoxPro

```
objectPtr = null
```

or

```
ObjectPtr.RELEASE
```

Final Words of Caution

The language comparison section ends with several dos and don'ts as you translate your understanding from one language to C#. These are special areas of concern since the C# language feature probably has familiarity in another language, yet performs differently in C#!

1. In C# there is only one location where `Static` is used by itself to declare a variable—inside a procedure.
2. In Visual Basic, procedures declared with the `Sub` keyword cannot return values. If a procedure is to return a value, you must declare it with the `Function` keyword.
3. `Me` is *not* resolved at compile time, so you can use it as the return value of a property or method.
4. While the `substr` function is still supported in C#, it is no longer the preferred way to access characters within a string.
5. In Visual Basic, constructors for classes derived from `.NET Framework System.Object` are always named `New`.
6. Overloading is not allowed on constructors in JScript.
7. In C++ an abstract class includes at least one pure virtual member.
8. Arrays in JScript are always sparse and dynamic.
9. A function or class declared as a friend has access to all of the private members of the class that contains the declaration.

10. Static local variables of non-shared class methods are stored per class instance in Visual Basic rather than sharing a single copy as in other languages.

11. All objects have synchronization features built in.

Conditional Controls

The C# language supports four basic conditional statements that have been briefly discussed earlier in this chapter: the `if`, the `if-else`, the conditional `?`, and the `switch`. Before we begin a detailed discussion of the individual conditional statements, however, one general rule needs to be highlighted.

Most of the conditional statements can be used to selectively execute either a single line of code or multiple lines of related code (called a *block*). Whenever a conditional statement is associated with only one line of executable code, braces (`{}`) are *not* required around the executable statement. However, if the conditional statement is associated with multiple executable statements, braces are required to relate the block of executable statements with the conditional test. For this reason, `switch` statements are required to have an opening and a closing brace.

if

The `if` statement can be used to conditionally execute a segment of code. The simplest form of the `if` statement is

```
if (expression)
  true_action;
```

You will notice that the expression must be enclosed in parentheses. To execute an `if` statement, the expression must evaluate to either `true` or `false`. If `expression` is `true`, `true_action` will be performed and execution will continue on to the next statement following the action. However, if `expression` evaluates to `false`, `true_action` will *not* be executed, and the statement following `action` will be executed. For example, the following code segment will print the message "Have a great day!" whenever the variable `ioutside_temp` is greater than or equal to 72:

```
if(ioutside_temp >= 72)
  Console.WriteLine("Have a great day!");
```

The syntax for an `if` statement associated with a block of executable statements looks like this:

```
if ( expression ) {
  true_action1;
  true_action2;
  true_action3;
```

```
      true_action4;
  }
```

The syntax requires that all of the associated statements be enclosed by a pair of braces ({}) and that each statement within the block must also end with a semicolon (;).

if-else

The if-else statement allows a program to take two separate actions based on the validity of a particular expression. The simplest syntax for an if-else statement looks like this:

```
if (expression)
  true_action;

else
  false_action;
```

In this case, if expression evaluates to true, true_action will be taken; otherwise, when expression evaluates to false, false_action will be executed. Here is a coded example:

```
if(ckeypressed == UP)
  iy_pixel_coord++;

else
  iy_pixel_coord--;
```

This example takes care of either incrementing or decrementing the current horizontal coordinate location based on the current value stored in the character variable *ckeypressed*.

Of course, either true_action, false_action, or both could be compound statements, or blocks, requiring braces. The syntax for these three combinations is straightforward:

```
if (expression) {
  true_action1;
  true_action2;
  true_action3;
}
else
  false_action;


if (expression)
  true_action;
else {
  false_action1;
  false_action2;
  false_action3;
}
```

```
if (expression) {
  true_action1;
  true_action2;
  true_action3;
}
else {
  false_action1;
  false_action2;
  false_action3;
}
```

Remember, whenever a block action is being taken, you do not follow the closing brace (}) with a semicolon.

Nested `if-elses`

When `if` statements are nested, care must be taken to ensure that you know which `else` action will be matched up with which `if`. Look at an example and see if you can figure out what will happen:

```
if(iout_side_temp < 50)
if(iout_side_temp < 30) Console.WriteLine("Wear the down jacket!");
else Console.WriteLine("Parka will do.");
```

The listing was purposely misaligned so as not to give you any visual clues as to which statement went with which `if`. The question becomes, What happens if `iout_side_temp` is 55? Does the "Parka will do." message get printed? The answer is no. In this example, the `else` action is associated with the second `if` expression. This is because C# matches each `else` with the first unmatched `if`.

To make debugging as simple as possible under such circumstances, the C# compiler has been written to associate each `else` with the closest `if` that does not already have an `else` associated with it.

Of course, proper indentation will always help clarify the situation:

```
if(iout_side_temp < 50)
  if(iout_side_temp < 30) Console.WriteLine("Wear the down jacket!");
  else Console.WriteLine("Parka will do.");
```

The same logic can also be represented by the alternate listing that follows:

```
if(iout_side_temp < 50)
  if(iout_side_temp < 30)
    Console.WriteLine("Wear the down jacket!");
  else
    Console.WriteLine("Parka will do.");
```

Each particular application you write will benefit most by one of the two styles, as long as you are consistent throughout the source code.

See if you can figure out this next example:

```
if(test1_expression)
  if(test2_expression)
    test2_true_action;
else
  test1_false_action;
```

You may be thinking this is just another example of what has already been discussed. That's true, but what if you really did want `test1_false_action` to be associated with `test1` and not `test2`? The examples so far have all associated the `else` action with the second, or closest, `if`. (By the way, many a programmer has spent needless time debugging programs of this nature. They're intended to work the way you are logically thinking, as was the preceding example, but unfortunately, the compiler doesn't care about your "pretty printing.")

Correcting this situation requires the use of braces:

```
if(test1_expression) {
  if(test2_expression)
    test2_true_action;
  }
else
  test1_false_action;
```

The problem is solved by making `test2_expression` and its associated `test2_true_action` a block associated with a `true` evaluation of `test1_expression`. This makes it clear that `test1_false_action` will be associated with the `else` clause of `test1_expression`.

if-else-if

The `if-else-if` statement combination is often used to perform multiple successive comparisons. The general form of this statement looks like this:

```
if(expression1)
  test1_true_action;

else if(expression2)
  test2_true_action;

else if(expression3)
  test3_true_action;
```

Each action, of course, could be a compound block requiring its own set of braces (with the closing brace *not* followed by a semicolon). This type of logical control flow evaluates each expression until it finds one that is `true`. When this occurs, all remaining test conditions are bypassed. In the preceding example, if none of the expressions evaluated to `true`, no action would be taken.

Consider the next example and see if you can guess the result.

```
if(expression1)
  test1_true_action;

else if(expression2)
  test2_true_action;

else if(expression3)
  test3_true_action;

else
  default_action;
```

This differs from the previous example. This `if-else-if` statement combination will always perform some action. If none of the `if` expressions evaluate to `true`, the `else default_action` will be executed. For example, the following program checks the value assigned to `econvert_to` to decide which type of conversion to perform.

```
if(econvert_to == YARDS)
  fconverted_value = length / 3;

else if(econvert_to == INCHES)
  fconverted_value = length * 12;

else if(econvert_to == CENTIMETERS)
  fconverted_value = length * 12 * 2.54;

else if(econvert_to == METERS)
  fconverted_value = (length * 12 * 2.54)/100;

else
  Console.WriteLine("No conversion required");
```

If the requested `econvert_to` is not one of the ones provided, the code segment prints an appropriate message.

The Conditional (?) Operator

The conditional statement `?` provides a quick way to write a test condition. Associated actions are performed depending on whether `test_expression` evaluates to `true` or `false`. The operator can be used to replace an equivalent `if-else` statement. The syntax for a conditional statement is

```
test_expression ? true_action : false_action;
```

The ? operator is also sometimes referred to as the ternary operator because it requires three operands. Examine this statement:

```
if(fvalue >= 0.0)
  fvalue = fvalue;
else
  fvalue = -fvalue;
```

You can rewrite the statement using the conditional operator:

```
fvalue = (fvalue >= 0.0) ? fvalue : -fvalue;
```

In this situation, both statements yield the absolute value of fvalue. The precedence of the conditional operator is less than that of any of the other operators used in the expression; therefore, no parentheses are required in the example. Nevertheless, parentheses are frequently used to enhance readability.

The following C# program uses the ? operator to cleverly format the program's output:

```
using System;
public class Class1
{
  public static int Main(string[] args)
  {
    // conditional.cs
    // A simple C# application demonstrating
    // the use of the conditional operator ?:
    // Copyright (c) Chris H. Pappas and Willliam H. Murray, 2001
    //

    string str;
    decimal dbalance, dpayment;

    Console.Write("Enter your loan balance: ");
    str = Console.ReadLine();
    dbalance = decimal.Parse(str);

    Console.Write("\nEnter your loan payment amount: ");
    str = Console.ReadLine();
    dpayment = decimal.Parse(str);

    Console.Write("\n\nYou have ");
    Console.Write( ((dpayment > dbalance) ?
                    "overpaid by $" : "paid $") );
```

```
      Console.Write( (dpayment > dbalance) ?
                     Math.Abs(dbalance - dpayment) :
                     dpayment);
      Console.Write(" on your loan of ${0}.", dbalance);

      return(0);
   }
}
```

The program uses the first conditional statement inside a `Console.WriteLine` statement to decide which string—"overpaid by $" or "paid $"—is to be printed. The following conditional statement calculates and prints the appropriate dollar value.

switch-case

It is often the case that you will want to test a variable or an expression against several values. You could use nested `if-else-if` statements to do this, or you could use a `switch` statement. Be very careful, though, the C# `switch` statement has a few peculiarities. The syntax for a `switch` statement is

```
switch (integral_expression) {
 case constant1:
   statements1;
   break;
 case constant2:
   statements2;
   break;
   .
   .
   .
 case constantn:
   statementsn;
   break;
 default: statements;
}
```

The redundant statement you need to pay particular attention to is the `break` statement. In the preceding syntax, if the `break` statement had been removed from `constant1`'s section of code, a match similar to the one used in the preceding paragraph would have left `statements2` as the next statement to be executed. It is the `break` statement that causes the remaining portion of the `switch` statements to be skipped. Let's look at a few examples.

Examine the following portion of `if-else-if` code:

```
if(emove == SMALL_CHANGE_UP)
   fycoord =    5;
```

```
else if(emove == SMALL_CHANGE_DOWN)
  fycoord =  -5;

else if(emove == LARGE_CHANGE_UP)
  fycoord =  10;

else
  fycoord = -10;
```

This code can be rewritten using a switch statement:

```
switch(emove) {
  case  SMALL_CHANGE_UP:
    fycoord =    5;
    break;
  case  SMALL_CHANGE_DOWN:
    fycoord =   -5;
    break;
  case  LARGE_CHANGE_UP:
    fycoord =   10;
    break;
  default:
    fycoord = -10;
    break;
}
```

The value of *emove*, in this example, is consecutively compared to each case value looking for a match. When one is found, fycoord is assigned the appropriate value. Then the break statement is executed, skipping over the remainder of the switch statements. However, if no match is found, the default assignment is performed (fycoord = -10). Since this is the last option in the switch statement, there is no need to include a break. A switch default is optional.

Proper placement of the break statement within a switch statement can be very useful. Examine the following example:

```
using System;
public class Class1
{
  public static int Main(string[] args)
  {
    // switch.cs
    // A simple C# application demonstrating
    // the drop through feature of cases
    // Copyright (c) Chris H. Pappas and William H. Murray, 2001
    //

    char c = 'a';
```

```
      int ivowelct = 0, iconstantct = 0;

      switch(c) {
        case 'a': goto case 'A';
        case 'A': goto case 'e';
        case 'e': goto case 'E';
        case 'E': goto case 'i';
        case 'i': goto case 'I';
        case 'I': goto case 'o';
        case 'o': goto case 'O';
        case 'O': goto case 'u';
        case 'u': goto case 'U';
        case 'U': ivowelct++;
          break;
        default : iconstantct++;
          break;
    }

   return(0);
   }
 }
```

This program actually illustrates two characteristics of the `switch` statement: the enumeration of several test values that all execute the same code section and the *non-existent* drop-through characteristic so familiar to C/C++ programmers. Unlike the C++ `switch` statement, C# does not support an explicit fall-through from one case label to another. If you want, you can use `goto` with a switch-case, or `goto default`.

Other high-level languages have their own form of selection (the case statement in Pascal and the select statement in PL/I) which allows for several test values, all producing the same result, to be included on the same selection line. C# however, requires a separate `case` for each. But notice in this example how the same effect has been created by using `goto` statements until all possible vowels have been checked. Should c contain a constant, all of the vowel case tests will be checked and skipped until the `default` statement is reached.

If `expression` does not match any *constant-expression*, control is transferred to the `statement`(s) that follow the optional `default` label. If there is no `default` label, control is transferred outside the `switch`.

Jump Control

C# has three control statements that could, if misused, easily break the design principles of top-down programming. In other words, one entry point and one exit point. However, if `break`, `continue`, and `goto` are used in their C# context, these control flow options can make for very eloquent algorithms.

break

The break statement can be used to exit a loop before the test condition becomes false. The break statement is similar in many ways to a goto statement, only the point jumped to is not known directly. When breaking out of a loop, program execution continues with the next statement following the loop itself, as in:

```
int itimes = 1, isum = 0;

while(itimes < 10){
    isum += isum + itimes;
    if(isum > 20)
        break;
    itimes++;
}
```

Use the integrated debugger to trace through the program. Trace the variables isum and itimes. Pay particular attention to which statements are executed after isum reaches the value 21.

What you should have noticed is that when isum reached the value 21, the break statement was executed. This caused the increment of itimes to be jumped over itimes++, with program execution continuing on the line of code below the loop. In this example, the next statement executed was the return.

continue

There is a subtle difference between the break statement and the continue statement. As you have already seen from the last example program, break causes the loop to terminate execution altogether. In contrast, the continue statement causes all of the statements following the continue statement to be ignored but does *not* circumvent incrementing the loop control variable or the loop control test condition. In other words, if the loop control variable still satisfies the loop test condition, the loop will continue to iterate.

The following program demonstrates this concept, using a number guessing game:

```
using System;
public class Class1
{
    public static int Main(string[] args)
    {
        // continue.cs
        // A C# program demonstrating the use of the continue
        // statement.
        // Copyright (c) Chris H. Pappas and William H. Murray, 2001
        //
```

```
int  ilucky_number = 77,
     iinput_val,
     inumber_of_tries = 0;
bool iam_lucky = false;

while(iam_lucky == false){
  Console.Write("Please enter your lucky guess: ");
  iinput_val = int.Parse(Console.ReadLine());
  inumber_of_tries++;
  if(iinput_val == ilucky_number)
    iam_lucky = true;
  else
    continue;
  Console.WriteLine("It only took you {0} tries to get lucky!",
  inumber_of_tries);
}

return(0);
  }
}
```

As an exercise, enter the preceding program and trace the variables `iinput_val`, `inumber_of_tries`, and `iam_lucky` in the debugger. Pay particular attention to which statements are executed after `iinput_val` is compared to `ilucky_number`.

The program uses a `while` loop to prompt the user for a value, increments the `inumber_of_tries` for each guess entered, and then determines the appropriate action to take based on the success of the match. If no match was found, the `else` statement is executed. This is the `continue` statement. Whenever the `continue` statement is executed, the `Console.WriteLine()` statement is ignored. Note, however, that the loop continues to execute. When `iinput_val` matches `ilucky_number`, the `iam_lucky` flag is set to `true` and the `continue` statement is ignored, allowing the `Console.WriteLine()` statement to execute.

goto

The `goto` statement transfers the program control directly to a labeled statement and has only three forms:

```
goto myLabel;
goto case constantValue;
goto default;
```

You will most likely encounter the last two categories of `goto`, both of which can justifiably appear within the context of a `switch-case`.

Iteration Control

C# includes the standard set of repetition control statements: `for` loops, `while` loops, and `do-while` loops (called repeat-until loops in several other high-level languages). You may be surprised, however, by the ways a program can leave a repetition loop. C# provides three methods for altering the repetitions in a loop. All repetition loops can naturally terminate based on the expressed test condition. In C#, however, a repetition loop can also terminate because of an anticipated error condition by using either a `break` or `goto` statement. Repetition loops can also have their logic control flow altered by a `break` statement or a `continue` statement.

The basic difference between a `for` loop and a `while` or `do-while` loop has to do with the "known" number of repetitions. Typically, `for` loops are used whenever there is a definite predefined required number of repetitions, and `while` and `do-while` loops are reserved for an "unknown" number of repetitions.

for

The syntax for a `for` loop is

```
for(initialization_exp; test_exp; increment_exp)
  statement;
```

When the `for` loop statement is encountered, the `initialization_exp` is executed first. This is done at the start of the loop, and it is never executed again. Usually, this statement involves the initialization of the loop control variable. Following this, `test_exp`, which is called the *loop terminating condition*, is tested. Whenever `test_exp` evaluates to `true`, the statement or statements within the loop are executed. If the loop was entered, then after all of the statements within the loop are executed, `increment_exp` is executed.

However, if `test_exp` evaluates to `false`, the statement or statements within the loop are ignored, along with `increment_exp`, and execution continues with the statement following the end of the loop. The indentation scheme applied to `for` loops with several statements to be repeated looks like this:

```
for(initialization_exp; test_exp; increment_exp) {
  statement_a;
  statement_b;
  statement_c;
  statement_n;
}
```

In the case where several statements need to be executed, a pair of braces is required to tie their execution to the loop control structure. Let's examine a few examples of `for` loops.

The following example sums up the first five integers. It assumes that isum and ivalue have been predefined as integers:

```
isum = 0;
for(ivalue = 1; ivalue <= 5; ivalue++)
   isum += ivalue;
```

After isum has been initialized to zero, the for loop is encountered. First, ivalue is initialized to 1 (this is done only once); second, ivalue's value is checked against the loop terminating condition, <= 5. Since this is true, a 1 is added to isum. Once the statement is executed, the loop control variable (ivalue) is incremented by 1. This process continues four more times until ivalue is incremented to 6 and the loop terminates.

In C#, the same code segment could be written as follows. See if you can detect the subtle difference:

```
for(int ivalue = 1; ivalue <= 5; ivalue++)
   isum += ivalue;
```

C# also allows the loop control variable to be declared and initialized within the for loop. This brings up a very sensitive issue among structured programmers, which is the proper placement of variable declarations. In C#, you can declare variables right before the statement that actually uses them. In the preceding example, since ivalue is used only to generate an isum, with isum having a larger scope than ivalue, the local declaration for ivalue is harmless. However, look at the following code segment:

```
int isum = 0;
for(int ivalue = 1; ivalue <= 5; ivalue++)
   isum += ivalue;
```

This would obscure the visual "desk check" of the variable isum because it was not declared below the function head. For the sake of structured design and debugging, it is best to localize all variable declarations. It is the rare code segment that can justify the usefulness of moving a variable declaration to a nonstandard place, in sacrifice of easily read, easily checked, and easily modified code.

The value used to increment for loop control variables does not always have to be 1 or ++. The following example sums all the odd numbers up to 9:

```
iodd_sum = 0;
for(iodd_value = 1; iodd_value <= 9; iodd_value += 2);
   iodd_sum += iodd_value;
```

In this example, the loop control variable iodd_value is initialized to 1 and is incremented by 2.

while

The C# `while` loop is a *pretest loop* just like the `for` loop. This means that the program evaluates `test_exp` before entering the statement or statements within the body of the loop. Because of this, pretest loops may be executed from zero to many times. The syntax for a C# `while` loop is

```
while(test_exp)
    statement;
```

For `while` loops with several statements, braces are needed:

```
while(test_exp) {
    statement1;
    statement2;
    statement3;
    statementn;
}
```

Typically, `while` loop control structures are used whenever an indefinite number of repetitions is expected. The following C# program uses a `while` loop to control the number of times `ivalue` is shifted to the right. The program prints the binary representation of a signed integer.

```
using System;
public class Class1
{
    public static int Main(string[] args)
    {
        // while.cs
        // A C# program demonstrating pretest while loops
        // Copyright (c) Chris H. Pappas and William H. Murray, 2001
        //

        int ivalue = 128, ibit_position = 1;
        ushort umask = 1;
        const short WORD = 16;
        const short ONE_BYTE = 8;

        Console.WriteLine("The following value {0},\n",ivalue);
        Console.WriteLine("in binary form looks like: ");

        while(ibit_position <= WORD) {
            if(((ivalue >> (WORD - ibit_position)) & umask) == 1)
                Console.Write("1");
            else
                Console.Write("0");
            if(ibit_position == ONE_BYTE)
                Console.Write(" ");
```

```
            ibit_position++;
        }

    return(0);
        }
    }
```

This application begins by defining two constants, WORD and ONE_BYTE, that can be easily modified for different architectures. WORD will be used as a flag to determine when the while loop will terminate. Within the while loop, ivalue is shifted, compared to umask, and printed from most significant bit to least. This allows the algorithm to use a simple Console.Write() statement to output the results.

NOTE

C/C++ programmers would have written the if test condition in the following accepted form:

```
if((ivalue >> (WORD - ibit_position)) & umask)  // legal C/C++
```

This line of code is shown without the C# required Boolean test (== 1)!

do-while

The do-while loop differs from the for and while loops. The do-while loop is a *post-test loop*. In other words, the loop is always entered at least once, with the loop condition being tested at the end of the first iteration. In contrast, for loops and while loops may execute from zero to many times, depending on the loop control variable.

Since do-while loops always execute at least one time, they are best used whenever there is no doubt you want the particular loop entered. For example, if your program needs to present a menu to the user, even if all the user wants to do is immediately quit the program, he or she needs to see the menu to know which key terminates the application.

The syntax for a do-while loop is

```
do
 action;
while(test_condition);
```

Braces are required for do-while statements that have compound actions:

```
do {
 action1;
 action2;
 action3;
 actionn;
} while(test_condition);
```

foreach, in

C#'s foreach statement goes one better than a simple array-element extraction by repeating a group of statements for each element in the array to get the matching criterion. It is a logical misuse of foreach if the embedded statements attempt to change the contents of the array. The syntax for foreach and its accomplice keyword, in, looks like:

foreach (datatype identifier **in** expression) statement(s)

identifier is the name you choose for the iteration variable representing the array element, datatype is naturally identifier's type, in the co-required keyword, expression represents the object collection or array expression, and statement(s), the statement(s) to be executed. The statement(s) are executed for each element in the array.

The following example program, foreach1.cs, queries each initialized array element in dArray to see if it meets the condition of being 2 raised to some power:

```
using System;
public class Class1
{
    public static int Main(string[] args)
    {
        // foreach1.cs
        // A C# application illustrating the new foreach keyword
        // Copyright (c) Chris H. Pappas and William H. Murray, 2001
        //

        int iPowerOf2 = 0, iNotPowerOfTwo = 0, iRaisedTo = 0;
        double[] dArray = new double[] {1,2,3,4,5,6,7,8};

        foreach( double dInArray in dArray )
        {
            if(Math.Round(Math.Pow(2,iRaisedTo))==
              (Math.Round(dInArray)))
            {
                iPowerOf2++;
                iRaisedTo++;
            }
            else
                iNotPowerOfTwo++;
        }

        Console.WriteLine("Found {0} values equal to a " +
                           "power of two,",iPowerOf2);
        Console.WriteLine("and {0} values not equal" +
                           " to a power of two.",
                           iNotPowerOfTwo);

        return 0;
    }
}
```

A more advanced use of `foreach` and `in` is used with collections. To iterate through a collection, the collection must be one of three types: `interface`, `class`, or `struct` and must include two methods, one named `GetEnumerator()` returning a type, for example, a method named `Enumerator()` must contain a property named `Current` that returns `elementType` or a type that can be converted to it. A second method must be of type `bool` named `MoveNext()`, that increments the item counter and returns `true` if there are more items in the collection.

This next program, `foreach2.cs`, creates the required `GetEnumerator()` and `MoveNext()` syntax requirements for traversing collections.

```
using System;
public class aCollection
{
    double[] dArray = new double[8] {1,2,3,4,5,6,7,8};

    public enumerateIt GetEnumerator()
    {
        return new enumerateIt(this);
    }

    public class enumerateIt
    {
        int iOffset;
        aCollection edC;

        public enumerateIt(aCollection dC)
        {
            edC = dC;
            iOffset = -1;
        }

        public bool MoveNext()
        {
            iOffset++;
            return(iOffset < edC.dArray.GetLength(0));
        }

        public double Current
        {
            get
            {
                return(edC.dArray[iOffset]);
            }
        }
    }
}
```

```
public static int Main(string[] args)
{
    // foreach2.cs
    // A C# application illustrating the new foreach keyword
    // Copyright (c) Chris H. Pappas and William H. Murray, 2001
    //

    int iPowerOf2 = 0, iNotPowerOfTwo = 0, iRaisedTo = 0;
    aCollection dc = new aCollection();

    foreach( double dInArray in dc )
    {
        if(Math.Round(Math.Pow(2,iRaisedTo))==
          (Math.Round(dInArray)))
        {
            iPowerOf2++;
            iRaisedTo++;
        }
        else
            iNotPowerOfTwo++;
    }

    Console.WriteLine("Found {0} values equal to " +
                      " a power of two,",iPowerOf2);
    Console.WriteLine("and {0} values not equal to " +
                      "a power of two.",iNotPowerOfTwo);

    return 0;
    }
}
```

NOTE

Not all classes support the `foreach` *and* `in` *statements. Only classes that support a method with the signature of* `GetEnumerator()`, *and the* `struct`, `class`, *or* `interface` *returned by it must have the public method* `MoveNext()`, *and the public property* `Current`.

The next example, `hashtable.cs`, uses just such a class, the predefined Hashtable collection class:

```
using System;
using System.Collections; //

public class Class1
```

```
{
  public static int Main(string[] args)
  {
    // hashtable.cs
    // A C# program demonstrating foreach
    // with Hashtable
    // Copyright (c) Chris H. Pappas and William H. Murray, 2001

    Hashtable Ht = new Hashtable();
    Ht.Add("607", "Binghamton, NY");
    Ht.Add("570", "Montrose, PA");
    Ht.Add("412", "Ambridge, PA");
    Ht.Add("843", "Myrtle Beach, SC");

    Console.WriteLine("Number of Entries in Hash Table - {0}\n\n",
                      Ht.Count );
    Console.WriteLine("Key\tCity/State\n");

    foreach(string areaCode in Ht.Keys)
    {
      Console.WriteLine(areaCode + '\t' + Ht[areaCode]);
    }

    return 0;
  }
}
```

You gain access to the Hashtable definitions via the using System.Collect-ions; statement in your program. The program hashtable.cs simply employs the pre-defined method Add() to insert entries into the Ht Hashtable instance. The foreach identifier *areaCode* is of type string and is used on the Ht.Keys hashcode key member. The output from the program takes the following form:

```
Number of Entries in Hash Table - 4


Key     City/State

607     Binghamton, NY
412     Ambridge, PA
570     Montrose, PA
843     Myrtle Beach, SC
```

Can you account for the ordering of the results?

Summary

This chapter has concentrated on a variety of C# control statements. These statements include `if`, `if-else`, and `switch` statements in addition to `for`, `while`, and `do-while` loops.

In the next chapter, we'll examine a very important concept for C# programmers—arrays. You'll start to see how the concepts of this chapter can be linked in programs relating to arrays.

CHAPTER 6

Arrays

$\mathbf{Y}$ou can think of *arrays* as variables containing several homogeneous data types. Each individual data item can be accessed by using a subscript, or index, into the variable. In the C# language, an array is not a standard data type; instead, it is an aggregate type made up of any other type of data. It is possible to have an array of anything: characters, integers, floats, doubles, arrays, (called *jagged arrays*) structures, classes, and so on.

NOTE

Good news for C/C++ programmers. First, you no longer need to use arrays-of-char to store string data—with the predisposition for memory leaks created by the forgotten null-string terminator '\0'. C# has a standard string data type for this purpose. Secondly, C# always performs bounds checking on array indices. It is no longer possible to use that "extra" array element n, when the array actually has n-1 elements. This makes it impossible to overwrite unallocated memory!

Array Properties

There are four basic properties to an array:

- The data items in an array are called *elements*.

- Elements must all be of the same data type.

- Elements are stored contiguously in memory. The subscript (or index) of the first element is zero.

- The array's name is a pointer or address. This pointer or address is the location of the first element in the array.

Since all elements of an array are assumed to be the same size, arrays cannot be defined by using mixed data types. Without this assumption, it would be very difficult to determine where any given element was stored. Since the elements are all the same size and since that fact is used to help determine how to locate a given element, it follows that the elements are stored contiguously in the computer's memory (with the lowest address corresponding to the first element, the highest address to the last element). This means that there are no gaps or spaces between elements. They are physically adjacent to each other in storage.

Arrays can themselves be part of an array, in other words, multidimensional arrays. An array element can also be a structure. If the element is a structure, then mixed data types can exist in the array because they exist within the structure itself.

Arrays are considered data structures. As data structures they can use member variables to access array indices. The array variables are often called *elements* of the array. These elements are of the same data type and this data type becomes the element type of the array.

Arrays have a *rank*. The rank is used to find the number of indices associated with each array element. The rank of an array is also referred to as the array's *dimensions*. Arrays with a rank of one are called *single-dimensional arrays* (or *vectors*). If an array has a rank greater than one it is sometimes referred to as a *multidimensional array*.

An array's dimensions have an associated integer length that is zero or greater. These dimensions are specified when an instance of the array is created at runtime. Thus, for a length *n,* the indices range from 0 to *n*–1 inclusive. The number of array elements is simply the product of each array dimension. If any array dimension is zero, the array is considered empty.

Array types

A C# array is declared with an `element_type` followed by the array's dimensions, the array's name, and any initializers, which are optional. C# arrays are one-dimensional but their `element_type` can be multidimensional. Here is the syntax for an array:

```
element_type [dimension(s)] array_name [= optional_initializers];
```

The `element_type` type can be an integer, string, or any type of object with the exception that it cannot be an `array_type`. The `dimension(s)` of an array are enclosed in a pair of square brackets `[]`. If the array is multidimensional, the comma operator is used to separate `dimension(s)` `[,]`. The `array_name` is the name assigned by the programmer. The array_name is followed by any values used to initialize the array.

The array's leftmost dimension determines the array's rank. Thus, if the dimension is specified as [ ], the array will have a rank of one. If the dimension is specified as [ ] [,], the array will be a single dimension array composed of two-dimensional arrays. Finally, if the dimension is specified as [ ] [, ,] [,], the array is a single dimensional array of three-dimensional arrays of two-dimensions.

Arrays As Objects

A one-dimensional array declaration takes this form:

```
int[] iArray_1D;
```

A two-dimensional array declaration looks like:

```
int[][] iArray_OfiArrays;
```

A three-dimensional array declaration takes this form:

```
int[,,] iArray_Multidimensional;
```

In C# arrays are objects and must always be instantiated. In order to allocate memory for the previous declarations you would need appropriate calls to the C# keyword new. For example:

```
int[] iArray_1D = new int[10];
int[][] iArray_OfArrays = new int[3][];
for (int i = 0; r < iArray_OfArrays.Length; i++)
    iArray_OfArrays[i] = new int[10];

int[,] iArray_Multidimensional = new int[3,5];
```

The following program uses these declarations and then prints several of the arrays' lengths:

```
using System;

namespace ArrDec
{
    /// <summary>
    /// Summary description for Class1.
    /// </summary>
    class Class1
    {
        static void Main(string[] args)
        {
            // one-dimensional array declaration
            int[] iArray_1D = new int[10];
```

```
// two-dimensional array-of-arrays declaration
int[][] iArray_OfiArrays = new int[5][];
// completing the second dimension
for (int i = 0; i < iArray_OfiArrays.Length; i++)
    iArray_OfiArrays[i] = new int[10];
// Print length of iArray_OfArrays + each row's length
for (int i = 0; i < iArray_OfiArrays.Length; i++)
{
    Console.WriteLine("The Number of Rows = {0}",
        iArray_OfiArrays.Length);
    Console.WriteLine("The Length of row {0} is {1}",
                    i, iArray_OfiArrays[i].Length);
}

// two-dimensional array declaration
int[,] iArray_Multidimensional = new int[3,5];
// Print length of iArray_Multidimensional
Console.WriteLine("The Number of Rows = {0}",
    iArray_Multidimensional.Length);
        }
    }
}
```

The output from this code segment reports the following information:

```
The Number of Rows = 5
The Length of row 0 is 10
The Number of Rows = 5
The Length of row 1 is 10
The Number of Rows = 5
The Length of row 2 is 10
The Number of Rows = 5
The Length of row 3 is 10
The Number of Rows = 5
The Length of row 4 is 10
The Number of Rows = 15
```

Unlike a C++ STL (Standard Template Library) dynamic array—called *vector*, a C# array instance maintains the rank and length of each dimension as declared remaining constant for the entire lifetime of the instance. Unlike an STL vector, it is not possible to change the rank of an existing array instance, nor is it possible to resize its dimensions. Elements of arrays created are always initialized to their default value.

Initializing Arrays

Arrays are zero indexed; that is, the array indexes start at zero. Arrays in C# work similarly to how arrays work in most other popular languages There are, however, a few differences that you should be aware of. When declaring an array, the square brackets [] must come after the type, not the identifier. Placing the brackets after the identifier is not legal syntax in C#. The following example highlights this difference between C# and C/C++:

```
int[10] iArray; // legal C# syntax
iArray int[10]; // legal C/C++ syntax
```

Since the C# compiler, like many other compilers, checks the data type between a formal argument and its matching actual argument in a subroutine call (function or method), you need to understand how C# views an array's type. In C# the size of an array is *not* part of its type as it is in the C/C++ language. This allows you to declare an array and assign any array of int objects to it, regardless of the array's length.

```
int[] iArray; // declare numbers as an int array of any size
iArray = new int[5];    // iArray with five elements
iArray = new int[50];   // iArray redefined with fifty elements
```

You may initialize a C# array in one of three ways—by using an in-field declaration, a local variable declaration, or within the array declaration itself. The syntax for initializing array elements during array declaration takes on the following form:

```
element_type array_name = [value] [{ [value,...] }];
```

Here, the array_name appears to the left of the assignment operator. To the right of the assignment operator is either a single initialization value, or optionally, multiple values, separated by commas. These values are all encapsulated with a pair of French braces {} and terminated with the semicolon statement terminator (;).

Explicit Array Initialization

Where and how you declare an array determines which type of initialization is appropriate. For example, when an array is initialized as it is being defined, the element_type precedes the initialization values. In a field or variable declaration, the array type is the type of the field or variable being declared. When an array initializer is used in a field or variable declaration, such as:

```
int[] iArray = {1, 3, 5, 7};
```

it is simply shorthand for an equivalent array creation expression:

```
int[] iArray = new int[] {1, 3, 5, 7};
```

The initialization values are applied in a left-to-right direction. This left-to-right direction means that storage occurs from the lowest memory address reference to highest address reference. The number of explicit values used in the array's initialization determines the length of the array. For example, the array declaration/initialization above creates an integer array instance of length 4 and then initializes the instance with the following values:

```
iArray[0] = 1;
iArray[1] = 3;
iArray[2] = 5;
iArray[3] = 7;
```

In cases of multidimensional arrays, the array initializer has as many levels of nesting as there are dimensions in the array. The outermost nesting level corresponds to the leftmost array dimension and the innermost nesting level corresponds to the rightmost array dimension. The length of each array dimension is dependent upon the number of elements at the particular nesting level. For example:

```
int[,] iArray = {{1, 1}, {2, 2}, {3, 3}, {4, 4}};
```

Here, a two-dimensional array is created with a length of five for the leftmost dimension and a length of two for the rightmost dimension:

```
int iRow = 4, iColumns = 2;

int[,] iArray = new int[iRows, iColumns];
```

The array is then initialized with the following values:

```
iArray[0, 0] = 1;
iArray[0, 1] = 1;
iArray[1, 0] = 2;
iArray[1, 1] = 2;
iArray[2, 0] = 3;
iArray[2, 1] = 3;
iArray[3, 0] = 4;
iArray[3, 1] = 4;
```

Dimensioning and explicitly initializing an array can be tricky. The array's dimension *must* be a constant value and the number of elements at each nesting level *must* match the corresponding dimension length. For example:

```
int ivalue = 4;
int[] iArrayA = new int[4] {0, 1, 2, 3};       // correct
int[] iArrayB = new int[ivalue] {0, 1, 2, 3};  // incorrect
int[] iArrayC = new int[4] {0, 1, 2}           // incorrect
```

The first array is correctly declared iArrayA since the number of explicit values {0, 1, 2, 3} matches the dimension of 4. The second array declaration is incorrect. Here, *iArrayB* is incorrect because the dimension specified by the variable ivalue is *not* a constant. The third declaration is also incorrect. Here, iArrayC is incorrect because the number of explicit values {0, 1, 2} does not match the dimension of 4.

Notice that the element type and number of dimensions make up the array's type. However, the length of each dimension is not part of the array's type. For example:

```
float[,] fArray_2D = new float[34.3, 29.4];
```

Here you see an array of type float[,] and an array creation expression of new float[34.3,29.4].

Local or Internal Array Declaration Shorthand

C# allows you to use a special syntax for variable and field declarations contained within the body of a subroutine. When using this syntax it is not necessary to restate the array's type. For example, a normal declaration might appear as:

```
int[] iArray = new int[] {1, 3, 5, 7, 9, 11};
```

The shorthand version then becomes:

```
int[] iArray = {1, 3, 5, 7, 9, 11};
```

C# views these two equivalent statements as structurally and internally identical.

Array Initializer Context

There is more to an array's initializer than just using shorthand abbreviations. Also important is the context in which the array initializer is used as in the previous two statements. The *context* actually determines the type of the array being initialized. Examine the following portion of code:

```
class ArrayContext
{
    static void Main() {
        int[] iArray = {1, 3, 5, 7, 9, 11};
        int32[] i32Array = {1, 3, 5, 7, 9, 11};
        long[] lArray = {1, 3, 5, 7, 9, 11};
    }
}
```

Here, the identical intializer is applied in three different arrays. This is an important concept since it is not possible to use an array initializer in an expression context. Consider the following example:

```
class IllegalArrayInitializer
{
    static void initArray(int[] dummyArgument) {}
```

```
static void Main() {
    initArray({1, 2, 3, 5, 7, 9, 11});
}
}
```

Actually, if you know any programming language, the syntax of the offending statement is obvious.

```
initArray({1, 3, 5, 7, 9, 11});
```

Most programming languages, C# included, cannot handle the translation of {1, 3, 5,
7, 9, 11} to the dummyArgument. The exception being a macro expansion or C/C++'s ellipsis operator (. . .). In this example, the initArray() does not contain a valid expression.

However, C# *does* provide a unique and clever workaround. The following code segment demonstrates the correct syntax:

```
class LegalArrayInitializer
{
    static void initArray(int[] arr) {}
    static void Main() {
        initArray(new int[] {1, 3, 5, 7, 9, 11});
    }
}
```

Here, a call using the new keyword dynamically allocates memory. The C# compiler
then calculates the required storage based on the initializers and allocates the memory. The
address to the first byte, passing this value to the method initArray(), is then returned.

One-Dimensional Arrays

The following section includes a simple one-dimensional array example followed by syntax
options for declaring multidimensional arrays. One-dimensional arrays are the most frequently used arrays. Consider the following portion of code:

```
int[] iArray = new int[9];
for (int offset = 0; offset < iArray.Length; offset++)
    iArray[offset] = offset * offset;
for (int offset = 0; offset < iArray.Length; offset++)
    Console.WriteLine("iArray[{0}] = {1}", offset,
                    iArray[offset]);
```

Here, a single-dimensional array of integer values initializes the array elements and
then prints out each of them. The output from the code segment takes on this form:

```
iArray[0] = 0
iArray[1] = 1
iArray[2] = 4
```

```
iArray[3] = 9
iArray[4] = 16
iArray[5] = 25
iArray[6] = 36
iArray[7] = 49
iArray[8] = 64
```

The type, `int[]`, used in the previous code segment, is an example of an array type.

Multidimensional Arrays

From earlier discussions you have learned that an array's type is declared with an element type. For example, the array's type could be `int` followed by one or more rank specifiers. This next code segment declares several different array types:

```
int[] iArray1          //one-dimensional array of type int
int[,] iArray_2D1      //two-dimensional array of type int
int[,,] iArray_2D2;    //three-dimensional array of type int
int[][] iArray_2Dj;    //jagged array of (array of type int)
int[][][] iArray_3Dj; //array of (array of (array of type int))
```

Technically, array identifiers like `iArray1`, `iArray_2D1`, . . ., and `iArray_3Dj` are reference types. This means that the declaration of an array variable sets aside space for the reference to the array. Reference types are another way to say pointers. Array instances are actually created via array initializers and array creation expressions. Consider the following portion of code:

```
int[] iArray1 = new int[] {1, 3, 5, 7, 9, 11};
int[,] iArray_2D1 = new int[,] {{1, 3, 5}, {7, 9};
int[,,] iAray_2D2 = new int[9, 18, 27];
int[][] iArray_2Dj = new int[5][];
j2[0] = new int[] {1, 3};
j2[1] = new int[] {1, 3, 5};
j2[2] = new int[] {1, 3, 5, 7};
j2[3] = new int[] {1, 3, 5, 7, 9};
j2[4] = new int[] {1, 3, 5, 7, 9, 11};
```

The variables `iArray1`, `iArrY_2D1`, and `iArray2D2` are examples of *rectangular arrays*. The variable `iArray_2Dj` declares a *jagged array*. The terms rectangular and jagged are based on the shapes of the arrays. Rectangular arrays always have a rectangular shape. Given the length of each dimension of the array, its rectangular shape is clear. For example, the length of `iArray_2D2`'s three dimensions are 9, 18, and 27. This means that this array has $(9 \times 18 \times 27)$ elements.

Now consider the variable `iArray2Dj` that denotes a jagged array, or an array of arrays. Specifically, `iAray2Dj` declares an array of an array of `int`, or a single-dimensional array of type `int[]`. Each of these `int[]` variables can be initialized individually, and this allows the array to take on a jagged shape. The example gives each of the `int[]` arrays a different length. Specifically, the length of `iArray_2Dj[0]` is 5, the length of `iArray_2Dj[1]` is 3, and the length of `iArray_2Dj[4]` is 6.

Array of (array of (array of `int`)) versus Array of `int`

The program in this section contrasts the two types of C# array syntax. The first portion of code uses the array of (array of (array of int)) declaration, `int[][][]`. The second portion of code uses C#'s array of `int` syntax for a three-dimensional cube, or `int[,,]`.

The code allows the user to digitally encrypt a musical score by using each row to represent one of the musical instruments in the score—each column representing an instance in time, with the planes or z dimension detailing how each note, on each instrument, is being played. For example, a piano can play the same note for a long period of time, a short period of time, loudly, or softly. A three-dimensional array is the ideal model for this encryption algorithm.

First, let's examine the entire program:

```
public class Class1
{
    enum NOTE { Ab, A, As, Cb, C, Cs };
    enum OCCIDENTAL { Forte, Pianissimo };
    enum INSTRUMENT { String, Horn, Piano, Organ };
    enum DURATION { Snote, Enote, Qnote, Hnote, Fnote };

    public static int Main(string[] args)
    {
        // array3Denum1.cs
        // A C# program demonstrating three dimensional
        // array instantiation, enumerated type definitions
        // Copyright (c) Chris H. Pappas and William H. Murray, 2001
        //

        // DME = Digital Music Encryption
        const int BEATS = 5; // Kept small for trace purposes
        int [][][] DME = new int[3][][];

        for( int plane = 0; plane < 3; plane++ )
            DME[plane] = new int[4][];

        for( int plane = 0; plane < 3; plane++ )
            for( int instrument = 0; instrument < 4; instrument++

                DME[plane][instrument] = new int[BEATS];

        // Plane 0 holds which NOTE is being played
```
)

```
// by which INSTRUMENT, columns are for the
// instance in time the INSTRUMENT is playing the NOTE
DME[0][0][0] = (int) NOTE.Ab;
DME[0][1][0] = (int) NOTE.Cs;
DME[0][2][0] = (int) NOTE.Cb;
DME[0][3][0] = (int) NOTE.A;

// Plane 1 describes how each NOTE
// is being played by each instrument
DME[1][0][0] = (int) OCCIDENTAL.Forte;
DME[1][1][0] = (int) OCCIDENTAL.Forte;
DME[1][2][0] = (int) OCCIDENTAL.Pianissimo;
DME[1][3][0] = (int) OCCIDENTAL.Pianissimo;

// Plane 2 describes the DURATION of each NOTE
DME[2][0][0] = (int) DURATION.Enote;
DME[2][1][0] = (int) DURATION.Fnote;
DME[2][2][0] = (int) DURATION.Qnote;
DME[2][3][0] = (int) DURATION.Snote;

        return 0;
    }
}
```

The program begins with four enumerated type declarations placed above the Main() method. These are used to initialize the *DME* array to demonstrate enumerated type use and three-dimensional cube referencing:

```
enum NOTE { Ab, A, As, Cb, C, Cs };
enum OCCIDENTAL { Forte, Pianissimo };
enum INSTRUMENT { String, Horn, Piano, Organ };
enum DURATION { Snote, Enote, Qnote, Hnote, Fnote };

public static int Main(string[] args)
{
```

Next, the three-dimensional *DME* array reference pointer is declared and the instance memory allocation for a three-plane cube is created with the call to new.

```
int [][][] DME = new int[3][][];
```

This step, however, does *not* detail the number of rows or columns used by each plane. The next for loop determines just how many rows there are in each plane by traversing the number of planes, in this case *3*, and deciding, with a call to new, the row's dimension, or *4* rows:

```
for( int plane = 0; plane < 3; plane++ )
   DME[plane] = new int[4][];
```

The complete memory allocation terminates with the second `for` loop which now selects the number of columns. This statement uses the `const int` BEATS. BEATS is left intentionally small, 5, to create a reasonably understood debug trace.

```
const int BEATS = 5; // Kept small for trace purposes
   .
   .

   .
for( int plane = 0; plane < 3; plane++ )
  for( int instrument = 0; instrument < 4; instrument++ )
    DME[plane][instrument] = new int[BEATS];
```

An array of (array of (array of `int`)) element selection begins with the name of the array, *DME*, followed by three pairs of square brackets [ ], selecting, in order, the plane, then the row, then the column. The first plane, at an offset of 0, details the particular note an instrument is playing:

```
// Plane 0 holds which NOTE is being played
// by which INSTRUMENT, columns are for the
// instance in time the INSTRUMENT is playing the NOTE
DME[0][0][0] = (int) NOTE.Ab;
DME[0][1][0] = (int) NOTE.Cs;
DME[0][2][0] = (int) NOTE.Cb;
DME[0][3][0] = (int) NOTE.A;
```

The `(int)` cast is necessary to store the enumerated type in an array element of type `int`. The [0], [1], [2], [3] subscripts are selecting the row, or which instrument is playing the defined note. The next code segment clarifies how each note is being played using the second plane at an offset of 1:

```
// Plane 1 describes how each NOTE
// is being played by each instrument
DME[1][0][0] = (int) OCCIDENTAL.Forte;
DME[1][1][0] = (int) OCCIDENTAL.Forte;
DME[1][2][0] = (int) OCCIDENTAL.Pianissimo;
DME[1][3][0] = (int) OCCIDENTAL.Pianissimo;
```

The final code segment initializes the *DME* three-dimensional array's third plane, at an offset of *2*, with the duration of each instrument's note:

```
// Plane 2 describes the DURATION of each NOTE
DME[2][0][0] = (int) DURATION.Enote;
DME[2][1][0] = (int) DURATION.Fnote;
DME[2][2][0] = (int) DURATION.Qnote;
DME[2][3][0] = (int) DURATION.Snote;
```

In the next section, we'll use this code with the Microsoft Visual Studio.NET debugger.

Using the Microsoft Visual Studio Debugger

Since Microsoft created C#, you are most likely working in the Microsoft Visual Studio.NET environment as you investigate this new language. The Visual Studio Debugger, though richly powerful, can be easily tamed with just a few knowledgeable hot-key strokes.

To help you understand the differences between the two three-dimensional array type declarations, it is very helpful to view their structures with the debugger. To start debugging *any* program, line-by-line, you simply need your Project or Solution open, the Main() method in the active Edit pane, and then press the F10 key. It's that simple!

Assuming you have pressed F10, you should see a screen that looks similar to Figure 6–1.

You will always know when you are in the Debug mode by the addition of a trace arrow (usually yellow) on the left-edge of the Edit pane (see Figure 6–1). The *trace arrow* represents the line of code to be executed the *next time you press F10*! Figure 6–1 shows the trace arrow on the statement that will ultimately instantiate the first dimension of *DME*.

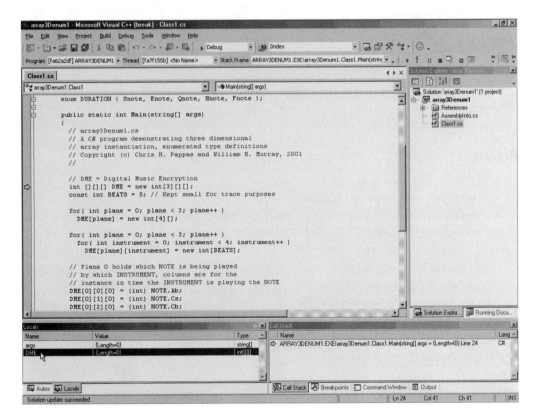

Figure 6–1   Single-step debug with Locals variables in view.

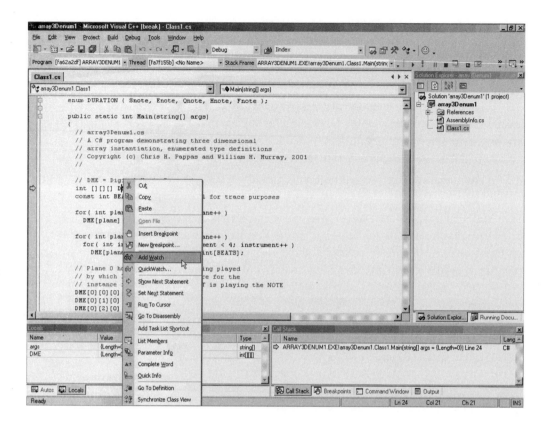

Figure 6–2   Right-click on *DME* to open Edit pane Local Menu—Add Watch.

If you look closely at the bottom left-edge of Figure 6–1, you will see the mouse-pointer to the right of *DME* in the Locals watch window. This window automatically tracks source code variables that are in scope. For our demonstration purposes, this will not do. Also, the Locals window is too small to display the entire *DME* cube.

To manually add any variable to the Watch window all you need to do is right-click the mouse button once on the variable you want to watch, as seen in Figure 6–2.

This opens up the Edit pane's Local menu. The item in this list you are interested in is Add Watch. Clicking on this option inserts the selected variable into the Watch window seen in Figure 6–3. The figure shows a manually expanded Watch window dimension with the, as yet, uninstantiated *DME* array.

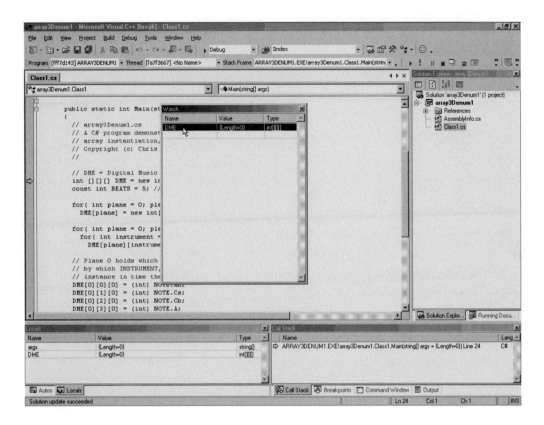

Figure 6–3   Expanded initial Watch window showing *DME* with Length = 0 int[][][].

Repeated presses of F10 cause the Debugger to advance to the beginning of the *second* `for` loop seen in Figure 6–4. This means the Debugger has traversed the *3* planes, allocating memory for *4* rows in each plane.

```
for( int plane = 0; plane < 3; plane++ )
    DME[plane] = new int[4][];

for( int plane = 0; plane < 3; plane++ )
    for( int instrument = 0; instrument < 4; instrument++ )
        DME[plane][instrument] = new int[BEATS];
```

Figure 6–4   Stopping Debug after executing the first `for` loop.

The repeated presses of F10 cause the Debugger to switch back to the Edit pane view of your program, hiding the Watch window. To quickly toggle back to the Watch window simply press the three keys Ctrl+Alt+W simultaneously. Figure 6–5 shows the updated contents of the Watch window with the first planes (offset *0*) of *4* rows visible.

Figure 6–5   Watch window showing three planes of four rows of `ints`.

Notice that while it is true each plane has four rows, none of the rows have any columns. That requires the code execution of the *second* `for` loop. However, to press F10 enough times to get the second loop executed would be boring. A more efficient approach requires the use of a breakpoint. Breakpoints allow the debugger to run full speed, instead of line-by-line, stopping at the breakpoint, allowing you to resume line-by-line tracing.

To set a breakpoint, right-click the mouse once, in the Edit pane, on whichever line you want the debugger to stop on. Figure 6–6 illustrates this step for the first line in the *second* `for` loop.

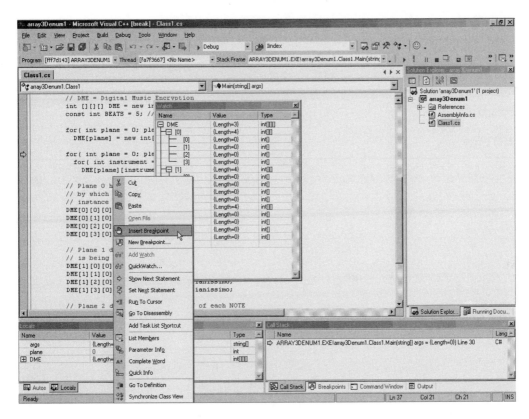

Figure 6–6   Right-click on *DME[0][0][0]* to open Edit pane Local menu—Insert Breakpoint.

When you want to execute your program full speed up to and stopping on a breakpoint, simply press F5. Figure 6–7 shows the resulting screen image.

Figure 6–7   Stopping debug after executing the second nested `for` loop pair.

There are a lot of things happening in Figure 6–7. First, you will notice the trace arrow sitting on top of the Breakpoint icon which resembles a small red stop sign. This lets you visually recognize your having successfully executed the second `for` loop.

Figure 6–7 also shows the dynamic memory allocated for each column. In the Watch window of Figure 6–7 you will notice plane *[0]*'s row *[0]* expanded displaying the new five columns.

NOTE

The Watch windows third column tells you a variable's type. This information can be invaluable when trying to match actual argument types with a subroutine's predefined formal argument type.

In this next program, `array3Denum2.cs`, the three-dimensional array *DME* is redefined using C#'s alternate syntax, `int[,,]`; the program looks like:

```
namespace array3Denum2
{
    using System;

    /// <summary>
    ///     Summary description for Class1.
    /// </summary>
    public class Class1
    {
      enum NOTE { Ab, A, As, Cb, C, Cs };
      enum OCCIDENTAL { Forte, Pianissimo };
      enum INSTRUMENT { String, Horn, Piano, Organ };
      enum DURATION { Snote, Enote, Qnote, Hnote, Fnote };

      public static int Main(string[] args)
      {
        // array3Denum2.cs
        // A C# program demonstrating three dimensional
        // array instantiation, enumerated type definitions
        // Copyright (c) Chris H. Pappas and William H. Murray, 2001
        //

        // DME = Digital Music Encryption
        const int BEATS = 5; // Kept small for trace purposes
        // int [][][] DME = new int[3][][]; now becomes
        int[,,] DME = new int [3,4,BEATS];

        /* for loops no longer needed for dimensioning
```

```
    for( int plane = 0; plane < 3; plane++ )
      DME[plane] = new int[4][];

    for( int plane = 0; plane < 3; plane++ )
      for( int instrument = 0; instrument < 4; instrument++ )
        DME[plane][instrument] = new int[BEATS];
*/

    // Syntax for element references changes
    // Plane 0 holds which NOTE is being played
    // by which INSTRUMENT, columns are for the
    // instance in time the INSTRUMENT is playing the NOTE
    DME[0,0,0] = (int) NOTE.Ab;
    DME[0,1,0] = (int) NOTE.Cs;
    DME[0,2,0] = (int) NOTE.Cb;
    DME[0,3,0] = (int) NOTE.A;

    // Plane 1 describes how each NOTE
    // is being played by each instrument
    DME[1,0,0] = (int) OCCIDENTAL.Forte;
    DME[1,1,0] = (int) OCCIDENTAL.Forte;
    DME[1,2,0] = (int) OCCIDENTAL.Pianissimo;
    DME[1,3,0] = (int) OCCIDENTAL.Pianissimo;

    // Plane 2 describes the DURATION of each NOTE
    DME[2,0,0] = (int) DURATION.Enote;
    DME[2,1,0] = (int) DURATION.Fnote;
    DME[2,2,0] = (int) DURATION.Qnote;
    DME[2,3,0] = (int) DURATION.Snote;

    return 0;
  }
 }
}
```

The redesigned syntax takes on quite a unique appearance from the declaration of the array itself:

```
// int [][][] DME = new int[3][][]; now becomes
int[,,] DME = new int [3,4,BEATS];
```

Notice that the array loses the three pairs of square brackets and now uses only one pair. Note also that the three dimensions are instantiated, rather than just the first.

The following two for loops become superfluous since the instantiation of *DME* now contains the three lengths:

```
/* for loops no longer needed for dimensioning
for( int plane = 0; plane < 3; plane++ )
  DME[plane] = new int[4][];

for( int plane = 0; plane < 3; plane++ )
  for( int instrument = 0; instrument < 4; instrument++ )
    DME[plane][instrument] = new int[BEATS];
*/
```

The final syntax change addresses the requirements for elemental access:

```
// Plane 0 holds which NOTE is being played
// by which INSTRUMENT, columns are for the
// instance in time the INSTRUMENT is playing the NOTE
DME[0,0,0] = (int) NOTE.Ab;
DME[0,1,0] = (int) NOTE.Cs;
DME[0,2,0] = (int) NOTE.Cb;
DME[0,3,0] = (int) NOTE.A;
```

Once again, the code modification follows a similar syntax by requiring only one set of square brackets to detail an element's location within the cube.

However, after executing the algorithm through to the last statement, you may be surprised to see just how the debugger displays *DME* in the Watch window, as seen in Figure 6–8.

Figure 6–8 shows an exploded view of the array. Did you notice anything interesting about the visual representation? By expanding and collapsing the tree hierarchy you can easily view planes, rows, and columns. Remember, the key to understanding the visual representation begins with one fact: All arrays, regardless of rank, contain consecutively allocated, homogenous element types stored *linearly* in memory. Any dimensionality is a mapping the programmer places over this linear allotment.

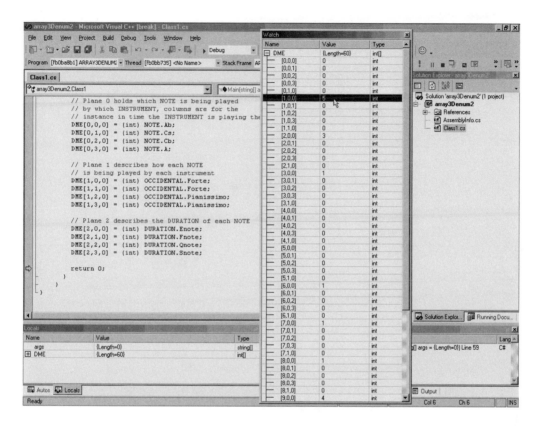

Figure 6–8   *DME* as a three-dimensional cube of `int`.

Array Element Access

In order to access array elements an *element access* expression is needed. This expression takes the form `array_name[d₁, d₂, ..., dₙ]`. Here, `array_name` is an expression of an array type and each $d_1 \ldots d_n$ is an expression of type `int`. The result of an array element access is a variable. The variable is the array element selected by the indices.

The `while` Statement

One way to simply process elements within an array is with the C# `while` loop. A `while` loop may execute a loop from zero to many times—as long as a Boolean test is true.

```
using System;

namespace whileArray
{
    class Class1
    {
        static int Locate(int ivalue, int[] iArray)
        {
            int offset = 0;
            while (iArray[offset] != ivalue)
            {
                if (++offset > iArray.Length)
                    throw new ArgumentException();
            }
            return offset;
        }

        static void Main(string[] args)
        {
            Console.WriteLine(Locate(9,
                            new int[] {10, 9, 8, 7, 6, 5}));
        }
    }
}
```

This program uses a while statement to find the first occurrence of a value in an array. For this example, the value returned is one (1).

The foreach Statement

An alternate approach to listing each element of an array is with the C# foreach keyword. A foreach statement enumerates the elements of a collection, executing a statement for each element in the container. Examine the following program:

```
using System;
using System.Collections;

class myContainer
{
    static void PrintObjs(ArrayList theList)
    {
        foreach (object theObj in theList)
            Console.WriteLine(theObj);
    }
    static void Main()
    {
        ArrayList theList = new ArrayList();
```

```
        for (int offset = 0; offset <= 10; offset++)
            theList.Add(offset);
        PrintObjs(theList);
    }
}
```

This program uses a `foreach` statement to iterate over the elements of a list. In this case the values 0,1,2,3,4,5,6,7,8,9,10 will be returned.

HELP with Subscripts!

If the first programming language you learned was C or C++, you had an unnecessarily steep learning curve when encountering the topic of arrays. Why? Because by design C/C++ were created to never get in a programmer's way. That means the C/C++ compilers faithfully try to execute just about any code statement you can generate.

If you first learned the topic of arrays from some older high-level language like Pascal, you were comforted by a compiler that, *at compile time*, warned you of an array element subscript that was out of bounds! Well, good news—C# will also warn you when an array subscript contains an illegal reference. However, the warning is a little different than you might expect.

Look at this next code segment. Notice that the array `inot_enough_room` is instantiated with `iMAX` or `10` elements. However, the `for` loop attempts to iterate `iOUT_OF_RANGE` or `50` times:

```
public static int Main(string[] args)
{
/* NOrun.cs
 *  Do NOT run this C# program
 *  Copyright (c) Chris H. Pappas and William H. Murray, 2001
 */
   const int iMAX = 10;
   const int iOUT_OF_RANGE = 50;

   int[] inot_enough_room = new int[iMAX];

   for(int offset = 0; offset < iOUT_OF_RANGE; offset++)
     inot_enough_room[offset] = offset;

   return 0;
}
```

Figure 6–9 shows the algorithm started in the Microsoft Visual Studio's debugger. Notice the trace arrow on the left-edge of the Edit pane.

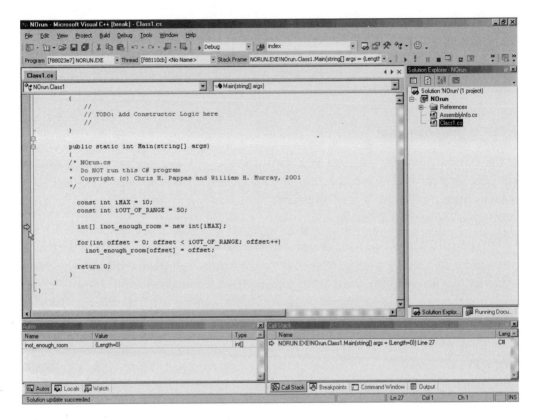

Figure 6–9   Instantiation of *inot_enough_room* array.

Figure 6–10 shows the debugger stopped in the `for` loop with *offset* set to *9*, the value at which you need to slow the debugger trace down so that you can test *offset* about to go out of bounds.

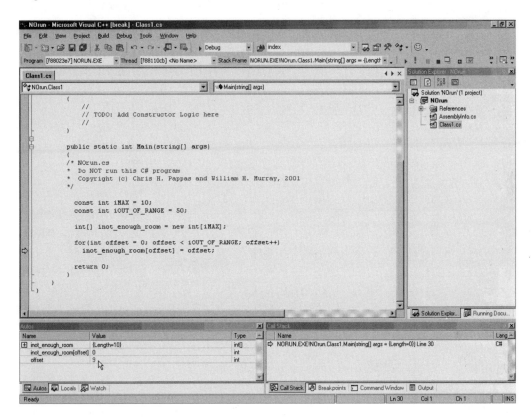

Figure 6–10   *offset* still legal at this point.

Figure 6–11 expands the Autos portion of Figure 6–10 for easy viewing of *offset*'s current value of *9*.

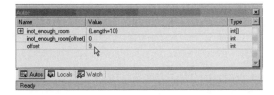

Figure 6–11   Close-up view of the debugger's Autos window with *offset* at *9*.

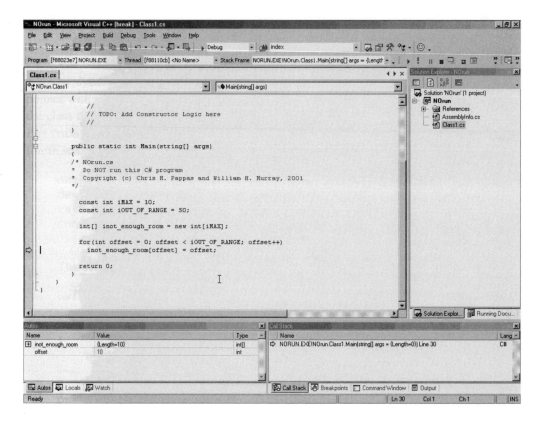

Figure 6–12   *offset* set equal to *10,* an illegal offset range.

With one more iteration of the `for` loop, the debugger displays *offset* set to *10* (see Figure 6–12). This is an illegal offset for an array of ten elements, which can only be accessed with legal *offset* values of 0 through 9.

Once again for easy viewing, Figure 6–13 expands the critical Autos window showing the preset value of *offset* to *10*, getting the C# compiler ready to flag the problem.

Figure 6–13   *offset* not updated to an about-to-be illegal range of *10.*

Figure 6–14   Microsoft Visual Studio debugger flagging illegal array *offset.*

Attempting to enter the `for` loop with an eleventh iteration and an illegal *offset* value of *10* invokes the exception warning message seen in Figure 6–14.

The good news is that C# caught the illegal reference; the bad news is that it was *not* at compile time but at runtime—somewhere in the middle of the non-existent compiler help missing in C/C++ and the full *compile-time* help found in Pascal.

Static Arrays?

This next example is included to guide the experienced C/C++ programmer away from pit-falls encountered when translating C/C++ syntax and experience into C# code design. In particular, the example highlights the differences between the C# keyword `static` versus C/C++'s use of their respective keyword `static`. Examine the following program and pay particular attention to the commented code:

```
// initar.cs
// Defines the entry point for the console application.
// A C# program verifying array initialization
// Copyright (c) Chris H. Pappas and William H. Murray, 2001
//

using System;

namespace initar
{
    class Class1
    {
        static void Main(string[] args)
        {

            // #define statement location/syntax
            //#define iSTATIC_ARRAY_SIZE 10

            // legal in C/C++, illegal in C#
            //#define iNON_STATIC_ARRAY_SIZE 20

            // following C# declaration defines the
```

```
                // two array dimension constants
                const int iSTATIC_ARRAY_SIZE = 10,
                        iNON_STATIC_ARRAY_SIZE = 20;

                // legal C/C++ syntax
                //int non_static_iArray[iSTATIC_ARRAY_SIZE];
                int[] non_static_iArray = new
                    int[iNON_STATIC_ARRAY_SIZE]; // in C# syntax

                // legal C/C++ static array
                //static int static_iArray[iSTATIC_ARRAY_SIZE];

                // illegal in C#
                // static int[] static_iArray = new
                //                            [iSTATIC_ARRAY_SIZE];
                // A constant or type declaration is implicitly a
                // static member.
                int[] static_iArray = new int[iSTATIC_ARRAY_SIZE];

                Console.WriteLine("non_static_iArray[0]: {0}",
                            non_static_iArray[0]);
                Console.WriteLine("static_iArray[0]: {0}",
                            static_iArray[0]);
            }
        }
    }
```

First, notice the legal C/C++ #define statement is *illegal* in C#:

```
//#define iSTATIC_ARRAY_SIZE 10
//#define iNON_STATIC_ARRAY_SIZE 20
```

These now syntactically become:

```
const int iSTATIC_ARRAY_SIZE = 10,
        iNON_STATIC_ARRAY_SIZE = 20;
```

The two array declarations also change dramatically:

```
//int non_static_iArray[iSTATIC_ARRAY_SIZE];
int[] non_static_iArray = new int[iNON_STATIC_ARRAY_SIZE];

//static int static_iArray[iSTATIC_ARRAY_SIZE];
//static int[] static_iArray = new [iSTATIC_ARRAY_SIZE];
// A constant or type declaration is implicitly a static member.
int[] static_iArray = new int[iSTATIC_ARRAY_SIZE];
```

The difference between C/C++ and C# is that C# views any constant or type declaration as an implicit static member.

Array Covariance

The term *array covariance* describes a potential relationship between two arrays. Array covariance exists when a value from `array1[d]` can be a reference to an instance of `array2[d]`. For this to be valid, an implicit reference conversion must exist from `array2` to `array1`.

Assignments to elements of reference type arrays include a runtime check, which validates that the value being assigned to the array element is of an appropriate type. Examine the following short code segment:

```
static void initArray(int iArray[] , int offset,
                      int SIZE, int ivalue) {
    for (int i = offset; i < SIZE-1;
        i++) array[i] = ivalue;
}
static void Main() {
    int[] iArray = new int[100];
    Fill(iArray, 0, 100, -1);
    Fill(iArray, 0, 100, null);
    Fill(iArray, 90, 10, "illegal_string_type");
}
```

The static method `initArray()` includes a runtime check insuring that the value passed to the `ivalue` variable is either `null` or an instance of a type compatible with the actual element type of `iArray`. In `Main()` (remember C/C++ programmers, not `main()` but `Main()`), the first two calls to `initArray()` are successful because all three formal arguments, for each call, are of an appropriate data type. However, the third call to `init-Array()` fails because the third formal argument type is that of `string`. The third call to `initArray()` forces the C# compiler to throw an `ArrayTypeMismatchException` because of the data type mismatch. Note that array covariance does *not* extend to arrays of *value-type*s so, for example, there is no conversion between an array-of-integers and an array-of-objects.

The `System.Array` Type

As it is not assumed you are already familiar with object-oriented programming, this chapter's discussion of C# arrays ends here. However, C# does provide an abstract array class definition in its `System.Array` type. The C# `System.Array` type is the abstract base type used by all array types. An implicit reference conversion exists from any array type to `System.Array`, and an explicit reference conversion exists from `System.Array` to any array type. Note that Sys-

`tem.Array` is itself not an *array_type*. Rather, it is a *class-type* from which all *array_type*s are derived. At runtime, a value of type `System.Array` can be null or a reference to an instance of any array type. Chapter 11, "Advanced C# Programming Considerations," takes another look at the topic of arrays using this powerful and portable set of definitions.

Summary

This chapter presented all of the details and nuances of arrays in C#, including new concepts such as jagged arrays and the popular dynamic array extensions. For most array-based applications you will not need to use these esoteric additions. However, if these new C# subtleties didn't surprise you, wait until you see what Chapter 7 shows you about C#'s unique approach to pointers!

Saying Goodbye to Pointers

Pointers, hmmm, if you have never submitted to a Data Structures course, the topic of pointers is a mystery. If you have had a formal course on advanced programming fundamentals, or have had experience with pointers, then you know what a headache they can be!

The difference between an algorithm that does *not* use pointers and one that does is similar to the difference between driving a car with an automatic shift versus one that has a standard shift. The key structural programming difference between non-pointer and pointer-enabled algorithms is that the algorithm's logic and syntax pull into the foreground something that is normally hidden and protected—namely, the physical addresses to your data and code.

The following discussions briefly present the topic of pointers, their dos and don'ts, and how C# attempts to improve upon an "advanced programming fundamental." Even if you are familiar with the topic of pointers and dynamic memory allocation, you may wish to read these sections to make certain you understand the differences engendered between C# and today's current language of choice, C/C++.

Static Variables

All programming languages have the category of variables known as static. This is *not* to be confused with the C/C++ keyword `static` or the one found in C#. Instead, *static* variables are those variables that are under load-time control. Examine the following simple C/C++ code segment:

```
int main(int argc, char *argv[])
{
  int iArray[10];
    .
    .
    .
```

The variable `iArray` is created when the program loads. The array, `iArray` continues to exist for the lifetime of the program. The programmer or user at runtime cannot increase its dimension(s) or delete the variable. This is an example of a static variable.

Pointer Variables

Technically speaking, pointer variables can also fall under the previous category of static. Look at this next example:

```
int main(int argc, char *argv[])
{
  int *pi;
    .
    .
    .
```

Here, the pointer variable `pi` has been defined as a variable that can hold the address to any memory location containing an integer. The variable `pi` is static, in other words, it too is created at load time.

Logical program design errors begin immediately if the algorithm attempts to syntactically and legally use the pointer variable. For example:

```
cout << *pi; // syntactically-legal, logically-fatal use of
unitialized pi
```

Here, an attempt is made to use a pointer variable without having previously given the pointer a valid address to a memory location of integer precision. The logical fix takes on this form:

```
int main(int argc, char *argv[])
{
  int iValue = 10,
     *pi = &iValue;
    .
   . .
    .
  cout << *pi;   // syntactically/logically-legal
                 // use of initialized pi
```

Now, two static variables, the pointer pi, and the integer-sized and initialized iValue are created. Then pi is initialized to hold a copy of the address to iValue. With an initialized pi, the cout statement can correctly access the iValue of 10.

Dynamic Memory Allocation

The previous example, while both logically and syntactically correct, could easily leave the unwary programmer asking, "So what is the advantage of pointers over static variables?" The answer for the previous example is "None!" As a matter of fact, *not* using pointers would have made the previous example much simpler.

```
int main(int argc, char *argv[])
{
   int iValue = 10;

   .
   .

   .
   cout << iValue;   // much simpler without pointers
```

The true power of pointer variables becomes evident when they are combined with the topic of dynamic memory allocation. Unlike static variables (remember, this is not the C#/C/C++ keyword static), which are under load-time control, dynamic variables are under runtime control. Look at this next C/C++ code segment:

```
int main(int argc, char *argv[])
{
   // int iArray[10]; static version
   // using dynamic or runtime memory allocation
   int *pi, iNumberToTrack;
   .

   .
   cout << "How many integers would you like to store? " << endl;
   cin >> iNumberToTrack;
   pi = new int[iNumberToTrack];

   for(int offset = 0; offset < iNumberToTrack; offset++)
     cin >> *pi++;   // dereference pointer for input, then
                     // increment pointer
   .
   .
   .
```

There is a lot happening here. The algorithm first creates two static variables, the pointer pi and the integer iNumberToTrack. This last variable will hold the runtime user's response to how many integers they would like to store. Notice that this variable's contents are under the control of the user at *runtime*. The user could type 0, 1, 10, 100, 100,000, etc.

The statement that kicks in the category of dynamic, or runtime, memory allocation is:

```
pi = new int[iNumberToTrack];
```

Here, you will notice the use of the C/C++ keyword `new` (also the C# keyword with the same use). The keyword `new` calculates the number of consecutive memory bytes necessary to store the requested data structure, in this case `iNumberToTrack`, times the system-dependent size of an integer (`sizeof(int)`). The pointer variable `pi` is assigned the address of the first byte of the allocated contiguous memory.

You can quickly see that this algorithm, with user-interactive runtime responsiveness, has many advantages. The biggest advantage is that the algorithm never wastes memory and, in theory, never runs out of memory. Rather than guessing how big the array should be at code time, in this case, the user decides at runtime.

Pointer Variables and Migraines

There is one serious problem with pointers and dynamic memory allocation, namely, what happens when an algorithm loses the address to a memory location. Take a second look at the following C/C++ code segment with the added last statement (in **bold**):

```
int main(int argc, char *argv[])
{
  // int iArray[10]; static version
  // using dynamic or runtime memory allocation
  int *pi, iNumberToTrack;
  .
  .
  cout << "How many integers would you like to store? " << endl;
  cin >> iNumberToTrack;
  pi = new int[iNumberToTrack];

  for(int offset = 0; offset < iNumberToTrack; offset++)
    cin >> *pi++;  // dereference pointer for input, then
                   // increment pointer

  cout << *pi; // syntactically legal, logically fatal
  .
  .
  .
```

The use of the dereferenced pointer `*pi` in the bolded `cout` statement is syntactically legal and compiles without any warnings or errors (again in C/C++). However, the previous `for` loop left the address in `pi` pointing *one past the end* of the dynamically allocated array!

Obvious, you say; okay, how about this next example. See if you can find the quicksand:

```
int *myMethod(void)
{
  int iInternalVariable = 5;
  .
  .
  .
  return (&iInternalVariable);
}
```

Once again you have a code segment that compiles without any warnings or errors. The problem is the iInternalVariable only exists for the lifetime of the subroutine. Returning the address to iInternalVariable sets the calling routine up for an inevitable crash.

The final insult presented to code developers involving pointers and dynamic memory allocation revolves around an algorithm that hangs on to a bad address, as in:

```
int main(int argc, char *argv[])
{
  int *pi;   // declare the integer pointer
  .
  .
  .
  pi = new int;   // initialize the pointer
  cin >> *pi;     // use the valid address to store data
  cout << *pi;    // use the valid address to retrieve data
  delete pi;      // tell the O.S. it can reuse the memory
  cin >> *pi;     // LOOK OUT, syntactically legal use
                  // of BAD address
  .
  .
  .
```

This final example shows the proper declaration for the pointer variable pi, its proper initialization and use for I/O, and one new statement. The C/C++ keyword delete tells the operating system that the previously allocated memory is now reusable. However, the algorithm syntactically and legally reuses this bad address in the next statement to input a second integer! All of this works (well, sort of) until another request is made for dynamic memory allocation with a call to new.

From the program's point of view, the last integer entered by the user was a success. Logically, however, if the program were to make a call to new, it is likely that the deleted memory location will be the first reallocated. When the algorithm reuses this address, the second input integer may become visible, or may be overwritten by the third value. In the latter case, the algorithm has lost valid data through a misuse of pointers—all without any compiler warnings or errors, just a runtime crash!

C# Has No Pointer Variables?

The lofty goal of C# is to solve the development problems created by today's programming environment. The typical application these days needs to be Windows-based, user-friendly, easily designed/implemented, easily modified, robust, and delivered on time, with the emphasis on robust.

Pointer variables and dynamic memory allocation combined can taunt an application developer with extremely efficient algorithm design at the cost of delays in development, debugging, and robustness. The previous discussions and code segments demonstrate just how easy it is to write syntactically correct code, using pointers and dynamic memory allocation, that is logically incorrect, predisposing an algorithm to a runtime break.

Well, C# Does Have Pointers but Don't Tell

Actually, C# does have pointer variables and dynamic memory allocation. However, for the purposes of robustness, the language inherently discourages their use. Instead, C# uses something called *automatic garbage collection*. Automatic garbage collection recovers dynamically allocated memory whenever an object goes out of scope.

Just Tell Me When I Can and Cannot Access a Variable

As a C# programmer you will have to become familiar with a few new concepts such as, *value types*, *reference types*, *pointer types*, *boxing*, *unboxing*, *safe code*, *unsafe code*, and *fixed* code. All of these topics deal directly or indirectly with when and how you access a variable's contents. Let's begin with the easier concepts—value types versus reference types.

Value Types

The difference between value types and reference types is straightforward. Value types always hold data, while reference types hold addresses to data, the latter known as *objects*. C# has three value types:

1. Simple types
2. `struct` types
3. Enumerated types

One feature of C# you will immediately appreciate is the compiler's ability to flag the misuse of an uninitialized value type variable! A value type is either a `struct` type or an enumerated type. C# provides a set of predefined `struct` types called the simple types. The simple types are identified through reserved words, and are further subdivided into numeric types, integral types, and floating-point types, as seen in Table 7–1.

Table 7–1   Value Types

value-type	struct-type, enum-type
struct-type	type-nam, simple-type
simple-type	numeric-type—bool
numeric-type	integral-type, floating-point-type, decimal
integral-type	sbyte, byte, short, ushort, int, uint, long, ulong, char
floating-point-type	float, double
enum-type	type-name

In C#, all value types derive from one class named `object`. Any variable of a value type must contain a value of that type. Unlike reference types, it is not possible for a value of a value type to be `null` or to reference an object of a more derived type. Any assignment made to a variable of a value type creates a *copy* of the value being assigned. However, any assignment made to a variable of a reference type copies the reference to an object.

Reference Types

When you copy a value type you are cloning a value from one memory location into another memory location at a different physical address. With reference types, you can have two variables reference the same object. Unlike a statement that modifies a cloned value type, which leaves the parent value type unscathed, reference types allow an algorithm to perform operations on one variable to affect the object referenced by the other variable. With value types, the variables each have their own copy of the data, and it is not possible for operations on one to affect the other. Legal reference types include class types, interface types, array types, or delegate types (see Table 7–2).

Table 7–2   Reference Types

reference-type	class-type, interface-type, array-type, delegate-type
class-type	type-name *object string*
interface-type	type-name
array-type	non-array-type rank-specifiers
non-array-type	type
delegate-type	type-name

C# allows you to treat a value of any type as an object. Every type in C# directly or indirectly is derived from the `object` class type where `object` is the parent class of all types. Values of reference types are treated as objects by viewing the values as type `object`. Values of value types are treated as objects by performing boxing and unboxing operations (discussed below). The value in a reference type is an address to an instance of the type. The special value `null` is compatible with all reference types. Here, `null` is a constant value that logically flags an algorithm to a reference variable pointing nowhere. For a discussion of C#'s `object` class to make sense, it is necessary to discuss two new C# fundamentals: boxing and unboxing.

Boxing and Unboxing

You will quickly discover that boxing and unboxing are integral components to C#'s type system. They provide a binding link between value types and reference types by permitting any value of a value type to be converted to and from type `object`. Boxing and unboxing enables a unified view of the type system wherein a value of any type can ultimately be treated as an object.

What To Do When You Must Use Pointers

The key here is to proceed with caution. Remember, the predominant source of C++ program breaks revolves around memory leaks—in other words, bad pointers. C# can and will minimize this source of logical errors if you take advantage of its safe code and automatic garbage collection. When you must circumvent these safeguards, there are a few C#-specific workarounds.

Understanding the Address Operator &

If you are familiar with C or C++, then you already know that the *address operator* & returns the address to a variable's (or object's) memory location (Note: The & operator also performs logical AND and bitwise functions identically in C#/C/C++). The syntax is straightforward, requiring you to precede an identifier with the operator itself, as in:

```
pointerToVariable = &addressOfVariable;
```

While the C# syntax is identical, the statement will not work by itself. The following program, addrsOpr.cs, details the C# syntax changes necessary to make the address operator (&) perform the same function as it does in C/C++:

```
using System;
public class addrsOpr
{
  public static int Main(string[] args)
  {
```

```
// addrsOpr.cs
// A C# program demonstrating how to use
// the Binary AND operator & to return
// the address of an unsafe value
// PROGRAM DOES NOT COMPILE - read last comment!!!
// Copyright (c) Chris H. Pappas and William H. Murray, 2001
//

Console.WriteLine("& used on true AND true  = {0}", true & true);
Console.WriteLine("& used on true AND false = {0}", true & false);

int iValue = 4;

/* this next statement seems OK but will not compile
   Console.WriteLine("& returning address of iValue 0x{0:x}",
                     &iValue);
*/

// the following "fixed" block IS correct - however,
// the program will NOT compile - WHY?
fixed(int *pi = &iValue)
{
   string hexAddress = int.Format((int)pi,"x");
   Console.WriteLine("& returning address of iValue: {0}",
                     hexAddress);

   //or the simpler version, not using the string variable
   Console.WriteLine("& returning address of iValue: {0}",
                     int.Format((int)pi,"x"));
}

// to get addrsOpr.cs to compile and execute
// you MUST remember - ANY method using unsafe pointers
// must include the "unsafe" keyword in the method prototype
// when you change Main()'s prototype to:
// unsafe public static int Main(string[] args)
// the program will compile and execute!

return 0;
   }
}
```

The first two uses of the & operator can be seen here:

```
Console.WriteLine("& used on true AND true  = {0}", true & true);
Console.WriteLine("& used on true AND false = {0}", true & false);
```

An attempt is made to perform a logical AND operator on two Boolean values causing the WriteLine() method to output 1 and 0, respectively, just as they would in a C/C++ algorithm.

Human nature being what it is, a seasoned C/C++ programmer learning C# would like these next two statements to be the C# equivalent for outputting the address to iValue in hexadecimal format:

```
int iValue = 4;

/* this next statement seems OK but will not compile
   Console.WriteLine("& returning address of iValue 0x{0:x}",
                      &iValue);
*/
```

C#, however, views this syntax as potentially dangerous, possibly generating a memory leak should the operating system decide to move iValue, and will not compile the statement.

The C# remedy begins with a new keyword called fixed:

```
// the following "fixed" block IS correct - however,
// the program will NOT compile - WHY?
   fixed(int *pi = &iValue)
{
```

The fixed keyword prevents the relocation of the specified variable. The syntax for fixed looks like:

```
fixed( type* ptrName = legalExpression ) someStatement;
```

The type may be any unmanaged type or void. The name, ptrName, is any name you give to the pointer variable. The legalExpression is any expression that ultimately returns a pointer to the specified type. Finally, someStatement is either a single executable statement or code block. The fixed statement sets a pointer to a managed variable and "pins" that variable during the execution of someStatement. Without fixed, pointers to managed variables would be of little use since garbage collection could relocate the variables unpredictably.

Additionally, pointers initialized in fixed statements cannot be modified and after someStatement is executed, any pinned variables are unpinned and subject to garbage collection. For this reason it is unadvisable to point to those variables outside the fixed statement.

As an example, consider this statement:

```
fixed(int *pi = &iValue)
{
```

You will see that even now the program will still fail to compile. Why? Just marking a variable as unmovable or fixed is not enough in C#. To legalize the syntax you must go one step further by marking the owning subroutine (function and/or method), in this case `Main()`, as unsafe with the keyword `unsafe`. To get `addrsOpr.cs` to compile an execute, you must change the prototype to `Main()` so that it looks like this:

```
unsafe public static int Main(string[] args)
```

Finally, make certain you recognize that any use of the pointer variable `pi`, from declaration to initialization to any use of it, *must* be within the scope of the `fixed` blocks French braces `{}`:

```
fixed(int *pi = &iValue)
    {
        string hexAddress = int.Format((int)pi,"x");
        Console.WriteLine("& returning address of iValue: {0}",
                          hexAddress);

        //or the simpler version, not using the string variable
        Console.WriteLine("& returning address of iValue: {0}",
                          int.Format((int)pi,"x"));
    }
```

The block contains two examples of how to syntactically output a pointer variable's address contents in hexadecimal. The `WriteLine()` uses a `string` class representation generated by a call to the `int` class method `Format()`. The first argument to `Format()` is the variable being converted, `pi`, and its interpretation via an integer cast `(int)`. The second argument instructs `Format()` to generate a hexadecimal representation for the address. The second `WriteLine()` example nests all of this within the `WriteLine()` statement itself. The output from the program looks like:

```
& used on true AND true  = True
& used on true AND false = False
& returning address of iValue: 12fc94
& returning address of iValue: 12fc94
```

The address operator `&` has one more additional use besides returning the address to a variable and performing the logical AND operation. You can use the `&` operator to perform a bitwise AND function as in:

```
Console.Write("0x{0:x}", 0xAB & 0x1D);
```

Here, the operator looks at the actual binary representations of the two hexadecimal values `AB` and `1D` and executes a bit-by-bit ANDing of the values.

Using `unsafe` and `fixed`

This next example builds upon your fresh understanding of how to legalize the use of pointers in C# with the use of keywords `fixed` and `unsafe`. The program begins by defining a
class called `classMembers` with two integer data members, `xValue` and `yValue`:

```
class classMembers
{
  // member data declarations
  public int xValue, yValue;
}
```

Within the body of `Main()`, `classMembers` is instantiated and each data member is
assigned initial values:

```
classMembers xyValue = new classMembers();
xyValue.xValue = 4;
xyValue.yValue = 5;
```

At this point the algorithm wants to pass these two data members to a method called
`CubeIt()` to generate their cubed values, respectively. The values are to be passed by reference so that the cubed calculation is reflected back in `Main()`. However, the use of pointers
generates unsafe code once again, requiring the use of the keyword `fixed`. The problem is
exaggerated by the fact that there are now two pointers and the `fixed` syntax deals with one
at a time. This explains the use of `fixed` twice in the following code segment:

```
// unsafe flagged pointer syntax with nested fixed addresses
unsafe
  {
    fixed(int *pixValue = &xyValue.xValue)
    {
      fixed(int *piyValue = &xyValue.yValue)
      {
        CubeIt(pixValue);
        CubeIt(piyValue);
      }
    }
  }
```

Did you notice the second `fixed` statement block is nested within the first set of
french braces {}? This nesting allows the consecutive calls to `CubeIt()` which uses the
two independently declared and initialized pointers `pixValue` and `piyValue`. Did you
also notice the outermost block owned by the keyword `unsafe`? Remember the two keywords work together. In this example, instead of the entire `Main()` method flagged as
`unsafe`, the algorithm selectively marked the unmanaged code segment as being `unsafe`.

Since the method `CubeIt()` doesn't declare any pointer variables, and only uses
passed references, only the method header needs the `unsafe` flag:

```
// necessary unsafe keyword legalizing pointer syntax
unsafe static void CubeIt(int *p)
{
  *p *= *p * *p;
}
```

The body of CubeIt() does not need to declare the pointer p fixed since the formal argument p is within the scope of the unsafe method's prototype. The complete program follows.

```
using System;
class classMembers
{
  // member data declarations
  public int xValue, yValue;
}
public class FIXED1
{
  // necessary unsafe keyword legalizing pointer syntax
  unsafe static void CubeIt(int *p)
  {
    *p *= *p * *p;
  }

  public static int Main(string[] args)
  {
    // fixed1.cs
    // A C# program demonstrating the arrow operator ->
    // Copyright(c) Chris H. Pappas and William H. Murray, 2001
    //

    classMembers xyValue = new classMembers();
    xyValue.xValue = 4;
    xyValue.yValue = 5;

    // unsafe flagged pointer syntax with nested fixed addresses
    unsafe
    {
      fixed(int *pixValue = &xyValue.xValue)
      {
        fixed(int *piyValue = &xyValue.yValue)
        {
          CubeIt(pixValue);
          CubeIt(piyValue);
        }
      }
      // pix and piy now unpinned
```

```
    }

    Console.WriteLine("Cubed xValue = {0}, Cubed yValue = {1}",
                    xyValue.xValue, xyValue.yValue);

    return 0;
    }
}
```

The output from the program looks like:

```
Cubed xValue = 64, Cubed yValue = 125
```

NOTE

The compiler's option to allow unsafe code must be set to true if this application is to compile without error. This can be done from the Solution Explorer by first right-clicking the mouse on the project's name. From the list shown, select Properties. Next, select the Configuration Build property and open the Build option. At this point it is possible to change the Allow Unsafe Code option from false to true.

unsafe Arrays and Pointer Syntax

The next example program puts a slight spin on the topic of fixed and unsafe code by restricting their use entirely within the body of a method (other than Main()). Main() begins by declaring an array, initializing it, and making a call to the method of interest, viewFixedAddress():

```
int[] iArray = new int[] {1, 3, 5, 7, 9, 11};

viewFixedAddress(iArray);
```

A close examination of Main() reveals no use of either the unsafe or fixed keywords. This is remedied by viewFixedAddress()'s prototype and the first statement in the method:

```
unsafe static void viewFixedAddress(int[] iArray)
{
    // unsafe method using fixed pointer
    // declaration/initialization

    fixed(int *pi = iArray)
    {
```

Within the scope of the `fixed` block are a few interesting C# array features. For example, the method `Length()` used on the array instance `iArray` returns the size of the array and is used as the `for` loop termination value. Notice also that the array element referencing is *not* performed using array subscript syntax, but instead is accomplished with the incremented pointer variable `pi`:

```
int *pRow = pi;
for(int offset = 0; offset < iArray.Length; offset++)
{
  int iValue = *pRow;
  string hexRowAddress = int.Format((int)pRow,"x");
  Console.Write("iValue at row {0}", offset);
  Console.WriteLine(" has a hex address of: {0}",
                    hexRowAddress);
  pRow++;
  }
 }
}
```

The `for` loop also makes repeated use of the integer class method `Format()` to generate the `string` version of each row's address for `Console.Write/Line()` output. The complete program follows:

```
using System;
public class FIXED2
{
  unsafe static void viewFixedAddress(int[] iArray)
  {
    // unsafe method using fixed pointer declaration/
initialization

    fixed(int *pi = iArray)
    {
      int *pRow = pi;
      for(int offset = 0; offset < iArray.Length; offset++)
      {
        int iValue = *pRow;
        string hexRowAddress = ((int)pRow).ToString("X");
        Console.Write("iValue at row {0}", offset);
        Console.WriteLine(" has a hex address of: {0}",
                          hexRowAddress);
        pRow++;
      }
    }
  }

  public static int Main(string[] args)
```

```
  {
    // fixed2.cs
    // A C# program demonstrating the use of
    // unsafe and fixed array-element pointer syntax
    // Copyright (c) Chris H. Pappas and William H. Murray, 2001
    //

    int[] iArray = new int[] {1, 3, 5, 7, 9, 11};

    viewFixedAddress(iArray);
    return 0;
  }
}
```

If you execute the algorithm you should see results similar to the following:

```
iValue at row 0 has a hex address of: BA1A70
iValue at row 1 has a hex address of: BA1A74
iValue at row 2 has a hex address of: BA1A78
iValue at row 3 has a hex address of: BA1A7C
iValue at row 4 has a hex address of: BA1A80
iValue at row 5 has a hex address of: BA1A84
```

Since arrays by definition are homogenous data types stored contiguously in memory, the consecutive four-byte address increments are self-explanatory.

NOTE

The compiler's option to allow unsafe code must be set to true if this application is to compile without error. This can be done from the Solution Explorer by first right-clicking the mouse on the project's name. From the list shown, select Properties. Next, select the Configuration Build property and open the Build option. At this point it is possible to change the Allow Unsafe Code option from false to true.

More on Unsafe Code

As you have discovered, C# provides the ability to write `unsafe` code. This code deals directly with pointer types and `fixed` objects, preventing the garbage collector from moving them. This `unsafe` code feature is, in fact, a safe feature from the perspective of both developers and users. This last example is for developers who are generally content with automatic memory management and only flags the methods `Main()` and `CubeIt()` as unsafe, leaving the variables `iValue` and `pToiValue` under automatic control:

```csharp
using System;
public class usesUNSAFE
{
  // note: required use of unsafe keyword
  unsafe static void CubeIt(int *pi)
  {
    // method using pointer type dummy argument
    // requires use of unsafe in method prototype!!!
    Console.WriteLine("\n\nEntering method CubeIt\n");
    Console.WriteLine("Initial Value of dereferenced pi: {0}",
                 *pi);
    *pi *= *pi * *pi;
    Console.WriteLine("Cubed Value of dereferenced pi  : {0}",
                 *pi);
    Console.WriteLine("\nExiting method CubeIt\n\n");
  }

  // note: required use of unsafe keyword
  unsafe public static int Main(string[] args)
  {
    // unsafe.cs
    // A C# application demonstrating unsafe keyword
    // making "standard pointer type" syntax/logic - legal
    // Copyright (c) Chris H. Pappas and William H. Murray, 2001
    //

    int iValue = 3;
    int *pToiValue = &iValue;

    Console.WriteLine("Entering Main()\n");
    Console.WriteLine("Current Value of iValue   : {0}", iValue);

    // converting address of iValue to string format for printing
    string spToiValue = ((int)pToiValue).ToString("X");
    Console.Write("Current Address of &iValue: ");
    Console.WriteLine("0x{0}", spToiValue);

    CubeIt(&iValue);

    Console.WriteLine("Final Value of iValue from Main() {0}",
                 iValue);

  return 0;
  }
}
```

Notice there is no use of the `fixed` keyword. The output from the program takes the following form:

```
Entering Main()

Current Value of iValue    : 3
Current Address of &iValue: 0x12F94C


Entering method CubeIt

Initial Value of dereferenced pi: 3
Cubed Value of dereferenced pi  : 27

Exiting method CubeIt


Final Value of iValue from Main() 27
```

NOTE

The compiler's option to allow unsafe code must be set to true if this application is to compile without error. This can be done from the Solution Explorer by first right-clicking the mouse on the project's name. From the list shown, select Properties. Next, select the Configuration Build property and open the Build option. At this point it is possible to change the Allow Unsafe Code option from false to true.

Automatic Garbage Collection

With manual memory management via pointers and dynamic memory allocation being so error prone, placing a high demand on programmer skill, automatic garbage collection makes sense. The following example program, `autommng.cs`, demonstrates how to rewrite your traditional linked-list stack algorithm incorporating this new C# feature.

The program necessarily begins with the definition of a node. The term *node* is a generic term that represents a structure or class that has as a minimum, two members—one holding data, the other containing a pointer to another node of the same type. The `autommng.cs` algorithm uses the following stack node definition:

```
class node
{
  public node nextNode;
  public object Value;

  // method for first node of empty list
```

```
    public node(object newValue):this(newValue,null) {}

    // method of adding nodes to existing list
    public node(object newValue, node oldTop)
    {
      nextNode = oldTop ;
      Value = newValue;
    }
}
```

The two constructors (remember, constructors are functions pulled into class definitions—changing their formal name from function to method, with the same name as the formal class and are automatically invoked) deal with a non-existent stack (first node constructor) and adding a new node to an existing stack (second constructor).

The class automemmng contains definitions for the top of the stack and is automatically initialized to null, indicating the reference pointer points nowhere officially. The method isEmpty() checks this value to see if the stack is empty, returning the C# Boolean value true or false.

```
public class automemmng
{
  private node top = null;

  public bool isEmpty
  {
    get { return( top == null ); }
  }
```

The traditional stack method push() adds the newValue to the top of the stack, with the new top node's nextNode pointer member set to the address of the oldTop. The method pop() returns the current Value in the stack's top node and updates the reference pointer top to the address of the node behind the current top:

```
private void push(object newValue)
{
    top = new node(newValue, top);
}

private object pop()
{
    object currentValue = top.Value;
    top = top.nextNode;
    return currentValue;
}
```

The `Main()` method instantiates the stack `sInstance`, while the `for` loop initializes the stack with five values. If you are familiar with object-oriented, pointer variable, and dynamic memory allocation stack algorithms, see if you can notice what is missing from the following entire code segment:

```
public static int Main(string[] args)
{
  // automemmng.cs
  // A C# program demonstrating automatic garbage collection
  // Copyright (c) Chris H. Pappas and William H. Murray, 2001
  //

  automemmng sInstance = new automemmng();

  for(int someValue = 0; someValue < 5; someValue++)
    sInstance.push(someValue);

  sInstance = null;

  return 0;
  }
}
```

Did you see it? Or better yet, did you notice what is *missing* from this traditional algorithm? There is no call to the keyword `delete`. Remember, `delete` flags the operating system to the reusability of dynamically allocated memory.

In C#/C/C++ the `node` instances are created in the `push()` method, but only in C# are they automatically garbage-collected when no longer needed. The `node` instance becomes eligible for garbage collection when it is no longer possible for any code to access it. For instance, when an item is removed from the `sInstance`, the associated `node` instance becomes eligible for garbage collection. Once the variable `sInstance` is assigned `null`, the stack and the associated five `nodes` are garbage collected. The garbage collector is permitted to clean up immediately, but is not required to do so.

The complete algorithm follows.

```
using System;
public class automemmng
{
    private node top = null;

    public bool isEmpty
    {
        get { return( top == null ); }
    }
```

```csharp
    private void push(object newValue)
    {
        top = new node(newValue, top);
    }

    private object pop()
    {
        object currentValue = top.Value;
        top = top.nextNode;
        return currentValue;
    }

    class node
    {
        public node nextNode;
        public object Value;

        // method for first node of empty list
        public node(object newValue):this(newValue,null) {}

        // method of adding nodes to existing list
        public node(object newValue, node oldFront)
        {
            nextNode = oldFront;
            Value = newValue;
        }
    }

    public static int Main(string[] args)
    {
        // automemmng.cs
        // A C# program demonstrating automatic garbage collection
        // Copyright (c) Chris H. Pappas and William H. Murray, 2001
        //

        automemmng sInstance = new automemmng();

        for(int someValue = 0; someValue < 5; someValue++)
            sInstance.push(someValue);

        sInstance = null;

        return 0;
    }
}
```

This application does not output any information to the command window. You can use the Microsoft Debugger to examine the step-by-step execution of the code if desired.

Understanding the Arrow Operator

There are two syntactically correct ways to use a reference type to point to a member—one cryptic but syntactically legal, the other is the more accepted way. Program `arrowOpr` highlights these two styles:

```
using System;
struct screenCoords
{
  public int xCoord, yCoord;
}
public class arrowOpr
{
  public static int Main(string[] args)
  {
    // arrowOpr.cs
    // A C# program demonstrating the arrow operator ->
    // Copyright(c) Chris H. Pappas and William H. Murray, 2001
    //

    screenCoords xyLocation = new screenCoords();
    unsafe
    {
      screenCoords *pxyLocation = &xyLocation;
      (*pxyLocation).xCoord = 640; // legal BUT who would want to?
      pxyLocation -> yCoord = 320; // BETTER, cleaner syntax!
    }

    Console.WriteLine("xCoord = {0}, yCoord = {1}",
                       xyLocation.xCoord, xyLocation.yCoord);
    return 0;
  }
}
```

Members are always accessed with the period member operator (.); however, when the member is being pointed to by a reference type, you need to dereference the pointer. This requires a cast of the pointer, as in (*pxyLocation). The combined syntax is verbose.

```
(*pxyLocation).xCoord = 640; // legal BUT who would want to?
```

The streamlined syntax is only made possible with an additional operator, called the arrow operator, which makes for a more readable code statement:

```
pxyLocation -> yCoord = 320; // BETTER, cleaner syntax!
```

Most programmers choose the more straightforward syntax. The output from the program looks like:

```
xCoord = 640, yCoord = 320
```

NOTE

The compiler's option to allow unsafe code must be set to true if this application is to compile without error. This can be done from the Solution Explorer by first right-clicking the mouse on the project's name. From the list shown, select Properties. Next, select the Configuration Build property and open the Build option. At this point it is possible to change the Allow Unsafe Code option from false to true.

Stack versus Heap Memory Allocation

In C# stackalloc is actually a language keyword and not a predefined function or method from some class. Use stackalloc to allocate a block of memory from the stack as opposed to the heap.

The syntax for stackalloc looks like:

```
type *ptrName = stackalloc type [optionalExpression ];
```

In the statement, type can be any unmanaged type, ptrName is the name for the variable being assigned the stack address, stackalloc is the keyword, and optional-Expression represents any statement returning an integral value. stackalloc is only valid in local variable declarations.

When you make a call to stackalloc, your program is assigned a block of memory equivalent to the size of type, or the size of type times the value returned from the optionalExpression. The memory is allocated on the stack, however, and not the heap. The address to the beginning of the block is stored in the pointer, ptrName.

Most importantly, since the memory is allocated from the stack, it is not subject to automatic garbage collection. You therefore do not need to flag the pointer or the instance with the fixed keyword. However, since you are still using pointers, the owning method must be declared as unsafe. The lifetime of the memory block is limited to the lifetime of the method in which it is defined.

The following program uses stackalloc to create an array of five integers. The pointer variable pToStackAlloc is assigned the address to the beginning of the memory block, with the pointer variable pi receiving a duplicate copy of the address. Look at the algorithm and see if you can discover why there are two pointer variables.

```
using System;
public class Class1
{
  unsafe public static int Main(string[] args)
  {
    // stackalloc.cs
    // A C# program demonstrating stack versus heap memory alloc.
    // Copyright(c) Chris H. Pappas and William H. Murray, 2001
    //

    int *pToStackAlloc = stackalloc int[5], pi = pToStackAlloc;

    *pi++ = 1;
    for(int offset = 1; offset < 5; offset++, pi++)
    {
      *pi = pi[-1] + offset;
    }

    for(int offset = 0; offset < 5; offset++)
    {
      Console.WriteLine(pToStackAlloc[offset]);
    }

    return 0;
  }
}
```

`Main()` with the following use of `stackalloc`:

```
int *pToStackAlloc = stackalloc int[5], pi = pToStackAlloc;
```

The first use of `pi`:

```
*pi++ = 1;
```

assigns a value of 1 to the first integer location and then updates `pi`'s contents with postfix increment ++ to the address of the next available integer location.

Next, the `for` loop

```
for(int offset = 1; offset < 5; offset++, pi++)
    {
       *pi = pi[-1] + offset;
    }
```

assigns the remaining elements, the last element's value plus the current `offset` value. The program terminates by outputting these values with the second `for` loop:

```
for(int offset = 0; offset < 5; offset++)
{
  Console.WriteLine(pToStackAlloc[offset]);
}
```

Have you detected the reason for the algorithm's declaration of two pointer variables? The answer is to simply demonstrate the alternate syntax available. The variable `pi` is a standard pointer variable used in a standard syntax for referencing consecutive memory allocations. The pointer variable `pToStackAlloc` was never incremented and therefore still holds the address to the front of the memory block allocated with `stackalloc`. The second `for` loop shows how you can combine the pointer variable with array subscript syntax and obtain the same consecutive memory accesses. The output from the program looks like:

```
1
2
4
7
11
```

Understanding C#'s Type System

Most experienced programmers separate what C# calls value types from reference types. Certainly the logical and syntactical dos and don'ts between the two types enforce this dichotomy. However, experienced programmers also realize that new languages are developed to solve new problems. Take, for example, the jump from non-structured ROM Basic to structured Pascal. Pascal was excellent for teaching and rehearsing a programmer novice in the ways of Top Down Design's one entry point, one exit point. The newer Pascal language was necessary as program sizes jumped from a whopping 16K to 256K.

The "new" problem presented by today's programming environment involves the coordination of the thousands of code statements necessary to *accurately* execute an algorithm on a plethora of unique architectures interacting in real-time with a graphical user-interface maximized by multitasking operating systems in every known written language with a global community over the Internet and/or Intranet!

While C++ could handle the majority of these "new" demands, it was lacking in innate Internet connectivity. Also, for anyone who has programmed for Microsoft Windows, generating the user-interface via dialog boxes (in particular) often left a bad taste in your mouth. Ergo, the migration over to Visual Basic for "quick 'n dirty" front end design, which necessitated the integration of C++ code and Visual Basic. Of course, even this symbiosis left the final executable non-Internet friendly which fed the need to combine C++, Visual Basic, and Java, or J++, or Jbuilder, depending on a programmer's particular persuasion. Yuk! Needless to say, designing a large-scale project incorporating the best of today's programming languages was a Herculean task.

C# *does* solve the nightmare scenario just presented. However, it also invokes the saying, "You don't get something for nothing." One of C/C++'s strengths was its closeness to the hardware and its grounds-up, designed-in main Achilles heel: never get in the programmer's way! The authors of C (Dennis Ritchie) and C++ (Bjarne Stroustrup) wanted a new language with minimal compile-time restrictions. This allowed a programmer to reinvent the languages as necessary. While this pivotal feature gives C/C++ their strength, it is also the single reason for code breaks. The burden of accurate code design is now on the programmer, not compile-time error diagnostics.

NOTE

If you are unfamiliar with object-oriented programming fundamentals and the use of classes, you may wish to skip the remainder of Chapter 7 until you finish reading the discussion of C# classes presented in Chapter 8. The following discussions present C#'s object *type and will only make sense if you know what an object (generic concept, not C#* object*) is in any OOP language.*

The first component of C# to minimize code breaks and increase accurate robust algorithms is its unified type system. In C# all types, including value types, derive from the type object. It is possible to call object methods on any value, even values of primitive types such as int. Examine this portion of code:

```
using System;
class toString
{
   static void Main() {
      Console.Write(5.ToString());
   }
}
```

This code invokes the object method ToString() on the constant value 5.

C# provides a new fundamental concept not previously available to any programming language, namely, boxing and unboxing (previously discussed in this chapter). First, a quick glance at the new syntax:

```
class Object
{
   static void Main() {
      int iValue = 777;
      object iObject = iValue;        // boxing iValue
      int iUnboxed = (int) iObject;   // unboxing iValue
   }
}
```

In this example, the integer `iValue` is being converted from a value type of `int` to an `object` type `iObject` called boxing. The last code statement reverses the processes by casting the object type `iObject` to a value type of `int`—called unboxing. When an algorithm needs to permute a variable or a value type needs to be converted to a reference type, an object box is allocated to hold the value and the value is copied into the box. Unboxing is just the opposite. When an object box is cast back to its original value type, the value is copied out of the box and into the appropriately sized memory location.

What? Why would I want to do that, you ask? Boxing in C# provides value types with the benefits of object capabilities without introducing unnecessary overhead. For programs that don't need `int` values to act like objects, `int` values remain simple 32-bit values. However, when an algorithm needs `int` values to behave like objects, this capability is available on demand.

To an experienced programmer this may sound like turning apples into oranges, but there are advantages. This ability to treat value types as objects bridges the gap that exists in most languages between value types and reference types. For example, a `Queue` class can provide *PushBack()* and *PopFront()* methods that take and return object values.

```
public class Queue
{
    public object PushBack() {...}
    public void PopFront(object oWhatEver) {...}
}
```

Because C# has a unified type system, the `Queue` class can be used for queues of any type, including value types like `int`.

A Closer Look at `object`

C#'s `object` type is based on the `System.Object` in the .NET framework. You can assign values of any type to variables of type `object`. All data types, predefined and user-defined, inherit from the `System.Object` class. The `object` data type is the type to and from which objects are boxed. The following example illustrates how a variable of type `object` can use `System.Object` methods.

In `Main()`, `dMain` is defined as an `object` type. The second statement boxes the value `12.345`. The first `WriteLine()` statement outputs the value as an integer type. The second `WriteLine()` invokes the `GetType()` method. The syntax highlights the treatment of `dMain` as a true object with its dot (.) member function syntax. The scenario is repeated in the third `WriteLine()` statement only using the `ToString()` method.

```
object dMain;
dMain = 12.345;    // boxing a double constant
Console.WriteLine("The value of dMain: {0}",dMain);
Console.WriteLine("\nThe type of dMain: {0}",dMain.GetType());
```

```
Console.WriteLine("dMain converted toString:
{0}",dMain.ToString());
```

The last four statements in Main() illustrate the reference component to object types by dynamically allocating an instance of the class DataMember, thereby updating the pointer with access to dMember. The second of the four statements instantiates an instance of the class DataMember, by the name refToDataMember. The third statement assigns the refToDataMember instance the unboxed dMain value via the (DataMember) cast. The fourth statement uses this reference to access the initialized dMember for output:

```
dMain = new DataMember();
DataMember refToDataMember;
refToDataMember = (DataMember)dMain; // unboxing dMain
Console.WriteLine("\nReferenced dMember: {0}",
                  refToDataMember.dMember);
```

The complete program is shown in the following listing:

```
using System;

public class DataMember
{
    public double dMember = 1.4953;
}

public class TestBoxing
{
    public static int Main()
    {
        // floatBoxing.cs
        // A C# program demonstrating boxing
        // and unboxing on double data and class members.
        // Copyright (c) Chris H. Pappas and William H. Murray, 2001
        //

        object dMain;
        dMain = 12.345;    // boxing double constant
        Console.WriteLine("The value of dMain: {0}",dMain);
        Console.WriteLine("\nThe type of dMain: {0}",
                          dMain.GetType());
        Console.WriteLine("dMain converted toString: {0}",
                          dMain.ToString());

        dMain = new DataMember();
        DataMember refToDataMember;
        refToDataMember = (DataMember)dMain; // unboxing dMain
        Console.WriteLine("\nReferenced dMember: {0}",
```

```
                              refToDataMember.dMember);

          return 0;
     }
}
```

The output from the program looks like:

```
The value of dMain: 12.345

The type of dMain: Double
dMain converted toString: 12.345

Referenced dMember: 1.4953
```

As you examine this output, recall that the purpose of the example is to illustrate how a variable of type `object` can use `System.Object` methods.

Boxing—In Detail

Technically, boxing involves an explicit conversion of a value type to an `object` type or to any interface type implemented by the explicit value type. Boxing the value of a value type causes the compiler to allocate an object instance and to copy the value into the new object, as in:

```
double dValue = 123.456;
object odObject = dValue;
double dV2 = (double)odObject;
```

Here, the object `odObject` is created on the stack referencing a value of the type `double`, on the heap. This value is a copy of the value type assigned to the variable `dValue`. The difference between the two variables, `dValue` and `odObject`, and the unboxed `dV2`, can be seen in Figure 7–1.

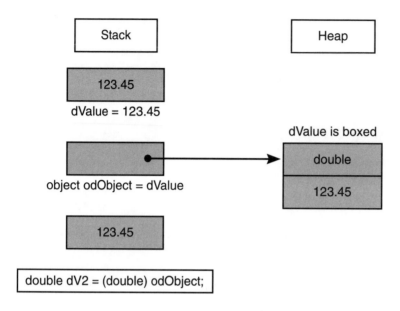

Figure 7–1   Example of Stack and Heap memory allocation with boxing.

This next example builds on the previous code segment by changing the value stored in the variable dValue from 123.45 to 678.900. Notice that the odObject retains the original value 123.45:

```
using System;
class testAgain
{
  public static int Main()
  {
    // testagain.cs
    // A C# program demonstrating how boxed references
    // retain their original "boxed" values.
    // Copyright (c) Chris H. Pappas and Willliam H. Murray, 2001
    //

    double dValue = 123.45;
    object odObject = dValue;    // implied boxing
    dValue = 678.900;                 // updating dValue
    Console.WriteLine("dValue contains         : {0}", dValue);
    Console.WriteLine("While odObject contains: {0}", odObject);

    return 0;
  }
}
```

The output from the program takes on the following form:

```
dValue contains        : 678.9
While odObject contains: 123.45
```

You should now be able to see how boxed references retain their original "boxed" values.

Unboxing—In Detail

As you would expect, unboxing is an explicit conversion from the type object to some legal value type. Actaully, it can also be from an interface type to a value type that implements the interface. The following rules must be met before any object may be unboxed. First, the object instance must contain a boxed value of the given value type; secondly, the unboxed value must be assigned into the value type variable (see Figure 7–1). Otherwise, if the source argument is null or a reference to an incompatible object, an InvalidCast-Exception is thrown.

Summary

In this chapter you learned how C# attempts to solve the problems created by traditionally combined pointer variables and dynamic memory allocation for the purposes of developing extremely efficient and robust algorithms. You also discovered how boxing and unboxing are ways of converting value types to C#'s object types for the purposes of data integrity.

In the next chapter you will learn about additional C# types. This too is an important chapter as it details the similarities and surprising differences between C/C++'s standard types and C#'s. Once again, skipping Chapter 8 will undoubtedly lead to code breaks and miscalculations if you are rolling your understanding of C/C++ over to C#!

CHAPTER 8

Last Stop before Objects

$\mathbf{T}$his chapter is your last stop before jumping into C#'s object-oriented programming (OOP) foundations. Successful OOP C# design depends exclusively on your proper use of its building blocks. This chapter finalizes your understanding of the C# keywords and concepts that make for robust algorithms. It also discusses new topics and highlights previous discussions with advanced details.

NOTE

There are details presented in this chapter, unique to C# application development that, if missed, will lead to program breaks and/or miscalculations.

Types

Forget how eloquent an algorithm may be, if it produces incorrect results, what good is it? In this section you will learn the nuances of C#'s standard data types.

sbyte

The `sbyte` keyword defines an integral type that stores values in the range of -128 to 127. This 8-bit integer has a .NET type representation of `System.Sbyte`. A sample declaration and initialization of an `sbyte` takes this form:

```
sbyte sbValue = -128;
```

Here, the integer literal −128 is converted from int to sbyte. The good news is, if you intended to limit integer ranges from −128 to +127, and attempted to assign an illegal range value, the compiler would flag this at compile time.

C# requires special syntax for overloaded functions and/or methods using sbyte and int permutations. First, look at the overloaded method headers:

```
public void MethodA( sbyte sbValue )
public void MethodB( int iValue )
```

Except for the unique formal argument type of sbyte, the overloaded headers look the same as in C/C++. The "special syntax" is only required when you invoke MethodA(). C# requires you to use a cast when calling overloaded methods.

```
MethodA( (sbyte) 5);  // Required cast for sbyte actual argument
MethodB( 5 );         // int default type for actual argument
```

Using the sbyte cast guarantees that the correct overloaded method is invoked.

There are also special C# considerations when using sbyte values in calculations. C# provides implicit conversions from sbyte to short, int, long, float, double, or decimal. Also, you cannot implicitly convert numeric types of larger storage size to sbyte.

The following example looks safe enough, yet generates a compiler error. See if you can't figure out why:

```
sbyte sbValue1 = 1, sbValue2 = 2;
sbyte sbSum = sbValue1 + sbValue2; // illegal statement
```

The compilation error results from the addition operator (+) formally returning the sum of int + int (by default), and not sbyte + sbyte. Once again, the corrected solution involves a cast:

```
sbyte sbSum = (sbyte)( sbValue1 + sbValue2 );
```

The reverse, however, does not require a cast. That is, when the destination variable has a higher precision than the source variables:

```
sbyte sbValue1 = 1, sbValue2 = 2;        // legal
int iResult = sbValue1 +  sbValue2;      // legal
double dResult = sbValue1 +  sbValue2;   // legal
float fResult = (sbyte) ( 1.0 + 2.0 );   // legal (cast)
```

the fourth statement is only legal when the (sbyte) cast explicitly demotes the two floating-point values to sbyte precision.

bool

While the C# bool keyword is identical to its C/C++ cousins, its .NET association is new. The .NET alias for bool is System.Boolean. Either is used to declare variables that hold either the constant true or false.

The two traditional uses for bool variables are to hold bool constants or the result of an expression as in:

```
bool bValue = false;   // bValue holds either true or false
```

or

```
bool bIsDigit = ( c >= 30 && c <= 39 );
```

C and C++ programmers must look out for a subtle difference between their bool and C#'s bool. C/C++ programmers are familiar with converting bool types to int and vice versa as in:

```
int iFalse = 0, iTrue = 1;
if( iTrue ) // legal in C/C++, ILLEGAL in C#!
```

In C#, there is no conversion between the bool type and other types. The fix takes this form:

```
If( iTrue == 1 ) // C# fix
```

The C# syntax requirement demands the variable be explicitly compared to some value.

byte

The C# byte keyword is similar to the 8-bit sbyte data type, except that the bit mapping applies to positive whole integers only. Legal assignments are restricted from 0 to 255 inclusive and have a .NET counterpart System.Byte. A sample declaration and initialization of an sbyte takes the following form:

```
byte byValue = 255;
```

Here, the integer literal 255 is converted from int to byte. The good news is, if you intended to limit integer ranges from 0 to +255, and attempted to assign an illegal range-value, the compiler would flag this at compile time.

C# requires special syntax for overloaded functions and/or methods using byte and int permutations. First, look at the overloaded method headers:

```
public void MethodA( byte byValue )
public void MethodB( int iValue )
```

Except for the unique formal argument type of `byte`, the overloaded headers look the same as in C/C++. The "special syntax" is only required when you invoke `MethodA()`. C# requires you to use a cast when calling overloaded methods.

```
MethodA( (byte)5 );    // Required cast for byte actual argument
MethodB( 5 );          // int default type for actual argument
```

Using the `byte` cast guarantees that the correct overloaded method is invoked.

There are also special C# considerations when using `byte` values in calculations. C# provides implicit conversions from `byte` to `short`, `int`, `long`, `float`, `double`, or `decimal`. Also, you cannot implicitly convert numeric types of larger storage size to `byte`.

The following example looks safe enough, yet generates a compiler error. See if you can't figure out why:

```
byte byValue1 = 1, byValue2 = 2;
byte bySum = byValue1 + byValue2; // illegal statement
```

The compilation error results from the addition operator (+) formally returning the sum of `int` + `int` (by default), and not `byte` + `byte`. Once again, the corrected solution involves a cast:

```
byte bySum = (byte)( byValue1 + byValue2 );
```

The reverse, however, does not require a cast. That is, when the destination variable has a higher precision than the source variables:

```
byte byValue1 = 1, byValue2 = 2;         // legal statement
int iResult = byValue1 +  byValue2;      // legal statement
double dResult = byValue1 +  byValue2;   // legal statement
float fResult = (byte)( 1.0 + 2.0 );     // legal statement with
(cast)
```

the fourth statement is only legal when the `(byte)` cast explicitly demotes the two floating-point values to `byte` precision.

double

The 64-bit `double` keyword defines a simple type that stores floating-point values in the range of $\pm 5.0 \times 10^{-324}$ to $\pm 1.7 \times 10^{308}$, with a .NET equivalent of `System.Double`. To avoid a plethora of compile-time error messages, you need to know that C#, by default, treats all real numeric literals on the right-hand side of an assignment operator as `double`. The following code segment illustrates this scenario:

```
float fValue = 1.1;
double dValue;
dValue = fValue; // precision???
```

The first data declaration illegally attempts to assign 1.1 (viewed by default as a double) to a `float` variable. The statement generates the following complaint from the C# compiler:

```
C:\C#\C#chp08\FloatWarning\Class1.cs(23): Cannot implicitly
convert type 'double' to 'float'
```

Statements of this type need the floating point designator, as in:

```
float fValue = 1.1f; // f or F
```

Of course, caution is also the word when attempting the assignment of a lower-precision variable to one that is higher, as seen in the third statement, which assigns a `float` precision to that of a `double`. Internal examination by the Visual Studio Debugger reveals fValue as containing the numeric representation 1.1. However, dValue internally contains 1.10000002384! If you want an integer treated as a `double`, use the following syntax:

```
double dValue = 1d;
```

In this case, simply follow the explicit value with a d or D.

false

C# allows you to use the `false` keyword as an overloaded operator or as a literal. When used as an overloaded operator, any user-defined type can define a `false` operator that returns the `bool` value `true`, when there is no match, or `false` otherwise, an ideal solution for user-defined types that represent `true`, `false`, or `null`. If a user-defined type overloads the operator `false`, it must also overload the operator `true`.

Consider the following portion of code:

```
using System;
class test
{
    public static void Main()
    {
        bool bTestReady = true;
        Console.Write("The test results are {0}",
          bTestReady ? "ready." : "not ready." );
    }
}
```

The output takes this form:

```
The test results are ready.
```

You can see that when `false` is used as a literal of type `bool` it simply represents a Boolean condition.

fixed

The C# keyword `fixed` is probably new to most programmers. Chapter 7, which dealt with pointers, exemplified its unique characteristics; however, a formal review of the keyword is noteworthy. The keyword `fixed` prevents the relocation of a variable by the automated garbage collector.

Remember from Chapter 7 that the `fixed` keyword is only permitted in an `unsafe` context. The `fixed` statement sets a pointer to a managed variable and "pins" that variable during the execution of code block. Without `fixed`, pointers to managed variables would be of little use since garbage collection could relocate the variables unpredictably. For example, the following data declaration defines a `classPointer` and initializes it to a managed instance:

```
Class classPointer = new Class();
```

Now assume that the formal definition for `Class` contains a `char` data member `cValue`. C# flags the following statement as illegal:

```
char* pc = &classPointer.cValue;
*pc = 'A';
```

The corrected C#-specific solution using `fixed` looks like:

```
fixed( char* pc = &classPointer.cValue; ) {
  *pc = 'A';
}
```

The `fixed` keyword allows you to initialize a pointer with the address of an array, as in:

```
fixed (float* pf = fArray)
fixed (float pf = &fArray[0]) // alternate syntax
```

or a string, as in:

```
fixed (char* ps = sMyStringr)
fixed (char* ps = &sMyString[0]) // alternate form
```

Multiple initializations of like-typed pointers can be combined using the comma operator, as in:

```
fixed (int* pi1 = iArray1, pi2 = iArray2)
```

Disparate pointer-type initializations require nested `fixed` declarations, as in:

```
fixed (int* pi = &iArray[0])
   fixed (double* pd = dArray)
      // *pi [some operation] *pd
```

The C# compiler will not allow any pointers initialized within a `fixed` statement to be modified. Also, never point to a pinned variable outside the `fixed` statement since any pinned variables are unpinned and subject to automatic garbage collection.

Also recall that the compiler must have the `/unsafe` option set to true in order for this type of program to correctly compile.

float

You are probably familiar with the standard `float` data type. The 32-bit floating point type stores values in the approximate range of $\pm1.5 \times 10^{-45}$ to $\pm3.4 \times 10^{38}$. However, by default, a real numeric literal on the right-hand side of the assignment operator is treated as a `double` *not* a `float`. For this reason, when you want the C# compiler to treat a `float` as a `float`, you need to use the suffix `f` or `F`, as in:

```
float fValue = 1.24596f;
```

If you forget to use the suffix, you will get a compilation error since the compiler will assume you are incorrectly trying to store a `double` value into a `float` variable.

int

The C# `int` data type mimics its 32-bit C/C++ counterpart, holding values in the range of –2,147,483,648 to 2,147,483,647. When an integer literal has no suffix, its type is the first of these types in which its value can be represented: `int`, `uint`, `long`, `ulong`.

C# implicitly converts from type `int` to `long`, `float`, `double`, or `decimal`, as in:

```
long lValue = 14;        // all use implicit conversion
float fValue = 11;       // of int to long, float
double dValue = 49;      // double
decimal decValue = 100;  // or decimal
```

There are also predefined implicit conversions from `sbyte`, `byte`, `short`, `ushort`, or `char` to `int`. Observe the following portion of code:

```
int iValue = 5.7;        // illegal statement
int iValue = (int)5.7;   // implicit cast required
```

Note that a cast is required to convert from floating-point to `int` in this code segment.

short

Today's 32-bit compilers default to a four byte integer data type. Older 16-bit compilers defaulted to a signed two byte integer, or 16-bits. This explained why `for` loops, which required an integer loop control variable, could not iterate more than 32,767 times. The 32-

bit compiler counterpart to this default 16-bit integer is short, with the anticipated range of -32,768 to 32,767.

Should you overload a function or method with an int and short formal argument list, you will always need to cast the formal argument past in order for the compiler to match the subroutine's signature, as in:

```
public void overloadedMethod(int iValue) ...    // int prototype
public void overloadedMethod(short sValue) ...  // short prototype
overloadedMethod(10);                           // making the int
                                                // call
overloadedMethod( (short)10 );                  // making the short
                                                // call
```

C# provides implicit conversions from type short to int, long, float, double, or decimal. However, by default, numeric integral calculations assigned to short variables are illegal since the C# compiler treats the result type as int, as in:

```
short sValue1 = 9, sValue2 = 6;
short sResult = sValue1 - sValue2;        // assumed int precision
```

As you might have anticipated, the fix involves an explicit cast:

```
short sResult = (short)( sValue1 - sValue2);   // explicit (short)
                                               // cast
```

Examine the following code segment:

```
short sValue = 5.2;          // illegal
short sValue = (short)5.2;   // explicit (short) cast
```

Notice that there are no implicit conversions from floating-point types to short. However, you can cast the expression, as shown in this code segment.

string

There is only one internal character representation for C# string data, the string type. Internally, strings are always stored as Unicode characters. string is an alias for System.String in the .NET framework. The equality and non-equality operators (==, !=) are overloaded to perform traditional string comparisons, as in:

```
string sGoodMorning = "Good Morning!";
string sAnotherOne = new string( "Good Morning!" );
Console.WriteLine( sGoodMorning == sAnotherOne );
Console.WriteLine( (object)sGoodMorning == sAnotherOne );
```

While the first WriteLine() returns true, the second statement outputs false because the two strings are not the same object! Additional string operators include concatenation +, and indexing [ ]. The latter allows you to treat the string like an array of characters, as in:

```
string sFirstName = "Race", sLastName = "Williams",
    sFullName = sFirstName + ' ' + sLastName;
char cFirstInitial = "Race"[0];
```

String literals are of type `string` and can be written in two forms: the traditional double-quoted examples seen above, or double-quoted but preceded by an at (@) symbol. At (@) symbol preceded strings differ from their simpler double-quoted counterparts in that escape sequences are *not* parsed:

```
string sUnicodeEscape = "\\\u0041\n";
```

Here, the `string` variable sUnicodeEscape contains a backslash (\), the Unicode value for "A", and a line-feed carriage return. At (@) symbol preceded strings look similar except for the leading @ symbol:

```
@"c:\rootDirectory\subDirectory\source.cs"
```

Their advantage, you ask? Look at the syntax required to parse the same literal using a standard C# `string` definition:

```
"c:\\rootDirectory\\subDirectory\\source.cs"
```

This more traditional C/C++ syntax requires the programmer to remember the lexical scanner's interpretation of a single backslash, that being that an escape sequence follows! While including a double-quote in a double-quoted `string` requires only a preceding backslash, @ symbol defined `strings` simply double the quote itself, as in:

```
"Then I was told, \"Your raise begins immediately!\"";
@"Then I was told, ""Your raise begins immediately!""";
```

The final use for @ symbol defined strings is their ability to reference identifiers that happen to be C# keywords.

true

In C#, `true` can be used as an overloaded operator or as a literal. For a description of its use, see the discussion of `bool` earlier in this chapter.

uint

Both `int` and `uint` default to a 32-bit precision in C#; only `uints` hold integral types in the size and range, from 0 to 4,294,967,295, as in:

```
uint uiValue = 1234567890;
uint uiValue = 1234u;
```

Adding a u or U to the explicit value defines either a uint or ulong depending on the value's precision. There are predefined implicit conversions from uint to long, ulong, float, double, or decimal. Also, you can implicitly convert from byte, ushort, or char to uint. Otherwise, you must use a cast, as in:

```
long lValue = 52;
uint uiValue = lValue;         // illegal no implicit conversion
uint uiValue = (uint)lValue;   // legal, with explicit cast
```

The same holds true for floating-point types:

```
uint uiValue = 21.0;           // illegal no implicit conversion
uint uiValue = (uint)21.0;     // legal with explicit conversion
```

ulong

Use ulong variables to define 64-bit integral types in the range 0 to 18446744073709551615 as in:

```
ulong ulValue = 123456789987654321;
```

The list of legal suffixes for ulong is quite exhaustive since the compiler does not care about the following upper/lower case or symbol order: UL, ul, Ul, uL, LU, lu, Lu, or lU.

Should you overload a function or method with an int and ulong formal argument list, you will always need to cast the formal argument past in order for the compiler to match the subroutine's signature, as in:

```
public void overloadedMethod(int iValue) ...     // int prototype
public void overloadedMethod(ulong ulValue) ...  // ulong prototype
overloadedMethod(10);                            // int call
overloadedMethod( (ulong)10 );                   // short call
overloadedMethod( 10ul);                         // alt form
```

Implicit conversions exist for values of ulong to float, double, or decimal. However, no implicit conversions exist for ulong to any integral type without an explicit cast.

ushort

ushort is the C# unsigned counterpart to short, holding 16-bit positive integer values in the range of 0 to 65535, as in:

```
ushort usValuet = 65535;
```

Specifying an illegal range value for ushort invokes a compilation error message.

Should you overload a function or method with an `int` and `ushort` formal argument list, you will always need to cast the formal argument past in order for the compiler to match the subroutine's signature, as in:

```
public void overloadedMethod(int iValue) ...      // int prototype
public void overloadedMethod(ushort sValue) ... // short prototype
overloadedMethod(10);                             // int call
overloadedMethod( (short)10 );                    // the short call
```

Implicit conversions exist for `ushort` values to `int`, `uint`, `long`, `ulong`, `float`, `double`, or `decimal`. No predefined implicit conversions exist from `byte` or `char` values to `ushort` without an explicit cast, as in:

```
ushort usValue1 = 10, usValue2 = 2;
ushort usResult = usValue1 - usValue2              // illegal
ushort usResult = (ushort)( usValue1 - usValue2); // explicit cast
```

Examine the following portion of code:

```
ushort usValue = 12.39;            // illegal
ushort usValue = (ushort)12.39;  // legal
```

Note that there is also no implicit conversion from floating-point types to `ushort` without an explicit cast.

void

The keyword `void` is used to specify a subroutine (function or method) that returns nothing.

Examine the following portion of code:

```
void mySubroutine(void) {} // illegal use of void as formal argument
```

Here, you can see that, unlike C/C++, C# does *not* allow `void` to appear as a subroutine's formal argument type.

User-Defined Types

There are two simple user-defined types: structures and enumerated types, represented by the C# keywords `struct` and `enum`, respectively. If you are already familiar with C/C++ structures and enumerated types, you'll find C#'s counterpart very similar. Actually, the `enum` keyword more closely matches C++'s use and syntax than C's with the additional requirement of a (type) cast before assigning integral values to an enumerated type.

struct

A structure is formed in C# by using the keyword `struct`, followed by a tag field, and then a list of members within the structure. The tag field is used to create other variables of the particular structure's type. A `struct` type is a value type that can contain constructors, constants, fields, methods, properties, indexers, operators, and nested types. It is an error to declare a default (parameterless) constructor for a `struct`. It is an error to initialize an instance field in a `struct`. Unlike C++, you cannot declare a class using the keyword `struct`. In C#, classes and structs are semantically different. A `struct` is a value type, while a `class` is a reference type.

The syntax for a structure with the optional tag field looks like this:

```
[attributes] [modifiers] struct tag_field [:interfaces] body [;]
```

A semicolon terminates the structure definition because it is actually a C# statement. The `struct` type is suitable for representing lightweight objects such as Point, Rectangle, and Color, or application-specific definitions such as:

```
struct stboat {
   char cModelCode;
   int iyear;
   long lmotor_hours;
   float fsaleprice;
};
```

The structure is created with the keyword `struct` followed by the tag field or type for the structure. In this example, `stboat` is the tag field for the structure.

This structure declaration contains several members: `cModelCode`, followed by an integer, `iyear`, a `long` integer, `lmotor_hours`, and a `float`, `fsaleprice`. The structure will be used to save sales information for a boat.

So far, all that has been defined is a new hypothetical structure type called `stboat`. However, no variable has been associated with the structure at this point. In a program, you can associate a variable with a structure by using a statement similar to the following:

```
stboat stused_boat;
```

The statement defines `stused_boat` to be of the type `struct stboat`. Notice that the declaration required the use of the structure's tag field. If this statement is contained within a function, then the structure variable named `stused_boat` is local in scope to that function. If the statement is contained outside of all program functions, the structure will be global in scope.

It is an error to initialize an instance field in a struct. Remember, unlike C++, you cannot declare a class using the keyword `struct`. In C#, classes and structs are semantically different. A `struct` is a value type, while a `class` is a reference type.

enum

The enumerated data type enum exists for one reason only: to make your code more readable. In other computer languages, this data type is referred to as a user-defined type. The general syntax for enumerated declarations looks like this:

```
enum op_tag_field { value1,. . .valuen } op_var_dec ;
```

Enumerated data types allow you to associate a set of easily understood human symbols—for example, Monday, Tuesday, Wednesday, and so on—with an integral data type. They also help you create self-documenting code. For example, instead of having a loop that goes from 0 to 4, it can now read from Monday to Friday:

```
enum eweekdays { Monday, Tuesday, Wednesday, Thursday, Friday };

/* Not using the enumerated type */
for(i = 0; i <= 4; i++)
        .
        .
        .

/* Using the enumerated type    */
for(ewToday = Monday; ewToday <= Friday; ewToday++)
```

C compilers, historically speaking, have seen no difference between the data types int and enum. This meant that a program could assign an integer value to an enumerated type. In C#, the two types generate a warning message from the compiler without an explicit type cast:

```
// legal in C not C# */
ewToday = 1;

// correcting the problem in C#
ewToday = (eweekdays)1;
```

The use of enum is popular in programming when information can be represented by a list of integer values such as the number of months in a year or the number of days in a week. This type of list lends itself to enumeration.

The following example, enum.cs, contains a list of the number of months in a year. These are in an enumeration list with a tag name emonths. The variable associated with the list is emcompleted. Enumerated lists will always start with zero unless forced to a different integer value. In this case, January is the first month of the year.

```
using System;
public class Class1
{
   enum emonths { January=1, February, March,
                  April, May, June,
                  July, August, September,
                  October, November, December };

  public static int Main(string[] args)
  {
    // enum.cs
    // A C# program shows the use of enum types.
    // Program calculates elapsed months in year, and
    // remaining months using enum type.
    //Copyright (c) Chris H. Pappas and William H. Murray, 2001
    //

    int ipresent_month;
    int isum,idiff;
    emonths emcompleted;

    Console.Write("\nPlease enter the present month (1 to 12): ");
    ipresent_month = int.Parse(Console.ReadLine();

    emcompleted = emonths.December;
    isum = ipresent_month;
    idiff = (int)emcompleted - ipresent_month;

    Console.WriteLine("\n{0} month(s) past,
                      {1} months to go.\n",isum,idiff);

    return (0);
  }
}
```

The enumerated list is actually a list of integer values, from 1 to 12, in this program. Since the names are equivalent to consecutive integer values, integer arithmetic can be performed with them. The enumerated variable, emcompleted, when set equal to December, is actually set to 12.

This short program will just perform some simple arithmetic and report the result to the screen:

```
Please enter the current month (1 to 12): 4
4 month(s) past, 8 months to go.
```

As an exercise, modify this application to return days left in the year instead of months.

Exception Handling

Exception handling is any compiler's ability to trap, and hopefully, eloquently recover from what would otherwise be a fatal crash. There are two phases to the cure; first, the syntax required to flag the specified otherwise-fatal condition (the C# throw keyword), and second, the syntax for recognizing the flagged condition and dealing with it (or C#'s catch, try-catch, or try-finally keywords).

throw

The use of C#'s throw statement is similar to that in C++. It is used to signal an abnormal situation or exception. The syntax for a throw statement looks like:

```
throw [throw_statement_expression];
```

The throw_statement_expression must be an object whose class is derived from System.Exception, as in:

```
class myExceptionClass : System.Exception {}
throw new myExceptionClass();
```

Usually, the throw statement is used with try-catch or try-finally statements. When an exception is thrown, the program looks for the catch statement that handles this exception.

The following program, throw.cs, demonstrates how to throw an exception using the throw statement:

```
using System;
public class Class1
{
  public static int divideIt(int x, int y)
  {
    if(y == 0)
    {
      throw new ArgumentException("Can't Divide by Zero (0)");
    }

    return x/y;
  }

  public static int Main(string[] args)
  {
    // throw.cs
    // A C# application demonstrating the
    // throw keyword.
    // Copyright (c) Chris H. Pappas and William H. Murray, 2001
    //
```

```
    int iValue1 = 10, iValue2 = 0;

    Console.WriteLine("iValue1/iValue2 = {0}",
                        divideIt(iValue1,iValue2)); // never
executed

    return 0;
  }
}
```

The output from the program looks like the following: (Note: this can be obtained from the MS-DOS prompt file pipe throw > output.dat during execution.)

```
Exception occurred: System.ArgumentException: Can't Divide by Zero (0)
    at Class1.divideIt(Int32 x, Int32 y)
      in c:\c#\c#chp08\throw\throw.cs:line 11
    at Class1.Main(String[] args) in
c:\c#\c#chp08\throw\throw.cs:line 23
```

The message details what the exception thrown was, and where it was thrown. A similar message is reported if you run the program from inside the debugger and generate a runtime exception error message window.

try-catch

The try-catch statement consists of a try block followed by one or more catch statements, catching each unique exception. The try-catch statement looks like:

  try *tryThis* **catch** (exception1) catch1 **catch** (exception2) catch2 ...

tryThis represents the statement possibly causing an exception. exception1 details the exception object declaration with catch1 containing the exception handler. There can be more than one catch block. In this case, the order of the catch clauses is important because the catch clauses are examined in order. Catch the more specific exceptions before the less specific ones.

The tryThis statement contains the guarded code that may cause the exception. tryThis is executed until an exception is thrown or it is completed successfully. The catch clause can be used without arguments, in which case it catches any type of exception, and is referred to as the general catch clause. It can also take an object argument derived from System.Exception, in which case it handles a specific exception.

Building on your understanding of throw statements, catch clauses often throw exceptions, as seen in this next program reThrow.cs:

```
using System;
public class someClass
{
  public void someMethod(string testString)
  {
    if(testString == null)
    {
      throw(new ArgumentNullException());
    }
  }

  public static int Main(string[] args)
  {
    // reThrow.cs
    // A C# application demonstrating
    // how to rethrow an exception.
    // Copyright (c) Chris H. Pappas and William H. Murray. 2001
    //

    someClass sC = new someClass();
    try
    {
      string testString = null;
      sC.someMethod(testString);
    }

    catch (Exception exception)
    {
      Console.WriteLine("Processing caught " +
                        "exception: {0}",exception);
    }

    return 0;
  }
}
```

The program's `try` statement invokes the `sC.someMethod()` that could cause the initial exception. The `catch` clause catches the exception, and `throws` the `ArgumentNull-Exception()` caught by the `Exception` catch displaying an appropriate message.

This next example, `catchOrder.cs`, contains two `catch` statements, demonstrating its syntax and order-of-precedence processing with the highest priority exception first.

```
using System;
public class someClass
{
  public void someMethod(string testString)
  {
    if(testString == null)
    {
```

```
        throw(new ArgumentNullException());
      }
      else if(testString == "Empty")
      {
        throw(new ArgumentOutOfRangeException());
      }
    }

    public static int Main(string[] args)
    {
      // catchOrder.cs
      // A C# program illustrating
      // how to order catch statements.
      // Copyright (c) Chris H. Pappas and William H. Murray, 2001
      //

      someClass sC = new someClass();
      try
      {
        string testString = "Empty";
        sC.someMethod(testString);
      }

      catch(ArgumentNullException exception)
      {
        Console.WriteLine("Processing Null exception: {0}",
                          exception);
      }

      catch(ArgumentOutOfRangeException exception)
      {
        Console.WriteLine("Processing Range exception {0}",
                          exception);
      }

      catch(Exception exception)
      {
        Console.WriteLine("Processing other exception {0}",
                          exception);
      }

      return 0;
    }
  }
```

This example builds on the previous algorithm by checking for a `null` string assignment, the highest-priority condition, followed by a check to see if the initialized string indicates a useless entry of `Empty`.

try-finally

Just as classes may contain destructors to deallocate any class-specific generated resource, the finally block cleans up any resources allocated in a try statement. finally statements are always processed regardless of how the try block executes. The syntax for try-finally looks like:

try *tryThis* **finally** *cleanUp*;

The tryThis statement, once again, represents statement expected to raise the exception with the cleanUp block detailing exception handler's cleanup algorithm. In this last example, tryFinally.cs, the program tries to cast a double to type char generating, and then catching, the InvalidCastException:

```csharp
using System;
public class Class1
{
   public static int Main(string[] args)
   {
     // tryFinally.cs
     // A C# demonstration of try-finally statements
     // Copyright (c) Chris H. Pappas and William H. Murray, 2001
     //

     double dValue = 1.23456789;
     char cValue;

     try
     {
       cValue = (char)dValue;
       throw new InvalidCastException();
     }

     catch(InvalidCastException exception)
     {
       Console.WriteLine("Invalid Cast Operation {0}",exception);
     }

     finally
     {
       Console.WriteLine("No matter what - DO THIS");
     }


     return 0;
   }
}
```

When you run the program, you get a runtime error message, but the `finally` clause will still be executed and display the output. Although the `InvalidCastException` is caught, the `finally` block executes outputting the *"No matter what—DO THIS!"* message.

Scope and Build Time Control

While the keywords `static` and `const` may be used to flag persistent values, they reflect an unobvious build sequence. `static` constructs are built before `Main()` even begins to execute, while `const` values are more likely substantiated at runtime.

static

See Chapter 7, "Saying Goodbye to Pointers," for a detailed discussion on this topic.

const

Use the C# `const` keyword to indicate locked, or unalterable, value contents, as in:

```
const string sCompanyTitle = "Where are we now Travel Agency!";
```

or in constant expressions like:

```
const int iValue1 = 1;
const int iDoubleValue1 = iValue1 + iValue1;
```

Identifiers marked `const` may *not* appear on the left-hand side of an assignment operator. Also, it is illegal to mark an identifier as both `const` and `static`.

Integer Conversions

C# provides two keywords, `checked` and `unchecked`, to help flag integer expressions returning inappropriate precisions for designated integral types at compile time or runtime.

checked

Use the `checked` keyword to flag integer arithmetic overflow conditions. It can be used as an operator or a statement, as in:

```
checked myBlock         // used as a statement
checked (myExpression)  // used as an operator
```

`myblock` represents the statement block that contains the expressions to be evaluated in a checked context, while the parenthesized block, `(myExpression)`, represents the expression to be evaluated in a checked context. Whenever an expression produces a value that is outside the range of the destination type, the result depends on whether the expression is constant or non-constant. Constant expressions cause compile time errors, while non-constant expressions are evaluated at runtime and raise exceptions.

The first program, `checkedExpressions.cs`, throws a `System.OverflowException` at runtime:

```
using System;
public class Class1
{
  // 65535 * 2 generates OverflowException for ushort
  // change uix to less than 36767 to remove error
  static ushort uix = 65535, uiy = 2;

  public static int timesTwo()
  {
    int iResult = checked( (ushort)(uix * uiy) );

    return iResult;
  }

  public static int Main(string[] args)
  {
    // checkedExpressions.cs
    // A C# illustration of checked expressions.
    // Copyright (c) Chris H. Pappas and William H. Murray, 2001


    Console.WriteLine("uix * uiy = {0}", timesTwo());

    return 0;
  }
}
```

The exception is thrown when the `checked` statement, inside the method `timesTwo()`, attempts to assign an incorrect cast precision of `ushort` into an `int` variable.

The second example, using an `unchecked` expression, employs an inaccurate, truncated value:

```
using System;
public class Class1
{
 // 65535 * 2 generates OverflowException for ushort
  // change uix to less than 36767 to remove error
  static ushort uix = 65535, uiy = 2;

  public static int timesTwo()
  {
```

```
    int iResult = unchecked( (ushort)(uix * uiy) );

    return iResult;
  }

  public static int Main(string[] args)
  {
    // uncheckedExpression.cs
    // A C# demonstration of unchecked statements.
    // Compare with checkedExpression.cs
    // Copyright (c) Chris H. Pappas and William H. Murray, 2001
    //

    Console.WriteLine("uix * uiy = {0}", timesTwo());

    return 0;
  }
}
```

The program does *not* flag any error conditions and simply forces an unacceptable precision for a type of ushort. The inaccurate result used by the program produces the following output:

```
uix * uiy = 65534
```

The third and last example, defaultChecking.cs, illustrates what happens when neither checked or unchecked are specified:

```
using System;
public class Class1
{
 // 65535 * 2 generates OverflowException for ushort
  // change uix to less than 36767 to remove error
  static ushort uix = 65535, uiy = 2;

  public static int timesTwo()
  {
    int iResult = (ushort)(uix * uiy);

    return iResult;
  }

  public static int Main(string[] args)
  {
    // defaultChecking.cs
    // A C# demonstration of unchecked statements.
    // Compare with uncheckedExpression.cs
```

```
// Copyright (c) Chris H. Pappas and William H. Murray, 2001
//

        Console.WriteLine("uix * uiy = {0}", timesTwo());

        return 0;
    }
}
```

Using default overflow checking, the third example behaves like its unchecked predecessor, producing the following inaccurate output:

```
uix * uiy = 65534
```

unchecked

The next three example programs are extensions of the previous three. The unchecked keyword performs the same overflow checking for integer arithmetic operations and conversions. In unchecked mode, expressions returning values outside the range of the destination's type are assigned truncated values. Omitting the keywords checked or unchecked invokes the compiler's default, compile-time, overflow checking. Otherwise, if the expression is non-constant, the runtime overflow checking depends on other factors such as compiler options and environment configuration, as illustrated in the next three algorithms. The three examples use constant expressions, for which the overflow checking is evaluated at compile time.

The first program, compileChecked.cs, uses an unchecked block:

```
using System;
public class Class1
{
  class compileChecked
  {
    const uint uix = 4294967295;
    const uint uiy = 2;

    public uint timesTwo()
    {
      unchecked
      {
        uint iResult = uix * uiy;
        return iResult;
      }
    }
  }

  public static int Main(string[] args)
  {
```

```
      // compileChecked.cs
      // A C# demonstration compile time overflow checking.
      // Copyright (c) Chris H. Pappas and William H. Murray, 2001
      //

      compileChecked cC = new compileChecked();

      Console.WriteLine("uix * uiy = {0}", cC.timesTwo());

      return 0;
    }
  }
```

which produces the runtime, truncated output of:

```
  uix * uiy = 4294967294
```

Only the last two algorithms, defaultCompileChecked.cs (seen next) and checkedOverflow.cs, produce compile-time errors.

NOTE

These errors are only generated when the project's compiler option is set to checked (see Microsoft Visual Studio Help on changing compiler options via the View ➤ Properties Window ➤ SolutionProperties tab).

```
using System;
public class Class1
{
  class compileChecked
  {
    const uint uix = 4294967295;
    const uint uiy = 2;

    public uint timesTwo()
    {
      uint iResult = uix * uiy;
      return iResult;
    }
  }

  public static int Main(string[] args)
  {
    // defaultCompileChecked.cs
    // A C# demonstration compile time overflow checking. The
    // program overflows at compile time if checked mode
    // from View | Properties Window menus - is active.
```

```
   // Copyright (c) Chris H. Pappas and William H. Murray, 2001
   //

   compileChecked cC = new compileChecked();

   Console.WriteLine("uix * uiy = {0}", cC.timesTwo());

   return 0;
   }
}
```

This last solution performs identically to its default predecessor, using the checked code block and generating a compile-time error:

```
using System;
public class Class1
{
  class compileChecked
  {
    const uint uix = 4294967295;
    const uint uiy = 2;

    public uint timesTwo()
    {
      checked
      {
        uint iResult = uix * uiy;
        return iResult;
      }
    }
  }

  public static int Main(string[] args)
  {
    // checkedOverflow.cs
    // A C# demonstration compile time overflow checking. The
    // program overflows at compile time if checked mode
    // from View | Properties Window menus - is active.
    // Copyright (c) Chris H. Pappas and William H. Murray, 2001
    //

    compileChecked cC = new compileChecked();

    Console.WriteLine("uix * uiy = {0}", cC.timesTwo());

    return 0;
  }
}
```

Parameters

You can pass actual arguments to subroutines one of two ways: call-by-value (a value copy) or call-by-reference (a pointer reference to the data using C# keyword ref). While C, C++, and now C# only have one formal category of subroutine, namely, a function (or method), many older high-level languages had a second subroutine category called a procedure.

Procedures varied from their function sibling in that they could return from zero to many arguments, with functions reserved exclusively for subroutines returning only one value. C# attempts to clandestinely return the two types to this new language with the out formal argument designator.

C# also adopts a concept originated in C—a subroutine desiring a varying length formal argument list, known in C as the ellipsis (. . .) operator. In C#, however, the syntax uses the new keyword params.

params

The params keyword is closest to the C/C++ ellipsis operator (. . .) and defines a subroutine parameter where the number of arguments is variable. Just like the ellipsis, once the subroutine's formal argument list uses the params keyword, no other formal argument types may follow.

```
using System;
public class Class1
{
  public static void like_C_ellipsis(params object[] va_list)
  {
    for(int offset = 0; offset < va_list.Length; offset += 2)
    {
      Console.Write("[{0}] {1}",offset,(object)va_list[offset]);
      Console.WriteLine(" {0}",(object)va_list[offset+1]);
    }
  }

  public static int Main(string[] args)
  {
    // params.cs
    // A C# application using the params
    // formal argument type.
    // Copyright (c) Chris H. Pappas and William H. Murray, 2001
    //

    like_C_ellipsis("int\t\t", 5, "char\t", 'c', "float\t", 2.3);

    like_C_ellipsis("2 * 2 = \t", 4);

    return 0;
  }
}
```

The output from the program takes this form:

```
[0]  int          5
[2]  char         c
[4]  float        2.3
[0]  2 * 2 =      4
```

As you study this code and output, can you see the similarity to the ellipsis operator (...)?

out

Nomenclature for C# subroutines fall under two categories: functions or methods. Traditionally speaking, "functions" by definition return *only one* value. Older high-level languages had an additional subroutine category called procedures. Procedures differed from functions in that procedures could return from zero to many values.

The C# out keyword turns a function (or method) *into* a procedure by allowing a method parameter to refer to the same variable that was passed into the method. Any changes made to the parameter in the method will be reflected in that variable when control passes back to the calling method. To confuse matters, a method that uses an out parameter can still return a value and may have more than one out parameter.

```
using System;
public class Class1
{
  public static int call_functionWithOutParameter(out int iValue)
  {
    iValue = 10;
    return -1;
  }

  public static int Main(string[] args)
  {
    // out.cs
    // A C# example program demonstrating
    // the out formal argument type
    // Copyright (c) Chris H. Pappas and William H. Murray, 2001
    //

    int iValue;

    // Following statement will not compile - no initial iValue
    // Console.WriteLine("Original Value of iValue {0}", iValue);
    Console.WriteLine("iValue returned:
      {0}",call_functionWithOutParameter(out iValue));
```

```
        Console.WriteLine("iValue in Main(): {0}", iValue);

        return 0;
    }
}
```

To use an `out` parameter, the argument must explicitly be passed to the method as an `out` argument.

The output from the program looks like:

```
iValue returned: -1
iValue in Main(): 10
```

The value of an `out` argument will not be passed to the `out` parameter. A variable passed as an `out` argument need not be initialized. However, the `out` parameter must be assigned a value before the method returns.

ref

The C# keyword `ref` tells the compiler that what is being sent over is the address to a memory location, rather than a copy of the contents of a memory location. Therefore, any changes made to the parameter in the called subroutine are reflected in the calling routine's formal argument. The following program, `ref.cs`, illustrates the syntax necessary when employing `ref` parameters:

```
using System;
public class Class1
{

    public static void withRefKeyword(ref int iValue)
    {
        iValue = -1;
    }

    public static void withoutRefKeyword(int iValue)
    {
        iValue = 55;
    }

    public static int Main(string[] args)
    {
        // ref.cs
        // A C# demonstration of ref formal arguments
        // Copyright (c) Chris H. Pappas and William H. Murray, 2001
        //
```

```
    int iValue = 6;

    Console.WriteLine("Original iValue: {0}", iValue);

    withoutRefKeyword(iValue);
    Console.WriteLine("iValue returned by withoutRefKeyword():
{0}",
                    iValue);

    withRefKeyword(ref iValue);
    Console.WriteLine("iValue returned by withRefKeyword(): {0}",
                    iValue);

    return 0;
  }
}
```

To use a `ref` parameter, the argument must be explicitly passed to the method as a `ref` argument. The value of a `ref` argument will be passed to the `ref` parameter. Any formal argument passed as a `ref` parameter must first be initialized. Contrast this prerequisite with the use of an `out` parameter, which does not require the variable to be explicitly initialized before being passed.

The output from the program looks like:

```
Original iValue: 6
iValue returned by withoutRefKeyword(): 6
iValue returned by withRefKeyword(): -1
```

Special Operators

The keywords `sizeof()` and `as` represent two C# operators. In the case of `sizeof()`, programmers are likely to misinterpret the syntax with the closing parenthesis `()`, as function syntax; however, `sizeof()` is an operator.

sizeof

Technically speaking, `sizeof()` is not a function or method, but a C# operator. You use `sizeof()` to return the number of bytes an object needs in memory. Unlike its C/C++ counterpart, the C# `sizeof` operator can be applied only to value types, not reference types, and *must be* used in `unsafe` mode only.

```
using System;
class StandardTypes
{
  unsafe public static void SizeofStandardTypes()
  {
```

```
    // C# requires unsafe mode when using sizeof()
    Console.WriteLine("sizeof char   : {0}", sizeof(char));
    Console.WriteLine("sizeof int    : {0}", sizeof(int));
    Console.WriteLine("sizeof double : {0}", sizeof(long));
  }

  public static int Main(string[] args)
  {
    // sizeof.cs
    // A C# program demonstrating the sizeof() operator
    // Copyright (c) Chris H. Pappas and William H. Murray, 2001
    //

    StandardTypes.SizeofStandardTypes();

    return 0;
  }
}
```

The output from the program looks like:

```
sizeof char   : 2
sizeof int    : 4
sizeof double: 8
```

Recall that the `unsafe` compile option must be set to `true` in order for this program to compile correctly.

as

Similar to `sizeof()`, the keyword `as` is an operator. You use `as` to convert between compatible types. The following program, `as.cs`, compares each `object testObjects[]`'s initialized element, `sC`, as compatible with `someClass`:

```
using System;
public class Class1
{
  public class someClass
  {
  }
  public static int Main(string[] args)
  {
    // as.cs
    // A C# demonstration of the as keyword
    // that returns a non-null value for compatible types
    // Copyright (c) Chris H. Pappas and William H. Murray, 2001
    //
```

```
object[] testObjects = new object[6];

testObjects[0] = new someClass();
testObjects[1] = "string";
testObjects[2] = 5;
testObjects[3] = 1.1;
testObjects[4] = true;
testObjects[5] = null;

for(int offset = 0; offset < testObjects.Length; offset++)
{
  someClass sC = testObjects[offset] as someClass;
  Console.Write("Row {0}: ",offset);
  if(sC != null)
  {
    Console.WriteLine("Compatible Type");
  }
  else
  {
    Console.WriteLine("Incompatible Type");
  }
}

return 0;
  }
}
```

The output from the program looks like:

```
Row 0: Compatible Type
Row 1: Incompatible Type
Row 2: Incompatible Type
Row 3: Incompatible Type
Row 4: Incompatible Type
Row 5: Incompatible Type
```

The `as` operator looks similar in syntax to a cast except that it returns `null` when the requested conversion fails instead of raising an exception.

Summary

This chapter was designed to prepare you for upcoming topics in object-oriented programming. The C# keywords and concepts form the foundation of a good understanding of OOPs concepts presented in subsequent chapters and are the key to successful OOP C#. Robust algorithms are based on two pivotal fundamentals: clean logic flow and accurate calculations. As an algorithm rolls over in complexity from a procedural approach to a more sophisticated and robust OOP design, additional design considerations are necessary to take advantage of the protection layers offered by OOP syntax.

Chapter 9 details the building blocks and syntax used by successful OOP algorithms. The chapter presents, in a step-by-step approach, how OOP design philosophy is one or two syntax layers away from what you already know as a procedural programmer!

Objects

If you are unfamiliar with object-oriented programming terminology, philosophy, design techniques, and syntax, there's great news—an object-oriented solution doesn't give your program any more horsepower than a procedural solution. The main difference between procedural and object-oriented solutions is packaging—in other words, syntax.

Giving an Application the Windows LOOK

Here's the problem. If you had to write and debug all of the code necessary to give your application the Microsoft Windows LOOK, you'd never get to write the code for the application itself. Think about it. You have framed windows, scroll bars, menus, dialog boxes, radio buttons, check boxes, fonts, multimedia, etc., all requiring (by Microsoft) a common look and user-interaction. Instead, you simply develop your application and plug into the code provided by Microsoft for the product-to-Windows interface.

For this scenario to actually work, the code for the interface must be generic, portable, extensible, and of course, robust. Here's where object-oriented syntax really shines over its procedural counterpart. Without getting heavily into object-oriented design philosophy, here's a simple test anyone could apply to an object-oriented solution to test the four fundamentals listed at the beginning of this paragraph.

Good Object Design

First, imagine you are observing the runtime of a fellow programmer's algorithm. You are particularly impressed with one of the program's features, for example, the program is a database, but one of the field options works just like a mini-word processor. You say to your friend, can you give me the code necessary to add that capability to my program. If the friend answers sure, you copy this one file (or possibly several), and you've got a well-designed object.

If, on the other hand, the answer sounds something like this: well, copy this file, edit out these lines, remember that you need a global variable to make the whole thing work, watch out for identifier collisions, oh, and you'll have to manually change all of the screen coordinates—look out! It sounds more like a procedural solution, or worse, a poorly implemented object.

So How Do I Create an Object?

If you are familiar with any high-level programming language, you are already familiar with three object-oriented building-block components: structures (or records), members of a structure (or fields within a record), and subroutines. Normal procedural solutions fracture structure definitions and subroutine bodies across the coded solution. This makes it difficult to clone. Add to that the various ways programming languages deal with visibility issues and you easily generate multiple side effects when sharing the algorithm with other applications.

Object-oriented syntax is really quite simple. You simply pull subroutine bodies into the structure. This syntactically isolates the subroutine code from external side effects and makes it very easy to clone. Of course, the encapsulated subroutines should only work on the structure's data members. That's it! And this definition for an object works whether you are programming in Ada, C++, any other object-oriented language, and now C#. While the syntax varies slightly between languages, the concepts are identical.

Family Trees

Actually, the statement made earlier about object-oriented solutions being identical in functionality to their procedural counterparts is not quite true. Objects do have one characteristic missing from non-object-oriented solutions, namely, inheritance.

If you had a good introductory programming course, not only did you study structures (or records) but also the concept of nesting structure definitions, where a member of one structure is of another previously defined structure. In non-object-oriented syntax, that is the definition of inheritance—one member's type inherits from another's.

Earlier, you discovered that an object is nothing more than the packaging of structure data member definitions with the subroutine bodies that work on said data members. However, just like one structure inheriting another's definition, one object's definition can inherit from another previously defined one. Only in the case of objects, the inherited members aren't just data members but subroutine code.

When one object's definition inherits from a previous one, the second definition is said to have been *derived* from a *base*, *parent*, or *root* object. The derived object is called a *child*, *descendant*, or *subclass*. From the child object's point-of-view, the parent, base, or root object is known as an *ancestor*. *Multiple inheritance* is the term applied to any object that has more than one base, parent, or root. While this feature makes for brilliant, eloquent, and sophisticated program solutions, it also brings design and debug nightmares. C# does *not* have this capability (not directly), and since multiple inheritance is superfluous for many applications, it is hardly missed.

Classes As C# Objects

C# inherits its object-oriented definition syntax from C++. Both languages use the keyword `class`. Without a `class`, no single C# program would compile. Since all C# classes are dynamically allocated, they fall under the C# *reference type* category—in other words, they are pointers to instantiated instances. While C# does not directly implement multiple inheritance, it does mimic this capability through multiple interfaces. Even if you are already familiar with object-oriented programming fundamentals, C# adds a few interesting features of its own, namely, indexers and events.

NOTE

If you are new to object-oriented terminology, study the following procedural statement:

```
int iValue;
```

This statement could be described as one that *creates* the *variable* `iValue` and that would be technically correct. However, in object-oriented terminology, the same process, i.e., allocating memory with a predefined mapping (`int`), becomes:

```
FORMALCLASS_DEFINITION anActualObject;
```

An object-oriented software engineer would describe this statement as one that *instantiates* the object `anActualObject`, with `anActualObject` technically known as an *instance*. So "creates" becomes "instantiates" and what you used to call a "variable" becomes an "instance." Both `int` and `FORMALCLASS_DEFINITION` remain the identifiers' types, respectively.

Constructors

When you syntactically pull a subroutine body into a formal class definition, you no longer call the subroutine a function technically speaking. To distinguish *stand-alone functions* from bundled class subroutines, the later category has its own name—*method* (or sometimes referred to as *member function*, *function member*, or *behavior*, as opposed to *member data*).

There are two special categories of methods known as *constructors* and *destructors*. They differ from regular methods in two areas. First, their headers have a unique syntax. Secondly, they are automatically invoked unlike a regular method, which must be called explicitly within the program.

A constructor method is automatically invoked whenever the object is instantiated. Likewise, a destructor is automatically invoked whenever the object instance goes out of scope.

The following code segment highlights the syntax difference between a `regular-Method()` and `classConstructor()`. See if you can detect the subtle compiler requirement:

```
class classConstructor
{
  public classConstructor()
  public regularMethod();
}
```

You can immediately recognize a class' constructor by its identifier or name. The name *must* match the formal identifier for the class. The previous code segment declared the class `classConstructor`, and the first method (constructor) is named `classCon-structor()`. Constructors do not have a return type and are usually declared `public`. The typical logical use for this automatically invoked method is to initialize variables.

This next code segment illustrates the syntax for a method (and constructor is just a specifically named method) header and the logical body of a constructor:

```
public classConstructor()
{
  // code to initialize variables here
}
```

By syntax requirement, constructors are not allowed to return a value. They are, however, allowed a full complement of formal arguments as needed, as in:

```
public classConstructor(int iValue, string sValue, double dValue)
{
  .
  .
  .
}
```

If a class contains only static members (you do not need to instantiate a class with static members and can access their definitions directly), you should use the `private` interface modifier, as in:

```
class classConstructor
{
  private classConstructor()
  . . .
}
```

While interface modifiers are discussed later in the chapter, simply stated, `private` marks a constructor that isn't visible or accessible from outside the class itself. Since it is, in effect, invisible to the `Main()` program, it cannot be legally called, and you cannot instantiate the object.

NOTE

Even if you do not explicitly declare a class constructor, the C# compiler automatically generates a default constructor (see section titled Instantiating Objects with new *later in this chapter).*

Default Constructors

If you do not explicitly include a class constructor, the C# compiler will automatically generate one. The default constructor simply invokes the parameter less constructor of the parent class. If the class is `abstract`, then the declared accessibility for the default constructor is `protected`. Otherwise, the declared accessibility for the default constructor is `public`. Thus, the default constructor is always of the form:

```
protected myClass(): base() {}
```

or

```
public myClass(): base() {}
```

Here, `myClass` serves as the name of the class. Examine the following code segment:

```
class DisplayString
{
    object messenger;
    string astring;
}
```

A default constructor is provided in this code segment because the class contains no constructor declarations. This is equivalent to the following portion of code:

```
class DisplayString
{
    object messenger;
    string astring;
    public DisplayString(): base() {}
}
```

The following program, `defaultConstructor.cs`, illustrates the hidden syntax for default constructors:

```
using System;
public class defaultConstructor
{
  object someClassObj;
  int iUsedBysomeClassObj;
  // auto-generated default constructor looks like
  // public defaultConstructor(); base() {}


  public static int Main(string[] args)
  {
    // defconstrut.cs
    // A simple C# application demonstrating the
    // hidden syntax for a default constructor
    // Copyright (c) Chris H. Pappas and William H. Murray, 2001
    //

    defaultConstructor AnInstanceOfdC;

    return 0;
  }
}
```

Notice that the class `defaultConstructor` has no formal constructor definition. Instead, the C# compiler automatically generates the `base()` equivalent.

Static Constructors

Use a *static constructor* method to initialize class member data. Static constructors are not inherited but are automatically invoked. However, static constructors cannot be invoked explicitly. When using static constructors, caution must be used since the timing and ordering of the constructors execution is not defined. Static constructors are processed using the following rules:

- Static constructors are executed before an instance of the class is created.

- Static constructors are executed before any static member of the class is referenced.

- Static constructors are executed before the static constructor of any of its child classes are executed.

- Static constructors are never executed more than once.

The following example program, `staticconstruct.cs`, defines two classes, *One* and *Two,* each with their own `static` constructors and respective sample methods `OneMethod()` and `TwoMethod()`:

```csharp
using System;
public class staticconstruct
{
  class One
  {
    static One()
    {
      Console.WriteLine("class One constructor invoked.");
    }

    public static void OneMethod()
    {
      Console.WriteLine("OneMethod entered");
    }
  }

  class Two
  {
    static Two()
    {
      Console.WriteLine("class Two constructor invoked.");
    }

    public static void TwoMethod()
    {
      Console.WriteLine("TwoMethod entered");
    }
  }

  public static int Main(string[] args)
  {
    // staticconstruct.cs
    // A simple C# application demonstrating the
    // characteristics of static constructors.
    // Copyright (c) Chris H. Pappas and William H. Murray, 2001
    //

    // Notice that static class declarations do not require
    // the instantiation of the object in order to legally
    // access internal class definitions!
    //

    One.OneMethod();
    Two.TwoMethod();

    return 0;
  }
}
```

Both classes not only flag the C# compiler to the presence of static constructors, but the two methods are also marked static. Because of this, there is no need for Main() to instantiate the objects. Static methods (constructor or otherwise) are placed into memory before any statement in Main() begins to execute. The output from the program looks like:

```
class One constructor invoked.
OneMethod entered
class Two constructor invoked.
TwoMethod entered
```

Try modifying this application so that it is unique to your needs.

Child Class Constructor Inheritance

The base keyword is used to access members of the base class from within a child, subclass, or derived class:

- Use the base keyword to call a method on the parent (base) class that has been overridden by another method.
- Use the base keyword to identify the parent (base) class constructor to be used when creating instances of the child class.

Base class access is allowed in a constructor, an instance method, or an instance property ancestor. The base keyword cannot be used from within a static method.

The following code segment defines a parent, Customer, and child, Bank_Customer, sharing the inherited method GetData():

```
using System;
    public class Customer
    {
        protected string pin = "871pun003";
        protected string FullName = "Lydia Smith";

        public virtual void GetData()
        {
            Console.WriteLine("Customer FullName: {0}", FullName);
            Console.WriteLine("PIN: {0}", pin);
        }
    }
    class Bank_Customer: Customer
    {
        public string RefNum = "ABC567EFG";

        public override void GetData()
        {
            // keyword base invoking parent method:
```

```
            base.GetData();
            Console.WriteLine("Bank_Customer ID: {0}", RefNum);
        }
    }

class TestClass {
    public static void Main()
    {
        Bank_Customer BC = new Bank_Customer();
        BC.GetData();
    }
}
```

By using the base keyword, it is possible to call the GetData() method on the base class Customer from within the child class Bank_Customer.

This sample shows how you can specify the base-class constructor called when creating instances of a child class.

```
using System;
public class Parent
{
   int iValue;
   public Parent() {
     Console.WriteLine("Parent() constructor invoked");
   }
   public Parent(int piParam)
   {
     iValue = piParam;
     Console.WriteLine("Parent(int piParam) overloaded constructor
invoked");
   }

   public int GetiValue()
   {
     return iValue;
   }
}

public class Child : Parent
{
   static int iValue = 0;

   public Child() : base()
   {
     // Child constructor invokes Parent()
   }
```

```
    public Child(int ciParam)   : base(ciParam)
    {
      // Child constructor invokes Parent(int piParam)
    }

    public static int Main()
    {
      // ovrldBase.cs
      // A C# application demonstrating an advanced
      // use of the keyword base combined with
      // overloaded and inherited constructors.
      // Copyright (c) Chris H. Pappas and William H. Murray, 2001
      //

      Child instance1 = new Child();
      Child instance2 = new Child(55);

      return 0;
    }
  }
```

In this program the `Parent` class defines two overloaded constructors: one without any formal arguments, the second expecting an `int` formal argument type. The `Child` subclass defines its own constructors which are quite happy to use the `Parents`' versions accessed through the use of C#'s `base` keyword.

The output from the program looks like:

```
Parent() constructor invoked
Parent(int piParam) overloaded constructor invoked
```

Syntactically, there are alternative forms to base constructor inheritance. The following program, `inheritedconstruct.cs`, demonstrates this alternate form. The algorithm begins by defining the parent class, `Base`, containing a constructor passed an integer and string formal argument.

```
class Base
{
  public Base(int iBaseValue, string sBaseValue)
  {
    Console.WriteLine("From Base  constructor iBaseValue: \t{0}",
                      iBaseValue);
    Console.WriteLine("                        sBaseValue: \t{0}",
                      sBaseValue);
  }
}
```

The constructor outputs the actual values passed to it when invoked. Next, the program defines a `Child` class with its own constructor. Look closely at the `Child()` constructor's header syntax (hint: the bolded code):

```
class Child : Base
{
   public Child(double dChildValue, int iChildValue,
         string sChildValue) : base(iChildValue, sChildValue)
   {
     Console.WriteLine("From Child constructor dValue    : \t{0}",
                    dChildValue);
   }
}
```

Did you notice the unique syntax? The subclass' constructor header syntax has an additional component:

```
: base(iChildValue, sChildValue)
```

Notice that the `Child()` constructor is passed *three* formal arguments: `double`, `int`, and `string`. Secondly, realize that the word used, `base`, is not `Base`. In other words, `base` is the C# keyword and *not* the name for the parent class `Base`. `base` accesses the parent `Base`'s constructor. Finally, the `Child()` constructor does output all three formal parameter values, however indirectly.

Examine the child class' header extension:

```
: base(iChildValue, sChildValue)
```

Note that it indirectly invokes the `Base`, or parent's constructor, which is responsible for outputting the integer and string component. Only the `Child()` constructor directly outputs the double formal argument. Such efficient inheritance is the underpinnings to an efficient family-tree development and efficient executables.

The complete algorithm follows:

```
using System;
public class inheritedconstruct
{
  class Base
  {
    public Base(int iBaseValue, string sBaseValue)
    {
      Console.WriteLine("From Base  constructor iBaseValue: \t{0}",
                    iBaseValue);
       Console.WriteLine("                       sBaseValue: \t{0}",
                    sBaseValue);
    }
```

```
    }

    class Child : Base
    {
      public Child(double dChildValue, int iChildValue,
             string sChildValue) : base(iChildValue, sChildValue)
      {
        Console.WriteLine("From Child constructor dValue    : \t{0}",
                        dChildValue);
      }
    }

    public static int Main(string[] args)
    {
      // A simple C# application demonstrating how
      // to use inherited base constructors
      // Copyright (c) Chris H. Pappas and William H. Murray, 2001
      //

      Child C = new Child(5.5,2,"Test");
      return 0;
    }
  }
```

The output from the program highlights just which constructor is responsible for printing the three actual arguments 5.5, 2, and Test:

```
From Base   constructor iBaseValue:      2
                        sBaseValue:      Test
From Child constructor dValue    :       5.5
```

Destructors

Similar to constructors, destructors are just special cases of class methods. If the logical idea behind a constructor involves all the code statements necessary to get an object up and running, then a destructor reverses the process. Destructor code can easily involve automated data dumps and the freeing of heap-allocated memory.

Once again, in the following code segment, see if you can detect the syntax requirement for a destructor (hint: it's subtle):

```
class classConDeStructor
{
  public classConDestructor();
  public ~classConDestructor();
  public regularMethod();
}
```

The first requirement for a destructor is that its identifier *must* match the identifier of the class, just like a constructor. However, the destructor method's name is preceded by a tilde (~).

In Chapter 7 you learned about C#'s automatic garbage collection. When an object instance goes out of scope, this is the ideal time for automated memory recovery. Unfortunately, garbage collection is only performed at certain intervals. For this reason, anytime an object instance procures significant system resources, you should explicitly release the resource through your own destructor.

```
class ~classConDeStructor()
{
   // code to explicitly release all instance resources
}
```

Remember, just like constructors, destructors are automatically invoked.

Methods

What's in a method? Nothing that isn't in a regular function! Remember, it's all packaging (new syntax). Functions have formal arguments and return types, as do methods. However, instead of the function prototype sitting somewhere in a header file, a method prototype is nested within some formal class definition. Examples of method headers look like:

```
public int TimesIt(int x, int y);
public void PrintString(string sSomeString);
private void UsedWithinClass(int Method1Calc, double Method2Calc);
```

Of course, the method prototypes would be nested within someClass definition:

```
public class someClass
{
   public int TimesIt(int x, int y);
   public void PrintString(string sSomeString);
   private void UsedWithinClass(int Method1Calc, double
Method2Calc);
}
```

In C++, a method body, unlike its prototype, usually sits outside the formal class definition and syntactically repeats the prototype, leaving off the ending semicolon and appending method body statements bracketed within a pair of French braces { . . . }:

```
private void UsedWithinClass(int Method1Calc, double Method2Calc)
{
   // method body statement(s)
}
```

C#'s code style reduces this fracturing of method prototypes and method bodies by combining the two within the formal class definition. Syntactically, you remove the prototype and simply insert the complete method header and body.

Virtual and Override Methods

If methods were compared to nouns, then virtual would be an adjective. Virtual methods are special categories of methods. When you precede a method's header with the `virtual` keyword, the method is said to be a *virtual method*. Without the keyword `virtual`, the method is said to be a *non-virtual method*. It is illegal to combine the `virtual` keyword with any one of the `static`, `abstract`, or `override` modifiers.

Non-virtual methods are inherited by any child subclasses, or descendants, "as is." However, virtual methods inherited within a family tree may be changed by the descendents. The process of changing the implementation of an inherited virtual method is known as *overriding* the method.

The decision as to which virtual method an algorithm invokes is based on the *run-time type* of the instance for which the method call takes place. In a non-virtual method call, the *compile-time type* of the instance is the determining factor.

Typically, the `virtual` keyword flags the C# compiler to a parent method that, when inherited by a child class, *may* be changed by the child class. When the child wants to modify the inherited `virtual` method, it must use the `override` keyword before the modified definition. The method is called an *override method* when a declaration includes an `override` modifier.

You can use an override method to override an inherited `virtual` method with the same signature. This is because an override method simply modifies an existing inherited `virtual` method. This is done by supplying a new implementation of the method.

Override method declarations cannot use `new`, `static`, or `virtual` modifiers, but can use an `abstract` modifier. The `abstract` modifier allows a `virtual` method to be overridden by an `abstract` method.

When a method uses an `override` declaration it is called an *overridden base method*. For example, if class *A* has a virtual method inherited by child class *B*, and child class *B* overrides the inherited virtual method, then child-child class *C* inherits not from class *A*'s implementation but from class *B*'s implementation. As such, `override` methods must satisfy the following conditions:

Parent virtual methods cannot use the `static` modifier and must use the `virtual` keyword.

The use of an override declaration cannot, in effect, change the accessibility of the virtual method.

The following program, `virtualMethod.cs`, uses both the `virtual` and override keywords to demonstrate their syntax and logic. The algorithm begins by defining a `Base` class with three `virtual` methods, `add()`, `sub()`, and `mul()`:

```
class Base
{
  public virtual int add(int a, int b)
  {
    Console.Write("Base add() invoked: ");
    return(a + b);
  }
  public virtual int sub(int a, int b)
  {
    Console.Write("Base sub() invoked: ");
    return(a - b);
  }
  public virtual int mul(int a, int b)
  {
    Console.Write("Base mul() invoked: ");
    return(a * b);}
}
```

Notice the placement of the `virtual` keyword in each prototype. The first sub-class defined is `ShowMath`:

```
class ShowMath : Base
{
  public override int mul(int a, int b)
  {
    Console.Write("ShowMath override mul() invoked: ");
    return(a * b);
  }
}
```

The definition for `ShowMath` indicates that the child class is content with inheriting the parent's `Base.add()` and `Base.sub()` methods, but wishes to rewrite or override the `Base.mul()` virtual method. The keyword `override` in `ShowMath.mul()`'s definition flags the C# compiler to the new meaning. In this definition, `mul()` is said to *hide* the parent's `mul()` method.

A *sibling*, or brother/sister subclass, is also defined and derives its meaning from the same ancestor class `Base`:

```
class PositiveSubt : Base
{
  public override int sub(int a, int b)
  {
    Console.Write("PositiveSubt override sub() invoked: ");
    return(Math.Abs(a - b));
  }
}
```

However, unlike its sibling ShowMath, PositiveSubt is happy to inherit Base.add() and Base.mul(), while choosing to recreate a unique sub() method. Notice the use of override in the method header, an interesting application for the Math.Abs() method for returning the absolute value of an expression.

It is important to realize that just marking a method virtual in a parent class does *not* mean you *must* override the method in a descendant. This is evident by each of the siblings selectively choosing which inherited method to keep "as is" and which to update.

The Main() program begins with an instantiation of the subclass ShowMath, called SM, invoking each of the three methods.

```
ShowMath SM = new ShowMath();

Console.WriteLine("Using ShowMath SM instance.");
Console.WriteLine("{0}",SM.add(562, 531));
Console.WriteLine("{0}", SM.sub(1500, 407));
Console.WriteLine("{0}\n", SM.mul(1093, 1));
```

The instance SM uses the Base inherited add() and sub() methods, but uses its own version of mul().

Main() then instantiates the subclass PositiveSubt with the instance name PS, repeating the method call sequence. In this case, PS uses the Base methods add() and mul(), but its own overridden method subt():

```
PositiveSubt PS = new PositiveSubt();

Console.WriteLine("Using PositiveSubt PS instance.");
Console.WriteLine("{0}", PS.add(892, 201));
Console.WriteLine("{0}", PS.sub(0, 1093));
Console.WriteLine("{0}", PS.mul(1, 1093));
```

The complete program follows:

```
using System;
public class virtualMethod
{
  class Base
  {
    public virtual int add(int a, int b)
    {
      Console.Write("Base add() invoked: ");
      return(a + b);
    }

    public virtual int sub(int a, int b)
    {
      Console.Write("Base sub() invoked: ");
```

```
      return(a - b);
    }

  public virtual int mul(int a, int b)
  {
    Console.Write("Base mul() invoked: ");
    return(a * b);}
}

class ShowMath : Base
{
  public override int mul(int a, int b)
  {
    Console.Write("ShowMath override mul() invoked: ");
    return(a * b);
  }
}

class PositiveSubt : Base
{
  public override int sub(int a, int b)
  {
    Console.Write("PositiveSubt override sub() invoked: ");
    return(Math.Abs(a - b));
  }
}

public static int Main(string[] args)
{
  // virtualmethod.cs
  // A more advanced C# application demonstrating the use of
  // virtual and override methods. The example also takes
  // advantage of the System Math class method Abs().
  // Copyright (c) Christ H. Pappas and William H. Murray, 2001
  //

  ShowMath SM = new ShowMath();

  Console.WriteLine("Using ShowMath SM instance.");
  Console.WriteLine("{0}",SM.add(562, 531));
  Console.WriteLine("{0}", SM.sub(1500, 407));
  Console.WriteLine("{0}\n", SM.mul(1093, 1));

  PositiveSubt PS = new PositiveSubt();

  Console.WriteLine("Using PositiveSubt PS instance.");
  Console.WriteLine("{0}", PS.add(892, 201));
  Console.WriteLine("{0}", PS.sub(0, 1093));
```

```
        Console.WriteLine("{0}", PS.mul(1, 1093));

        return 0;
    }
  }
}
```

While the calculated values shown in the output from the algorithm are identical, *how* they were derived is totally dependent on which `virtual` or child-`overriden` method was called:

```
Using ShowMath SM instance.
Base add() invoked: 1093
Base sub() invoked: 1093
ShowMath override mul() invoked: 1093

Using PositiveSubt PS instance.
Base add() invoked: 1093
PositiveSubt override sub() invoked: 1093
Base mul() invoked: 1093
```

Picking up on an early topic, an `override` declaration can access the overridden base method using the `base` keyword, as in the following code segment:

```
class Base
{
    int iBase;
    public virtual void DisplayValue() {
        Console.WriteLine("iBase = {0}", iBase);
    }
}
class Child: Base
{
    int iChild;
    public override void DisplayValue() {
        base.DisplayValue(); // keyword base not parent Base!
        Console.WriteLine("iChild = {0}", iChild);
    }
}
```

Here, the method `base.DisplayValue()` called from within the child class `Child` invokes the `DisplayValue()` method declared in `Base`. The keyword `base` disables the virtual invocation mechanism. By doing so, it treats the base method as a non-virtual method. Then, by including an `override` modifier, the method can override another method. In all other cases, a method with the same signature as an inherited method simply hides the inherited method, generating a compiler warning.

new Virtual Methods

In C#, the new keyword can be used as an operator or as a modifier. As an operator, new creates objects on the heap:

```
SomeClass anInstance  = new SomeClass();
```

and invokes constructors, as in:

```
int iValue = new int();
```

This statement invokes the base constructor for the value type int.

Use new as a modifier to explicitly hide a member inherited from a base class. To hide an inherited member, declare it in the child class using the same method name as if preparing to override it, but instead, precede the definition with new. The following program, newvirtmethod.cs, illustrates the syntax and logic.

The algorithm begins identically to its virtual/override counterpart previously discussed in the chapter—with a Base class and three virtual methods: add(), sub(), and mul(). So far, nothing new (no pun intended):

```
class Base
{
  public virtual int add(int a, int b)
  {
    Console.WriteLine("Base add() invoked: ");
    return(a + b);
  }
  public virtual int sub(int a, int b)
  {
    Console.WriteLine("Base sub() invoked: ");
    return(a - b);
  }
  public virtual int mul(int a, int b)
  {
    Console.WriteLine("Base mul() invoked: ");
    return(a * b);}
}
```

Additionally, the ShowMath and PositiveSubt descendants remain unaltered:

```
class ShowMath : Base
{
  public override int mul(int a, int b)
  {
    Console.WriteLine("ShowMath override mul() invoked: ");
    return(a * b);
  }
```

```
  }

class PositiveSubt : Base
{
 public override int sub(int a, int b)
   {
     Console.WriteLine("PositiveSubt override sub() invoked: ");
     return(Math.Abs(a - b));
   }
 }
```

To help clarify the logic variations between override and new inherited methods, the program defines a third sibling to ShowMath and PositiveSubt, called newVirtual-Add(), seen here:

```
class newVirtualAdd : Base
{
   new public virtual int add(int a, int b)
   {
     Console.WriteLine("New add() invoked: ");
     return(a + b);
   }
}
```

Notice the use of the keyword new in the method's header, *along with* the use of virtual!

The class newVirtualAdd() is used as a parent to the derived child override-newVirtualAdd(), listed next:

```
class overridenewVirtualAdd : newVirtualAdd
{
   public override int add(int a, int b)
   {
     Console.WriteLine("override of newVirutalAdd.");
     return(a + b);
   }
}
```

This is used to override its parent's newVirtualAdd.add() method.

The Main() program instantiates each of the four descendants as a reminder that the keyword new is also used to create instances of a class:

```
ShowMath SM = new ShowMath();
Console.WriteLine("Using ShowMath SM instance.");
SM.add(1,2);

PositiveSubt PS = new PositiveSubt();
```

```
Console.WriteLine("Using PositiveSubt PS instance.");
PS.add(3,4);

newVirtualAdd NVA = new newVirtualAdd();
Console.WriteLine("Using PositiveSubt NVA instance.");
NVA.add(5,6);

overridenewVirtualAdd ONVA = new overridenewVirtualAdd();
Console.WriteLine("Using PositiveSubt ONVA instance.");
ONVA.add(7,8);
```

The complete algorithm follows:

```
using System;
public class newvirtmethod
{
  class Base
  {
    public virtual int add(int a, int b)
    {
      Console.WriteLine("Base add() invoked: ");
      return(a + b);
    }

    public virtual int sub(int a, int b)
    {
      Console.WriteLine("Base sub() invoked: ");
      return(a - b);
    }

    public virtual int mul(int a, int b)
    {
      Console.WriteLine("Base mul() invoked: ");
      return(a * b);}
  }

  class ShowMath : Base
  {
    public override int mul(int a, int b)
    {
      Console.WriteLine("ShowMath override mul() invoked: ");
      return(a * b);
    }
  }

  class PositiveSubt : Base
  {
    public override int sub(int a, int b)
    {
      Console.WriteLine("PositiveSubt override sub() invoked: ");
```

```csharp
      return(Math.Abs(a - b));
    }
}

class newVirtualAdd : Base
{
  new public virtual int add(int a, int b)
  {
    Console.WriteLine("New add() invoked: ");
    return(a + b);
  }
}

class overridenewVirtualAdd : newVirtualAdd
{
  public override int add(int a, int b)
  {
    Console.WriteLine("override of newVirutalAdd.");
    return(a + b);
  }
}

public static int Main(string[] args)
{
  // newvirtmethod.cs
  // A more advanced C# application demonstrating the use of
  // new with virtual and override methods.
  // Copyright (c) Christ H. Pappas and William H. Murray, 2001
  //

  ShowMath SM = new ShowMath();
  Console.WriteLine("Using ShowMath SM instance.");
  SM.add(1,2);

  PositiveSubt PS = new PositiveSubt();
  Console.WriteLine("\nUsing PositiveSubt PS instance.");
  PS.add(3,4);

  newVirtualAdd NVA = new newVirtualAdd();
  Console.WriteLine("\nUsing PositiveSubt NVA instance.");
  NVA.add(5,6);

  overridenewVirtualAdd ONVA = new overridenewVirtualAdd();
  Console.WriteLine("\nUsing PositiveSubt ONVA instance.");
  ONVA.add(7,8);

  return 0;
  }
}
```

The output from the program looks like:

```
Using ShowMath SM instance.
Base add() invoked:

Using PositiveSubt PS instance.
Base add() invoked:

Using PositiveSubt NVA instance.
New add() invoked:

Using PositiveSubt ONVA instance.
override of newVirutalAdd.
```

Here, you can see that SM is used to invoke its parent's Base.add(), as did its sibling PS. However, the NVA instance accessed its own new virtual add() instead of an inherited Base.add(). Finally, the ONVA instance, derived from newVirtualAdd, uses and overrides newVirtualAdd.add()!

The Conditional Methods

Use the Conditional keyword to define a method that is only visible when a predefined symbol is active. If the symbol is defined, then the method's definition and any calls made to it are included. If the symbol is undefined, then all references are omitted.

In the following program, conditmethod.cs, notice the #define preprocessor directive defining the DEBUGON symbol. Pay particular attention to the algorithm's need to include the following statement:

```
using System.Diagnostics; // MUST be used to access Conditional
                          // keyword
```

This statement is needed to legalize access to the Conditional modifier:

```
#define DEBUGON
using System;
using System.Diagnostics; // MUST be used to access Conditional
                          // keyword
```

The syntax for Conditional is seen in the code statement preceding the DEBUGONmethod() header:

```
public class conditmethod
{
  [Conditional("DEBUGON")]
    public void DEBUGONmethod()
    {
      Console.WriteLine("conditionalMethod is active.");
    }
```

Forethought combined with the C# keyword `Conditional` allows you to easily optimize an executable code size by simply commenting out the controlling symbol's definition. This syntax allows the source code to retain any designed-in debug logic while not exploding the executable with unnecessary Release Version translations.

The complete program follows:

```
#define DEBUGON
using System;
using System.Diagnostics; // MUST be used to access Conditional
keyword
public class conditmethod
{
  [Conditional("DEBUGON")]
    public void DEBUGONmethod()
    {
      Console.WriteLine("conditionalMethod is active.");
    }


    public static int Main(string[] args)
    {
    // conditmethod.cs
    // A more advanced C# application demonstrating
    // the syntax and use for conditional methods.
    // Copyright (c) Chris H. Pappas and William H. Murray, 2001
    //

    conditmethod CM = new conditmethod();

    CM.DEBUGONmethod();
    return 0;
    }
}
```

In order to take advantage of a `Conditional` method, the following conditions must be satisfied:

- It should be a method of a class and *not* an `interface` method.
- It should not use the `override` modifier. It can, however, use a virtual modifier.
- It should use a `void` return type.

Indexers—New to C++ Programmers

Indexing allows you to access your class just like it was an array. The syntax is straightforward, as seen in the following syntax:

```
public someType this[int iOffset]
{
  get {...}
  set {...}
}
```

The indexer is `public`, `someType` is the type returned by the indexer, and the keyword `this` denotes the indexer on the default interface. The implementation rules for `get` and `set` allow you almost unlimited freedom in defining the parameter list in the square brackets.

The following program, `indexer.cs`, revisits a streamlined version of the stack algorithm discussed in Chapter 7, with the addition of an indexer. The indexer overrides the usual address to a stack's top and instead treats the stack like an array. The top of the stack is always at offset 0, and the bottom of the stack grows incrementally.

First, examine the following portion of the indexer code:

```
public object this[int index]
   {
     get {return getnode(index).Value;}
     set {getnode(index).Value = value;}
   }
```

Note that this code indirectly invokes the `getnode()` method to do the grunt work of locating specific stack-element positions and either return or set the new `Value`:

```
   private node getnode(int index)
   {
     node temp = top;
     while (index > 0)
     {
       temp = temp.nextNode;
       index--;
     }
     return temp;
   }
```

This uninteresting method, when combined with the indexer, allows the `Main()` program to treat the stack like an array. In the following code segment, cut from the algorithm, notice that the instance `S` is syntactically subscripted like an array, instead of the traditional `push()` and `pop()` address to stack entries:

```
Console.WriteLine("Value at TOP    of stack: {0}", S[0]);
Console.WriteLine("Value at BOTTOM of stack: {0}", S[3]);

S[0] = 99;  // update top from 44 to 99
S[3] = 0;   // bottom from 1 to 0

Console.WriteLine("New Value at TOP    of stack: {0}", S[0]);
Console.WriteLine("New Value at BOTTOM of stack: {0}", S[3]);
```

The first two output statements invoke the get indexer, while the next two assignment statements trigger the set indexer to update stack contents as if it were an array!

The complete algorithm follows:

```
using System;
class node
{
  public node nextNode;
  private object Value;
  private node top;

  // method for first node of empty list
  public node() {top = null;}

  // method of adding nodes to existing list
  public node(object newValue, node oldTop)
  {
    nextNode = oldTop ;
    Value = newValue;
  }

  private node getnode(int index)
  {
    node temp = top;
    while (index > 0)
    {
      temp = temp.nextNode;
      index--;
    }
    return temp;
  }

  private void push(object newValue)
  {
   top = new node(newValue, top);
  }

  private object pop()
  {
    object currentValue = top.Value;
    top = top.nextNode;
    return currentValue;
  }

  public object this[int index]
  {
    get {return getnode(index).Value;}
```

```
      set {getnode(index).Value = value;}
   }

   public static int Main()
   {
     // indexer.cs
     // A C# application demonstrating a new
     // feature to the language called indexing
     // Copyright (c) Chris H. Pappas and William H. Murray, 2001
     //

     node S = new node();

     S.push(11);
     S.push(22);
     S.push(33);
     S.push(44);

     Console.WriteLine("Value at TOP    of stack: {0}", S[0]);
     Console.WriteLine("Value at BOTTOM of stack: {0}", S[3]);

     S[0] = 99;   // update top from 44 to 99
     S[3] = 0;    // bottom from 1 to 0

     Console.WriteLine("New Value at TOP    of stack: {0}", S[0]);
     Console.WriteLine("New Value at BOTTOM of stack: {0}", S[3]);

     return 0;
   }
}
```

The output from the program looks like:

```
Value at TOP    of stack: 44
Value at BOTTOM of stack: 11
New Value at TOP    of stack: 99
New Value at BOTTOM of stack: 0
```

Delegates and Events

When any compiler processes a source file, all identifiers used in the algorithm are given a signature. The process is called mangling and each programming language uses a different set of rules regarding upper/lower case sensitivity along with other decorations. A C# delegate locks a method's signature. This makes them type-safe. A delegate is C#'s equivalent to function pointers. You can encapsulate both static and instance methods in a delegate instance. Although you can use delegates as is with methods, their main use is with a class' events. Events allow a class to flag the occurrence of a particular event. C++ programmers have done this for years with the use of function pointers. This exciting topic is explored in Chapter 11, "Advanced C# Programming Considerations."

Interfaces

An interface can be thought of as defining a contract. Classes or structures that use an interface must abide by the contract. Interfaces can contain events, indexers, methods, and properties as members, but they do not implement the members that they define. Interfaces require that members must be provided by classes (or interfaces) that use the interface.

Interfaces can inherit from one or more parent interfaces. In the following example, the interface iF3 inherits from two base interfaces, iF1 and iF2:

```
interface iF3: iF1, iF2
{
    void iF3m1();
    void iF3m2();
}
```

Formal class definitions may inherit interface contracts. The identifier of the implemented interface appears in the class base list. For example:

```
class myClass: iF1, iF2
{
    // myClass member definitions...
}
```

When a class base list contains a base class and interfaces, the base class comes first in the list. For example:

```
class myClass: Parent, iF1, iF2
{
    // myClass member definitions...
}
```

The following algorithm, interfacecast.cs, adds one more component to interface inheritance—*interface casting*. The program begins by defining two interfaces, IinFeet and IinInches, with syntax similar to a class definition, only the keyword is substituted with interface:

```
interface IinFeet
{
    float length();
    float width();
    float height();
    float volume();
```

```
}

interface IinInches
{
  float length();
  float width();
  float height();
  float volume();
}
```

Both interfaces define the same four methods: `length()`, `width()`, `height()`, and `volume()`. The interfaces are followed with an actual class definition, *dimensions*, which inherits the two interface contracts.

A class that implements an interface can explicitly implement a member of that interface. When a member is explicitly implemented, it cannot be accessed through a class instance but only through an instance of the interface. Notice, syntactically, how the interfaces `IinInches` and `IinFeet` are located identically, as if they were parent classes:

```
class dimensions : IinInches, IinFeet
{
  float lengthInFeet;
  float widthInFeet;
  float heightInFeet;
```

The formal class definition continues with a fleshing out of the eight interface-specific method bodies. This allows each interface-specific method body to effect the required conversions. Syntactically, each method body header *must* be preceded by the owning interface's name, either `IinFeet` or `IinInches`:

```
public dimensions(float length, float width, float height)
{
  lengthInFeet = length;
  widthInFeet = width;
  heightInFeet = height;
}

float IinFeet.length()
{
  return lengthInFeet;
}

float IinFeet.width()
{
  return widthInFeet;
}

float IinFeet.height()
```

```
    {
      return heightInFeet;
    }

    float IinFeet.volume()
    {
      return lengthInFeet * widthInFeet * heightInFeet;
    }

    float IinInches.length()
    {
      return lengthInFeet * 12;
    }

    float IinInches.width()
    {
      return widthInFeet* 12;
    }

    float IinInches.height()
    {
      return heightInFeet * 12;
    }

    float IinInches.volume()
    {
      return (lengthInFeet * 12) * (widthInFeet * 12) *
             (heightInFeet * 12);
    }
```

The `Main()` program instantiates the class `dimensions` by the name `sample` and passes three actual arguments to the constructor:

```
dimensions sample = new dimensions(30.0f, 20.0f, 10.0f);
```

Interface-specific views of the `sample` instance are generated by the following two statements involving an interface-cast (in bold) of `sample` to their respective types:

```
IinFeet VinFeet = (IinFeet) sample;
IinInches VinInches = (IinInches) sample;
```

`Main()` completes the demonstration by invoking each of the four respective views of `sample`:

```
System.Console.WriteLine("Length in feet: {0}", VinFeet.length());
System.Console.WriteLine("Width  in feet: {0}", VinFeet.width());
System.Console.WriteLine("Height in feet: {0}", VinFeet.height());
System.Console.WriteLine("Volume in cubic feet: {0}\n",
                         VinFeet.volume());
```

```
System.Console.WriteLine("Length in inches: {0}", VinInches.length());
System.Console.WriteLine("Width  in inches: {0}", VinInches.width());
System.Console.WriteLine("Height in inches: {0}", VinInches.height());
System.Console.WriteLine("Volume in cubic inches: {0}",
                        VinInches.volume());
```

This example program demonstrates how one class may inherit two interfaces that share the same member names and give each interface member a separate implementation. The two views of `sample` display their respective dimensions box in both feet and inches. Both interfaces have identical member names, `IinFeet` and `IinInches`.

The complete program follows:

```
using System;
interface IinFeet
{
    float length();
    float width();
    float height();
    float volume();
}

interface IinInches
{
    float length();
    float width();
    float height();
    float volume();
}

class dimensions : IinInches, IinFeet
{
    float lengthInFeet;
    float widthInFeet;
    float heightInFeet;

    public dimensions(float length, float width, float height)
    {
        lengthInFeet = length;
        widthInFeet = width;
        heightInFeet = height;
    }

    float IinFeet.length()
    {
        return lengthInFeet;
    }
```

```csharp
float IinFeet.width()
{
    return widthInFeet;
}

float IinFeet.height()
{
    return heightInFeet;
}

float IinFeet.volume()
{
    return lengthInFeet * widthInFeet * heightInFeet;
}

float IinInches.length()
{
    return lengthInFeet * 12;
}

float IinInches.width()
{
    return widthInFeet * 12;
}

float IinInches.height()
{
    return heightInFeet * 12;
}

float IinInches.volume()
{
    return (lengthInFeet * 12) * (widthInFeet * 12) *
           (heightInFeet * 12);
}

public static int Main()
{
    // interfacecast.cs
    // A C# application demonstrating interfaces and casting.
    // Copyright (c) Chris H. Pappas and William H. Murray, 2001
    //

    dimensions sample = new dimensions(30.0f, 20.0f, 10.0f);

    IinFeet VinFeet = (IinFeet) sample;
    IinInches VinInches = (IinInches) sample;
```

```
System.Console.WriteLine("Length in feet: {0}",
                         VinFeet.length());
System.Console.WriteLine("Width  in feet: {0}",
                         VinFeet.width());
System.Console.WriteLine("Height in feet: {0}",
                         VinFeet.height());
System.Console.WriteLine("Volume in cubic feet: {0}\n",
                         VinFeet.volume());

System.Console.WriteLine("Length in inches: {0}",
                         VinInches.length());
System.Console.WriteLine("Width  in inches: {0}",
                         VinInches.width());
System.Console.WriteLine("Height in inches: {0}",
                         VinInches.height());
System.Console.WriteLine("Volume in cubic inches: {0}",
                         VinInches.volume());

        return 0;
    }
}
```

The output from the program looks like:

```
Length in feet: 30
Width  in feet: 20
Height in feet: 10
Volume in cubic feet: 6000

Length in inches: 360
Width  in inches: 240
Height in inches: 120
Volume in cubic inches: 1.0368E+07
```

What applications can you envision creating with this new knowledge?

Class and Interface Modifiers

The following keywords are class and interface modifiers:

```
internal
new
private
protected
public
```

Each modifier subtly changes the visibility of class and interface members (data or subroutine) or modulates inheritance within a family tree. The internal modifier, for example, flags a class member as being only visible within the owning program. The new modifier is only permitted on nested interfaces. It states that the interface hides an inherited member by the same identifier name. The public, protected, internal, and private modifiers control the accessibility of the interface. Then, depending on the context in which the interface declaration occurs, only some of these modifiers may be permitted.

The following example program, puppropri.cs, concentrates on three of the most frequently used accessibility modifiers: public, protected, and private. The algorithm begins by defining a Base class with three methods. The first publicBase() method is flagged as public:

```
class Base
{
  public void publicBase(string whichClass)
  {
    Console.Write("publicBase() entered from ");
    Console.WriteLine("{0} instance.", whichClass );

    this.protectedBase();
    Console.WriteLine("{0} instance.", whichClass);

    this.privateBase();
    Console.WriteLine("{0} instance.", whichClass);

  }
```

You have learned that public methods have minimal scope and are easily accessed by any code within the translation unit. The method publicBase() invokes within its body, legally invoking both the protectedBase() and privateBase() methods.

The header for the next method, protectedBase(), is preceded by the keyword protected, marking the method as invisible outside the class, but visible within any derived subclasses:

```
protected void protectedBase()
{
  Console.Write("protectedBase{} entered from ");
}
```

The method privateBase() has a header initialized with the private keyword. This flags the scope as not only inaccessible to code outside the class, but to any child subclasses:

```
private void privateBase()
{
  Console.Write("privateBase() entered from ");
}
```

A `Child` subclass is defined with only one `public` method `publicBase()` containing a legal call to both the parent's public `publicBase()` and protected `protectedBase()` methods:

```
class Child : Base
{
  public void calls_publicBase(string whichClass)
  {
    this.publicBase(whichClass);
    // even access to a parent's protected methods are legal

    this.protectedBase();
```

The `Child.calls_publicBase()` method body contains a statement that if left in the code would be flagged as illegal, since it would be an attempt to access the parent's `private` non-inherited method `privateBase()`:

```
    // next statement is an illegal attempt to access privateBase()
    // Console.WriteLine("illegal access to Base method privateBase()");
    // this.privateBase();
    // however the comment in Main() highlights the indirect access
    // of this private method through the Base public method.
  }
}
```

The `Main()` program first instantiates b from the `Base` class definition and then calls `b.publicBase()`, with the `"Base"` string marker:

```
Base b = new Base();

Console.WriteLine("Base b instance instantiated.");
b.publicBase("Base");
// b.protectedBase(); illegal access to hidden class method
// b.privateBase(); another illegal attempt
```

The commented-out statements reflect the scope of a class' protected *and* private methods. From outside a family tree, the algorithm cannot distinguish between the two keywords, treating both cases as unaccessible.

Contrasting with what can and cannot be done on the `Base` class, the program continues with the instantiation of *c* from the derived subclass `Child`. The program terminates by invoking the `c.calls_publicBase()` child method, illustrating a subclass' ability to also access a parent's `public` methods. The call to `c.publicBase()` is a reminder of the parent method's visibility to code outside the family tree:

```
Child c = new Child();

Console.WriteLine("\nChild C instance instantiated.");
// notice the following call to the Child calls_publicBase()
// LEGALLY accesses the Base privateBase() method !!!
c.calls_publicBase("Child");

// so does this next statement
c.publicBase("Child");

// however both of the following attempts are flagged as illegal!
//c.protectedBase();
//c.privateBase();
```

The final two commented-out statements reflect the inability for internal access to either a child's inherited `protected` method, or the obvious illegal access to a `private` parent method.

The complete program follows:

```
using System;
public class pubpropri
{
  class Base
  {
    public void publicBase(string whichClass)
    {
      Console.Write("publicBase() entered from ");
      Console.WriteLine("{0} instance.", whichClass );

      this.protectedBase();
      Console.WriteLine("{0} instance.", whichClass);

      this.privateBase();
      Console.WriteLine("{0} instance.", whichClass);

    }

    protected void protectedBase()
    {
      Console.Write("protectedBase{} entered from ");
    }

    private void privateBase()
    {
      Console.Write("privateBase() entered from ");
    }
  }
```

```
class Child : Base
{
  public void calls_publicBase(string whichClass)
  {
    this.publicBase(whichClass);
    // access to a parent's protected methods are legal

    this.protectedBase();

    // next statement is an illegal attempt to access
    // privateBase()
    // Console.WriteLine("illegal access to Base method
    // privateBase()");
    // this.privateBase();
    // however the comment in Main() highlights the indirect
    // access
    // of this private method through the Base public method.
  }
}

public static int Main(string[] args)
{
  // pubpropri.cs
  // A simple C# application highlighting the
  // inheritance options provided by the keywords
  // public, protected, and private. To understand the keyword
  // private read comment in Main() and calls_publicBase().
  // Copyright (c) Chris H. Pappas and William H. Murray, 2001
  //

  Base b = new Base();

  Console.WriteLine("Base b instance instantiated.");
  b.publicBase("Base");
  // b.protectedBase(); illegal access to hidden class method
  // b.privateBase(); another illegal attempt

  Child c = new Child();

  Console.WriteLine("\nChild C instance instantiated.");
  // notice the following call to the Child calls_publicBase()
  // LEGALLY accesses the Base privateBase() method !!!
  c.calls_publicBase("Child");

  // so does this next statement
  // c.publicBase("Child");
```

```
            // however both of the following attempts are flagged as illegal!
            //c.protectedBase();
            //c.privateBase();

            return 0;
        }
}
```

The output from the program looks like:

```
Base b instance instantiated.
publicBase() entered from Base instance.
protectedBase{} entered from Base instance.
privateBase() entered from Base instance.

Child C instance instantiated.
publicBase() entered from Child instance.
protectedBase{} entered from Child instance.
privateBase() entered from Child instance.
protectedBase{} entered from
```

From this information, how do you think you can use the three most frequently used accessibility modifiers, public, protected, and private, in an application?

Abstract Classes

The abstract modifier is used to define a parent (base) class that will not be instantiated itself but used wholly for deriving child classes. Abstract classes are different from non-abstract classes.

An abstract class cannot be directly instantiated. A compiler error will be generated if there is an attempt to instantiate an abstract class with the new keyword. In the cases where there are variables whose compile-time types are abstract, those variables generally must be null. Abstract classes can contain abstract, class members. An abstract class may not be sealed (see next section).

Child classes that are derived from a parent abstract class should include implementations for inherited abstract members. This is generally achieved by overriding the abstract members. Examine the following portion of code as a demonstration of these concepts.

The abstractBase.cs algorithm begins with the definition for an abstract-Base class that includes one abstract BaseMethod():

```
abstract class abstractBase
{
    // note the absence of method body
    public abstract void BaseMethod();
}
```

Next, a definition for an abstract child class, abstractChild, is derived from its abstractBase parent. The subclass definition also includes an abstract Child-Method() unique to the subclass:

```
abstract class abstractChild : abstractBase
{
   public abstract void ChildMethod();
}
```

Next, the GrandChild class is derived from its parent, abstractChild, and *must* implement, via the keyword override, both the inherited abstract.Basemethod() and abstractChild.ChildMethod() if the program plans to instantiate the Grand-Child class:

```
class GrandChild : abstractChild
{
   public override void BaseMethod()
   {
      // implement inherited BaseMethod();
   }
   public override void ChildMethod()
   {
      // implement inherited ChildMethod();
   }
}
```

If a compilation is attempted, the C# compiler would flag the following two statements as illegal:

```
abstractBase AB = new abstractBase();
abstractChild AC = new abstractChild();
```

The compiler error results from an attempt to instantiate an abstract class. The following listing provides the whole application:

```
using System;
public class Abstract
{
   abstract class abstractBase
   {
      // note the absence of method body
      public abstract void BaseMethod();
   }

   abstract class abstractChild : abstractBase
   {
      public abstract void ChildMethod();
   }
```

```
class GrandChild : abstractChild
{
  public override void BaseMethod()
  {
    // implement inherited BaseMethod();
  }

  public override void ChildMethod()
  {
    // implement inherited ChildMethod();
  }
}

public static int Main(string[] args)
{
  // abstract.cs
  // A simple C# application demonstrating the
  // logic and syntax behind the C# abstract keyword.
  // Copyright (c) Chris H. Pappas and William H. Murray, 2001
  //

  // illegal attempt to instantiate abstract classes
  // abstractBase AB = new abstractBase();
  // abstractChild AC = new abstractChild();

  // legal instantiation of GrandChild inheriting from
  // two abstract ancestors:
  GrandChild GC = new GrandChild();
  return 0;
}
}
```

Note that there is no output from this example if you attempt to run the application.

Sealed Classes

The `sealed` modifier can be considered the logical compliment to `abstract`. For example, suppose an abstract class is created as the parent class. `Sealed` class definitions would then be used to create non-inheritable object definitions. You cannot use a sealed class as the parent class of another class.

In the following program, `sealedClass.cs`, the definition for class `sealed-Class` is preceded with the keyword `sealed`. This program will *not* compile because it includes an attempt to derive the class CANT_DO_THIS from `sealedClass`:

```
using System;
public class Sealed
{
    sealed class sealedClass
    {
        // TODO: class member declarations
    }

    class CANT_DO_THIS : sealedClass
    {
        // TODO: fill in inherited definitions.
    }

    public static int Main(string[] args)
    {
        // sealed.cs
        // A simple C# application demonstrating the
        // logic and syntax behind the C# keyword sealed.
        // View related "Build Error" message.
        // Copyright (c) Chris H. Pappas and William H. Murray, 2001
        //

        return 0;
    }
}
```

Should you try to compile the algorithm, you will see a compiler error message similar to:

```
C:\sealed\sealedClass.cs(9): 'Sealed.CANT_DO_THIS' : cannot
inherit from sealed class 'Sealed.sealedClass'
```

The main purpose of using a sealed modifier is to eliminate the possibility of an accidental derivation. Sometimes the sealed modifier is used to enable runtime optimizations.

Inheritance Reviewed

As you know, a class *inherits* the members of its parent class. This means that a class implicitly contains all members of its parent class. This is true for all members except constructors and destructors. Key features of inheritance include:

- A child class can hide inherited members. This is accomplished by creating new members with the same name.
- A child class extends its parent class. While new members can be added to the inherited members, inherited members cannot be removed.
- A class instance provides all instance fields declared in the class and any inherited fields from parent classes. In this manner, a reference to an instance of a child class instance is similar to a reference to a parent class instance.

- All class members are inherited by a child class regardless of their declared accessibility. The exception is that constructors and destructors are not inherited. However, the declared accessibility directly affects whether a member is accessible in a child class.

- Classes can contain virtual methods, properties, and indexers. Derived child classes can then override these members. This polymorphic capability allows a member's invocation to vary. It depends upon the runtime instance from which the member is invoked.

Classes Reviewed

Class members can include constants, constructors, destructors, events, fields, indexers, methods, operators, properties, and nested type declarations. Additionally, classes can be used to define new reference types. You have already learned that a class can inherit from another class. Classes exhibit a variety of accessibility types. Table 9–1 shows the standard accessibility types that can be used by a class.

Table 9–1   Accessibility for Classes

Form	Purpose
internal	The access is limited to the application.
private	The access is limited to the containing class.
protected	The access is limited to the containing class or children derived from the class.
protected internal	The access is limited to the application or children of the class.
public	The access is unlimited.

Each member has an associated accessibility, which controls the portions of the program that are able to access the class.

Summary

In this chapter you learned that the main difference between procedural and object-oriented solutions is packaging, in other words, syntax. You also discovered that three quarters of C#'s approach to object-oriented programming is derived directly from its C/C++ ancestors. You also learned that while C# does not have C++'s multiple-inheritance capabilities, it does use interfaces in a similar manner. For a breather, Chapter 10 drops the pace slightly by dealing with a simpler topic, namely, I/O in C#.

I/O in C#

$\mathbf{W}$hether it's C, C++, Java, Visual Basic, or now C#, I/O is always where the rubber meets the road. Each programming language is plagued with its own unique set of dos and don'ts when it comes to data throughput! In this chapter you will learn how to do keyboard and external file input, console and external file output, and how to output directly to a printer (in a Windows-based, Intel-architecture environment).

Console Class

If C has `stdin`, `stdout`, and `stderr`, and C++ has the equivalent `cin`, `cout`, and `cerr`, then C# has a matching `Console.In`, `Console.Out`, and `Console.Error` to perform its keyboard input, monitor-display output for program data, and debugging error streams. Table 10–1 lists the three streams.

Table 10–1   Console Class Input and Output Streams

Stream	Purpose
Error	`Error` is the C# equivalent to C++'s `cerr`, and C's `stderr`. It can be redirected via the `SetError` method.
In	`In` is the C# equivalent to C++'s `cin`, and C's `stdin`. It can be redirected via the `SetIn()` method.
Out	`Out` is the C# equivalent to C++'s `cout`, and C's `stdout`. It can be redirected via the `SetOut` method.

C#, like C and C++, allows a programmer to redirect any of the three streams using the Console methods SetIn(), SetOut(), and SetError(). All Console read methods read from Console.In by default, and are a more direct alternative to directly invoking a Console.In, that is a StreamReader. Console write methods write to Console.Out and are syntactically streamlined over the alternative to directly invoking them on Console.Out which is a StreamWriter (StreamReader and Stream-Writer are described later in this chapter under the section System.IO).

Console Class Members

The following tables provide an overview of the most frequently used Console class members. Take a minute to look over the member names and brief descriptions. Doing so will give you a rough idea of how C# implements the standard I/O requirements of any programming language, and enable you to understand the chapter's example programs.

Table 10–2 lists the static Console class members. Remember, static members represent definitions that do not require your program to actually instantiate an object in order to make full use of their code segments.

Table 10–2   Static Console Methods

Method	Purpose
OpenStandardError()	Returns the standard error stream.
OpenStandardInput()	Returns the standard input stream.
OpenStandardOutput()	Returns the standard output stream.
Read()	Reads the next character from the input stream.
ReadLine()	Reads the next line of characters from Console.In.
SetError()	Redirects Console.Error to the specified TextWriter, which by default is set to the system's standard error stream.
SetIn()	Redirects Console.In to the specified TextReader, which by default is set to the system's standard input stream.
SetOut()	Redirects Console.Out to the specified TextWriter, which by default is set to the system's standard output stream.
Write()	Writes the specified information to Console.Out.
WriteLine()	Writes information followed by a line terminator to Console.Out.

Unlike the `Console` methods listed in the previous table, those listed in Table 10–3 *do* require an application to instantiate a `Console` class instance before their use.

Table 10–3   Public Console Class Instance Methods

Method	Purpose
`Equals` (derived from `Object`)	Flags whether or not the specified `Object` is the same instance as the current `Object`.
`GetHashCode` (derived from `Object`)	Is a hash function for a particular type. Used by C# hashing algorithms and hash tables.
`GetType` (derived from `Object`)	Returns the type of an `Object`.
`ToString` (derived from `Object`)	Returns a `string` that represents the current Object.

Table 10–4 lists the protected Console class methods.

Table 10–4   Protected Console class methods

Method	Purpose
`Finalize` (derived from `Object`)	Launches an `Object`'s attempt to cleanup resources before the `Object` is reclaimed by the Garbage Collector or GC.
`MemberwiseClone` (derived from `Object`)	Duplicates the current `Object`.

`char`, `int`, `float`, `string` Console I/O

The following program, `charIntFloatIO.cs`, is designed to quickly cover standard `char`, `int`, `float`, and `string` type Console I/O. Once you see the basics, you will immediately recognize the logic and syntax necessary to rework the example into your programming needs.

The syntax for using `Console` class definitions simply requires you to use the

```
using System;
```

statement to pull in the class' formal definitions. The example program defines the

```
string sValue;
```

allowing the algorithm to accept any keyboard input, and then converting the anticipated type into its respective type-specific variable. The `Console.Write()` statements prompt the user with a runtime message as to just what type they are supposed to enter.

```
Console.Write("Enter a character -> ");
```

The `Console.ReadLine()` statements input *any* keyboard keystrokes and store them in `sValue`:

```
sValue = Console.ReadLine();
```

Next, each logical code-section equivalent defines its own type-specific variable and invokes a type-specific conversion method to turn the string `sValue` into its required type. All of the `FromString(sValue)` methods use a common syntax:

```
type tIdentifier = type.FromString(sValue);
```

In these instances, `type` is usually `bool`, `byte`, `char`, `int`, `float`, `Decimal`, `Double`, `DateTime`, `Enum`, `Int16`, `Int32`, `Int64`, `SByte`, `Single`, `UInt16`, `UInt32`, or `UInt64`. The example program first uses `Parse(sValue)` to convert the `char` type:

```
char cValue = char.Parse(sValue);
```

Then the following line of code demonstrates how `Console.Writeline()` displays the value back to the user:

```
Console.WriteLine("The character entered is: {0}", cValue);
```

This logical sequence then repeats for the remaining types:

```
Console.Write("\nEnter an integer  -> ");
sValue = Console.ReadLine();
int iValue = int.Parse(sValue);
Console.WriteLine("The integer entered is  : {0}", iValue);

Console.Write("\nEnter a float     -> ");
sValue = Console.ReadLine();
float fValue = float.Parse(sValue);
Console.WriteLine("The float entered is    : {0}", fValue);

Console.Write("\nEnter a string    -> ");
sValue = Console.ReadLine();
Console.WriteLine("The string entered is   : {0}", sValue);
```

The output from the program takes this form:

```
Enter a character -> A
The character entered is: A

Enter an integer  -> 1
The integer entered is  : 1

Enter a float     -> 2.2
The float entered is    : 2.2

Enter a string    -> hello
The string entered is   : hello
```

The complete program listing follows:

```csharp
using System;
public class charIntFloatIO
   {
   public static int Main(string[] args)
   {
     // charIntFloatIO.cs
     // A C# application demonstrating simple
     // console char, int, float, string Console IO.
     // Copyright (c) Chris H. Pappas and William H. Murray, 2001
     //

     string sValue;

     Console.Write("Enter a character -> ");
     sValue = Console.ReadLine();
     char cValue = char.Parse(sValue);
     Console.WriteLine("The character entered is: {0}", cValue);

     Console.Write("\nEnter an integer  -> ");
     sValue = Console.ReadLine();
     int iValue = int.Parse(sValue);
     Console.WriteLine("The integer entered is  : {0}", iValue);

     Console.Write("\nEnter a float     -> ");
     sValue = Console.ReadLine();
     float fValue = float.Parse(sValue);
     Console.WriteLine("The float entered is    : {0}", fValue);

     Console.Write("\nEnter a string    -> ");
     sValue = Console.ReadLine();
     Console.WriteLine("The string entered is   : {0}", sValue);

     return 0;
   }
}
```

Using System.IO

As with any programming language, standard I/O via keyboard and monitor is by far the syntactically easiest approach to user/program interaction. The minute you switch gears to interfacing with an external file there is a geometric increase in code complexity. C#'s `System.IO` namespace defines the types necessary to perform synchronous and asynchronous reading from and writing to data streams and files. The difference between a file and a stream is not always hard and fast, but the following distinctions are useful.

A file is an ordered and named collection of a particular sequence of bytes having persistent storage. Therefore, with files, one thinks in terms of directory paths, disk storage, and file and directory names. Unlike files, streams provide a way to write and read bytes to and from a backing store that can be one of several storage mediums. Just as there are several backing stores other than disks, there are several kinds of streams other than file streams. For example, there are network, memory, and tape streams.

C# begins its `Stream` class hierarchy with the base class `Stream` supporting the reading and writing of bytes. While the `Stream` base class supports asynchronous communication, it defaults to synchronous reads and writes in terms of their corresponding asynchronous methods. The `Stream` class and its descendant classes provide a generic view of data sources and destinations.

C# streams allow you to perform the anticipated set of fundamental operations. Streams can be read from and written to. Streams also support a seek operation that updates the current position of a stream I/O pointer. Depending on the underlying data source or destination, additional operations include: `NetworkStreams` (which, however, has no seek capability), and `CanRead`, `CanWrite`, and `CanSeek` properties to detect the operations available to a particular stream. There are even `BinaryReader` and `BinaryWriter` encoded strings and, along with primitive data types, interpretations into and from Streams.

The File Class

The `File` class defines static methods to create `FileStream` objects. `File` contains routines for creating, copying, deleting, moving, and opening files. A `FileStream` represents a disk file and includes random access support. `FileStream` objects implement their own standard in, standard out, and standard error streams. While `FileStream` objects support asynchronous communication, the default is synchronous. Additional `FileStream` enumerators, `FileAccess`, `FileMode`, and `FileShare` describe constants used by some `FileStream` objects and some of the `File.Open()` overloaded methods. These constants affect the way in which the underlying file is created, opened, and shared.

File Encoding

By default, `Stream` class I/O processes data in byte form. C# `TextReader` and `TextWriter` classes override the default byte orientation and instead process Unicode formats.

The `StringReader` and `StringWriter` classes read and write characters from and to `Strings` and allow you to treat `Strings` with any encoding or a `String`. These classes use `Encoding` to convert characters to and from bytes, triggering a constructor that will attempt to decipher which `Encoding` for a given `Stream` is being requested, based on the presence of `Encoding`-specific byte order marks (BOMs).

File Buffering

`BufferedStreams` add buffering to other `Streams` such as a `NetworkStream`, as opposed to `FileStreams` and `MemoryStreams` which are inherently buffered. You can tweak a `BufferedStream` object for performance purposes by specifying a specific type of stream. Buffers improve runtime efficiency by allocating blocks of bytes in memory. These blocks cache data and only dump when full, reducing the number of calls to the operating system.

`char`, `int`, `float`, `string` Printer Output

The `PrinterOutput.cs` algorithm that follows has two instructional goals, the first of which is to slowly wade into C#'s external file syntax. The second more obvious goal is the syntax requirements for outputting to the printer at runtime.

The first code change required is the `using System.IO;` statement seen below the usual `using System;` autograph.

```
using System;
using System.IO; // Necessary for FileStream definitions
```

Printers are treated syntactically and logically, just like external disk files. The following statement defines `fs` as a `FileStream` reference to an instance with the system-specific printer access nomenclature of `"lpt1"` the `FileMode` is `Open`, and `FileAccess` enumerator is `Write`:

```
// "lpt1" identifies the line printer as the external file
FileStream fs = new FileStream("lpt1",FileMode.Open,
                              FileAccess.Write);
```

The algorithm next instantiates a `StreamWriter` instance called `Printer` and is associated with the `fs` reference.

```
// create a StreamWriter called Printer
StreamWriter Printer = new StreamWriter(fs);
```

The code segment that follows mimics the logic from the first algorithm examined in this chapter, except for one addition: the additional statements duplicating the `Console` output to the `Printer`.

```
string sValue;

Console.Write("Enter a character -> ");
sValue = Console.ReadLine();
char cValue = char.Parse(sValue);
Console.WriteLine("The character entered is: {0}", cValue);
Printer.WriteLine("The character entered is: {0}", cValue);
```

The straightforward syntax necessary only involves the substitution of the `Printer` stream reference, instead of `Console`!

Do you have any idea why the program summarizes with this next statement?

```
Printer.Close();
```

The `Close()` method *forces* the dumping of the output buffer. While this would be performed automatically at program termination, it is an unwise and unprofessional design to rely on a system control.

The complete program follows:

```
using System;
using System.IO; // Necessary for FileStream definitions
public class Class1
{
  public static int Main(string[] args)
  {
    // PrinterOutput.cs
    // A C# application illustrating the syntax
    // necessary to output directly to an external printer.
    // Copyright (c) Chris H. Pappas and William H. Murray, 2001
    //

    // "lpt1" identifies the line printer as the external file
    FileStream fs = new FileStream("lpt1",FileMode.Open,
                                   FileAccess.Write);

    // create a StreamWriter called Printer
    StreamWriter Printer = new StreamWriter(fs);

    string sValue;

    Console.Write("Enter a character -> ");
    sValue = Console.ReadLine();
    char cValue = char.Parse(sValue);
    Console.WriteLine("The character entered is: {0}", cValue);
    Printer.WriteLine("The character entered is: {0}", cValue);
```

```
        Console.Write("\nEnter an integer  -> ");
        sValue = Console.ReadLine();
        int iValue = int.Parse(sValue);
        Console.WriteLine("The integer entered is  : {0}", iValue);
        Printer.WriteLine("The integer entered is  : {0}", iValue);

        Console.Write("\nEnter a float     -> ");
        sValue = Console.ReadLine();
        float fValue = float.Parse(sValue);
        Console.WriteLine("The float entered is   : {0}", fValue);
        Printer.WriteLine("The float entered is   : {0}", fValue);

        Console.Write("\nEnter a string    -> ");
        sValue = Console.ReadLine();
        Console.WriteLine("The string entered is   : {0}", sValue);
        Printer.WriteLine("The string entered is   : {0}", sValue);

        // close the Printer file dumping all buffers
        Printer.Close();

        return 0;
    }
}
```

The output from the program looks slightly different than the Console-only version since all prompts go to the Console, not the Printer file:

```
The character entered is: A
The integer entered is  : 1
The float entered is    : 2.2
The string entered is   : hello
```

Method to Output to External File or Printer

In the previous example program, output was *hardwired* in sequence and destination by the use of either the default Console stream, or Printer. What if you wanted to allow the user, at runtime, to select the output destination?

This next example, someExternalFile.cs, improves upon the previous algorithm by placing all of the output statements within a called method that is passed a selectable output Stream.

The algorithm looks identical to the last one until you reach the printToSome-ExternalFile() method body:

```
public static void printToSomeExternalFile(FileStream ss)
{
    // create a StreamWriter called SomeFile
    StreamWriter SomeFile = new StreamWriter(ss);
```

The dummy argument `ss` is formally defined as a `FileStream` reference. This placeholder will be passed either the reference to an external disk file reference or a reference to `lpt1`!

The internal workings of the method are identical in logic and syntax to those discussed previously, except for the generic `FileStream` reference to `SomeFile`, which is the instantiation of the requested output file.

```
string sValue;

Console.Write("Enter a character -> ");
sValue = Console.ReadLine();
char cValue = char.FromString(sValue);
SomeFile.WriteLine("The character entered is: {0}", cValue);
```

Finally, the anonymous `Close()` method is called to the instantiated `FileStream`:

```
// close the Printer file dumping all buffers
SomeFile.Close();
```

The `Main()` method is responsible for defining the two types of reference pointers, es and ps. es, is associated with an external disk file in the *C:* root directory called `"testOut.dat"`; ps is associated with `"lpt1"`. Both files use the `FileMode Create`, and `FileAccess` of `Write`.

By the way, did you notice the duplicate backslashes "\\" in the filename? It is a result of a collision between C being written for a UNIX environment and MS-DOS and today's Windows flavors—the backslash defines subdirectory paths!

Remember, C, C++, and C# view a single backslash as a flag to a control code, such as '\n' for new-line carriage return, and '\t' for tab control. To force the compiler to see a backslash as a backslash, you duplicate it.

```
// "c:\\testOut.dat" identifies a sample external file
FileStream es = new FileStream("c:\\testOut.dat",FileMode.Create,
                              FileAccess.Write);

// "lpt1" identifies the line printer as the external file
FileStream ps = new FileStream("lpt1",FileMode.Open,
                              FileAccess.Write);
```

With the reference pointers defined, all that is left is to decide which `FileStream` to pass to `printToSomeExternalFile()`. The example program illustrates the use of es:

```
printToSomeExternalFile(es); // external file reference
```

The complete program follows:

```csharp
using System;
using System.IO; // necessary to access FileStream definition
public class Class1
{
  public static void printToSomeExternalFile(FileStream ss)
  {
    // create a StreamWriter called SomeFile
    StreamWriter SomeFile = new StreamWriter(ss);

    string sValue;

    Console.Write("Enter a character -> ");
    sValue = Console.ReadLine();
    char cValue = char.FromString(sValue);
    SomeFile.WriteLine("The character entered is: {0}", cValue);

    Console.Write("\nEnter an integer  -> ");
    sValue = Console.ReadLine();
    int iValue = int.FromString(sValue);
    SomeFile.WriteLine("The integer entered is  : {0}", iValue);

    Console.Write("\nEnter a float    -> ");
    sValue = Console.ReadLine();
    float fValue = float.FromString(sValue);
    SomeFile.WriteLine("The float entered is    : {0}", fValue);

    Console.Write("\nEnter a string   -> ");
    sValue = Console.ReadLine();
    SomeFile.WriteLine("The string entered is   : {0}", sValue);

    // close the Printer file dumping all buffers
    SomeFile.Close();
  }

  public static int Main(string[] args)
  {
    // someExternalFile.cs
    // A C# application demonstrating how to pass
    // a file pointer to a method.
    // Copyright (c) Chris H. Pappas and William H. Murray, 2001
    //

    // "c:\\testOut.dat" identifies a sample external file
    FileStream es = new FileStream("c:\\testOut.dat",
                                   FileMode.Create,
                                   FileAccess.Write);
```

```
           // "lpt1" identifies the line printer as the external file
           FileStream ps = new FileStream("lpt1",FileMode.Open,
                                           FileAccess.Write);

           printToSomeExternalFile(es); // external file reference
           // before trying this next commented out method call
           // make certain you have the printer turned on,
           // you may need to turn printer offline then do a
           // page feed to force the printer to dump its buffer.
           // printToSomeExternalFile(ps); printer reference

           return 0;
       }
   }
```

`FileMode` Enumerators

Of course, there are more file modes in C# than `Create`. Table 10–5 lists `FileMode` enumerators and their specific meaning.

Table 10–5   `FileMode` Enumerators

Enumerator	**Purpose**
`Append`	Either opens a file if it exists and seeks to the end of the file, or creates a new file. `Append` can only be used in conjunction with `FileAccess.Write`.
`Create`	Instructs the operating system to create a new file. If the file already exists, it will be overwritten.
`CreateNew`	Instructs the operating system to create a new file. Specifies that the operating system should create a new file.
`Open`	Instructs the operating system to open an existing file.
`OpenOrCreate`	Instructs the operating system to open a file if it exists; otherwise, a new file should be created.
`Truncate`	Instructs the operating system to open an existing file. Once opened, the file should be truncated so that its size is zero bytes.

`FileAccess` Enumerators

The `FileAccess` enumerators define how a stream is accessed. Table 10–6 lists your code options.

Table 10–6   `FileAccess` Enumerators

Member	Purpose
`Read`	Defines read access. Include `Write` for read-write access.
`ReadWrite`	Defines read and write access. Data can be written to the file and read from the file.
`Write`	Defines write access. Include `Read` for read-write access.

`StreamWriter` and `StreamReader` Classes

The `StreamWriter` class defines a `TextWriter` used to write characters to a stream in a particular encoding, unlike subclasses of `Stream` which are specific to byte input and output. `StreamWriters` default to the UTF8 Encoding definition (Unicode) by default. The `StreamReader` class also defines a `TextReader` used to read characters from a byte stream in a particular encoding, unlike subclasses of `Stream`, which are specific to byte input and output.

Detecting End of File

The following program, `seekEOF.cs`, uses a `StreamReader` and the `Peek()` method to detect the end of an external input file. Once again, the application begins with the additional `using System.IO;` statement to pull in `FileStream` definitions:

```
using System;
using System.IO;
```

In a now familiar pattern, an external `FileStream` reference, `fs`, is created and instantiated:

```
FileStream fs = new FileStream("c:\\Text.fil", FileMode.Open,
                            FileAccess.Read, FileShare.Read);
```

Notice the `FileShare.Read` enumerator. This is followed by the creation of the `sr` `StreamReader` and associated with the `fs` `FileStream` instance:

```
StreamReader sr = new StreamReader(fs);
```

The `while` loop invokes the `StreamReader`'s `Peek()` method to look ahead, nondestructively, for the end of the file marker. Pay particular attention to C#'s requirement for a relational test to the method's returned value, that is, `> -1`. C and C++ would have been happy to just examine the method's return value for zeroness, `0`, or non-zeroness `!0`.

```
while( sr.Peek() > -1 )
{
  sOneLine = sr.ReadLine();
  Console.WriteLine(sOneLine);
}
```

If `Peek()` had actually gone out into the beginning or middle of an external file and extracted a byte, the input stream would be corrupted. Since `Peek()` does *not* do this, the first statement in the `while` loop is an actual `StreamReader ReadLine()` method call.

The complete algorithm follows:

```
using System;
using System.IO;

public class Class1
{
  public static int Main(string[] args)
  {
    // seekEOF.cs
    // A C# application demonstrating
    // the Peek() method detecting end of file
    // Copyright (c) Chris H. Pappas and William H. Murray, 2001
    //

    string sOneLine;
    FileStream fs = new FileStream("c:\\Text.fil", FileMode.Open,
                                       FileAccess.Read,
FileShare.Read);

    // Define StreamReader sr
    StreamReader sr = new StreamReader(fs);

    // While not eof
    while( sr.Peek() > -1 )
    {
      sOneLine = sr.ReadLine();
      Console.WriteLine(sOneLine);
    }
    sr.Close();

    return 0;
  }
}
```

The output from the program takes the following form:

```
Text.Fil
With several
lines of text of
varying lengths.
```

Can you think of any unique uses for `Peek()`?

Binary File I/O

Tangible example programs demonstrating the alternate external file manipulation of binary data are often glossed over by many textbooks. The following program, `BinaryFile.cs`, shows exactly how this is done in C#.

`BinaryFile.cs` begins in a predictable fashion, not requiring any new `using` statements perse to process a Binary file:

```
using System;
using System.IO; // necessary to use FileStream definitions
```

Even the declaration and instantiation of the `FileStream` reference looks familiar:

```
FileStream fs = new FileStream("c:\\Binary.fil", FileMode.Create);
```

What is new are the `BinaryReader br` and `BinaryWriter bw` statements:

```
BinaryReader br = new BinaryReader(fs);
BinaryWriter bw = new BinaryWriter(fs);
```

These two statements overlay an I/O interpretation of Binary upon the two streams. With external Binary files closely mimicking their raw internal memory source, they must be created in Binary mode. The following `for` loop accomplishes this task by creating an external file containing the Binary representations of 1 to 5:

```
// Create initial set of output data
for( int iValueToOutput = 1; iValueToOutput <= 5;
     iValueToOutput++ )
  bw.Write( iValueToOutput );
```

To input these newly created values, the input/output FileStream pointer must be repositioned to the beginning of the file. Use the `BinaryWriter`'s `Seek()` method to move the pointer:

```
// Reset the file pointer to beginning of file
bw.Seek(0,SeekOrigin.Begin);
```

The `SeekOrigin.Begin` enumerator instructs `Seek()` to move 0 (first argument) bytes from the beginning of the file. The echo-printing of the Binary files contents is accomplished with the second `for` loop:

```
// Input data from Binary.fil and output to Console
Console.Write("Int32 values interpreted as Int32: ");
for( int iValueToIO = 0; iValueToIO < 5; iValueToIO++ )
{
  Console.Write(" {0}", br.ReadInt32() );
}
```

The `Console.Write()` method formats the `BinaryReader`'s call to `ReadInt32()`, which simply grabs the external file's Binary bytes in groups of four. The complete program follows:

```
using System;
using System.IO; // necessary to use FileStream definitions
using System.Collections; // necessary to use Stack collection

public class Class1
{
  public static int Main(string[] args)
  {
    // BinaryFile.cs
    // A C# application demonstrating the syntax necessary
    // to create and read from a Binary file.
    // Copyright (c) Chris H. Pappas and William H. Murray, 2001
    //

    // "Create" FileStream fs
    FileStream fs = new FileStream("c:\\Binary.fil",
                                   FileMode.Create);

    // Define a BinaryReader/Writer
    BinaryReader br = new BinaryReader(fs);
    BinaryWriter bw = new BinaryWriter(fs);

    // Create initial set of output data
    for( int iValueToOutput = 1; iValueToOutput <= 5;
         iValueToOutput++ )
      bw.Write( iValueToOutput );

    // Reset the file pointer to beginning of file
    bw.Seek(0,SeekOrigin.Begin);

    // Input data from Binary.fil and output to Console
    Console.Write("Int32 values interpreted as Int32: ");
```

```
    for( int iValueToIO = 0; iValueToIO < 5; iValueToIO++ )
    {
      Console.Write(" {0}", br.ReadInt32() );
    }

    return 0;
  }
}
```

The `Console.Write()` output of the program looks like:

```
Int32 values interpreted as Int32:  1 2 3 4 5
```

However, the contents of `Binary.fil`, if viewed by a standard ASCII file text editor, looks like:

´ ˎ ˎ ˎ ˄ ˎ ˎ ˎ ˜ ˎ ˎ ˎ ˍ ˎ ˎ ˎ ˘ ˎ ˎ ˎ

Remember, a text file represents a *1* as the ASCII value 31h, while the Binary representation of a four-byte `Int32` is *0001* backwards, or *1000*!

Binary File I/O Byte-By-Byte

This next program, `BinaryByByte.cs`, illustrates the point that Binary file input can take on just about any form you can think of. The previous program grabbed a four-byte integer value in one felled swoop via `ReadInt32()`. `BinarybyBytes.cs` uses the same external file format and contents, only it inputs the four-byte integers one byte at a time.

Notice the third `using` statement found in the program's overhead:

```
using System;
using System.IO;           // to access FileStream definitions
using System.Collections;  // to access Stack definitions
```

The `Collections` class provides a full set of definitions to implement an efficient stack algorithm. Since Binary files are read in single bytes, or groups of bytes, and since the program will be inputting integer values one byte at a time, a stack is needed. Why, you ask? Because the Intel family of microprocessors stores low bytes at low addresses (or memory offsets), and high bytes at high addresses. Simply put, a four-byte representation of *1* would sit in memory as *1000*. If `BinaryFile.cs` were to simply echo-print the external file's binary contents to the `Console`, the integers would come out backwards. The fix involves the stack.

The code statements necessary to create the external Binary file, initialize its contents, and reposition the input/output pointer remains identical to the last application:

```
// "Create" FileStream fs
FileStream fs = new FileStream("c:\\Binary.fil",
                               FileMode.Create);
```

```
// Define a BinaryReader/Writer
BinaryReader br = new BinaryReader(fs);
BinaryWriter bw = new BinaryWriter(fs);

// Create initial set of output data
for( int iValueToOutput = 1; iValueToOutput <= 5;
     iValueToOutput++ )
  bw.Write( iValueToOutput );

// Reset the file pointer to beginning of file a second time
// to reread the file one byte at a time, each int is 4 bytes
bw.Seek( 0,SeekOrigin.Begin );
```

The next statement instantiates the stack reference to a Stack Collections:

```
// Define stack to hold/reverse byte ordering of Int32 Values
Stack stack = new Stack();
```

Nested within the second for loop are the statements needed to freshly push each four-byte's bytes, one-by-one, and then pop them out in reverse order:

```
// Outer loop processes the five Int32s
for( int oneInt32 = 0; oneInt32 < 5; oneInt32++ )
{
  // Inner loops store and then reverse backwards file ordering
  for( int byteNumber = 0; byteNumber < 4; byteNumber++ )
    stack.Push( br.ReadByte() );
  for( int byteNumber = 0; byteNumber < 4; byteNumber++ )
    Console.Write("{0}",stack.Pop() );
  Console.WriteLine();
 }
```

Notice the use of the BinaryReader's ReadByte() method call instead of the previous program's ReadInt32(), and the ease in using a Stack instance via Push() and Pop() method calls.

The complete algorithm follows:

```
using System;
using System.IO; // to access FileStream definitions
using System.Collections; // to access Stack definitions

public class Class1
{
  public static int Main(string[] args)
  {
    // BinaryByByte.cs
    // A C# application that reexamines an Int32
    // Binary I/O file, byte-by-byte.
    // Copyright (c) Chris H. Pappas and William H. Murray, 2001
    //
```

```
    // "Create" FileStream fs
    FileStream fs = new FileStream("c:\\Binary.fil",
                              FileMode.Create);

    // Define a BinaryReader/Writer
    BinaryReader br = new BinaryReader(fs);
    BinaryWriter bw = new BinaryWriter(fs);

    // Create initial set of output data
    for( int iValueToOutput = 1; iValueToOutput <= 5;
        iValueToOutput++ )
      bw.Write( iValueToOutput );

    // Reset the file pointer to beginning of file
    bw.Seek(0,SeekOrigin.Begin);

    // Reset the file pointer to beginning of file a second time
    // to reread the file one byte at a time, each int is 4 bytes
    bw.Seek( 0,SeekOrigin.Begin );

    // Define stack to hold/reverse byte ordering of Int32 Values
    Stack stack = new Stack();

    Console.WriteLine("Int32 Values interpreted byte-by-byte:");
    // Outer loop processes the five Int32s
    for( int oneInt32 = 0; oneInt32 < 5; oneInt32++ )
    {
      // Inner loops store then reverse backwards file ordering
      for( int byteNumber = 0; byteNumber < 4; byteNumber++ )
        stack.Push( br.ReadByte() );
      for( int byteNumber = 0; byteNumber < 4; byteNumber++ )
        Console.Write("{0}",stack.Pop() );
      Console.WriteLine();
    }

    return 0;
  }
}
```

The output from this application looks like:

```
Int32 Values interpreted byte-by-byte:
0001
0002
0003
0004
0005
```

Formatting Data

Have you had a gnawing question running through your mind every time you see an input statement in just about every example program examined so far, in every chapter, no less? Have you wondered why the input statements seem to always use string variable types? Well, there *is* a reason.

For input, the answer is straightforward. While the digits 0–9 can be viewed as the symbols "0"–"9", for example, "59 Main Street," the letters "A"–"Z" or "a"–"z" cannot be viewed as numbers. If you are trying to write a user-friendly, robust algorithm, string input accepts just about anything a user could enter, correctly or incorrectly. Proper interpretation of the user's input is up to the eloquence of the program's logic.

Using string type output has even more advantages. Strings are easily converted to other base types, and easily displayed and appended to messages. String type output conversions also allow an algorithm to use the highest precision data type for internal calculation accuracy while displaying results in a more user-friendly, familiar form. You can even reuse the algorithm by simply converting only the output to the desired form without having to rewrite the data types used in the entire calculation. C# even tops the output formatting options with dynamically modified, culture-specific Currency and DateTime. The .NET Framework provides methods in every base type that convert numeric data types to strings and strings to numeric data types.

This philosophy of using the highest-precision types within an algorithm and outputting the information in a culture-specific, architecture-specific, environment-specific form is so important to C#'s underpinnings that every .NET Framework base data type—Int32, Int64, single, double, DateTime, etc.—has its own format() and ToString() method returning a string-formatted representation of the original value. The format() method provides several formatting options and the ability to dynamically change output based on the current culture. The simpler-to-use ToString() method provides only one culture-independent formatting option.

The syntax for format() looks like:

```
static nType format(nType nValue, string sFormat);
static nType format(nType nValue, string sFormat,
                    NumberFormatInfo info);
static nType format(string sFormat, IServiceObjectProvider isop);
```

where nType is the name of the numeric base data type: The format() method takes a combination of three parameters: an nValue, a string sFormat specifier, and an IService-ObjectProvider interface, isop. isop selects the current culture detailing the characters to use for decimal and thousand separators and the spelling and placement of currency symbols. When set to null, it will use the characters specified by the current culture.

The Format method accepts two sFormat types: standard numeric format strings and picture numeric format strings. Standard format strings are built-in options that address the most common formatting requirements, while picture strings allow you to paint a picture of how you want the output to look. For example, the following `format()` statement displays the value of 20 as a currency-formatted string in the console's output window:

```
int iValue = 20;
iValue.Format("C", null);
// Displays the value: "$20.00"
```

The `format()` statement takes two arguments: the `format` string and `isop`. The format string specifies the value returned by `format()`. In this case, the string has a value of `"C"`, returning a currency representation of the original value. You can safely set the `isop` to `null`, instructing `format()` to default to the current culture. Note that `format()` returns a string data type, not a numeric value!

The next example is similar to the previous example, except for the formatting of a hard-wired value:

```
int.Format( 20, "C");
//Returns "$20.00"
```

The `ToString()` method quickly converts a .NET Framework base type value into a string. It requires no arguments and is easy to use. The following example converts an integer value of 22 into a string value:

```
int MyInt = 22;
string MyString =  MyInt.ToString();
//Mystring will have a string value of "22"
```

The `ToString()` method is a quick and easy way to convert numeric data into a string format.

Format Specifiers

Table 10–7 lists the seven built-in format characters that define the most commonly used .NET Framework numeric format types. The precision specifier controls the number of significant digits or zeros to the right of a decimal.

Table 10–7   Format Specifiers

Specifier	Meaning	Output Format (without a precision specifier)
C or c	Currency format	$nn,nn.nn ($nn,nnn.nn)
D or d	Decimal format	[-]nnnnnnn

Table 10–7   Format Specifiers *(Continued)*

Specifier	Meaning	Output Format (without a precision specifier)
E or e	Scientific (exponential) format	[-]n.nnnnnnE+xxx [-]n.nnnnnne+xxx [-]n.nnnnnnE-xxx [-]n.nnnnnne-xxx
F or f	Fixed-point format	[-]nnnnnnn.nn
G or g	General format	Variable. Either general or scientific.
N or n	Number format	[-]nn,nnn.nn
n or x	Hexadecimal format	Variable. Returns the minimum hexadecimal representation.

We'll show you several examples of how these work in the next few sections.

"C" Currency Specifier

The "C" format specifier returns a string representing the number as a currency value. The currency symbols used is determined by the current culture if a NumberFormatInfo object is not provided. Integers following "C" define the number of decimal places displayed; the default is two digits. Both forms are demonstrated in the two format() statements.

```
int MyInt = 12345;

MyInt.format( "c", null );
// Returns the currency string "$12,345.00"

MyInt.format( "c3", null );
// Returns the currency string "$12,345.000"
```

Now it is easy to format and print your net worth!

"D" Decimal Specifier

Use the "D" format specifier to convert an integer to a base 10 number. Only integral types support the "D" format code. A negative symbol is prefixed to the result if the value is negative. You can also specify the minimum number of decimal digits to display using a precision specifier.

```
int MyInt = 123;

MyInt.format( "d5", null );
// Returns the decimal string "00123"

MyInt.format( "d2", null );
// Returns the decimal string "123"
```

Now it is possible to "pad" numeric data. You will find this specifier useful when trying to get table columns to align.

"E" Exponential Specifier

Use the "E" format specifier to return a string formatted as a scientific or exponential number. The precision specifier determines the number of digits after the decimal point. The case of the exponent format character "E" or "e" selects the case of the formatted value.

```
int MyInt = 12345;

MyInt.format( "e", null );
// Returns the exponential string "1.234500e+004"

MyInt.format( "e3", null );
// Returns the exponential string "1.235e+004"
```

Use this specifier and eliminate your fear of really large numbers. What could be more compact than scientific notation?

"F" Fixed Point Specifier

The "F" format specifier converts nondecimal values into ones *with* a decimal point.

```
int MyInt = 12345;

MyInt.format( "f", null );
// Returns the string "12345.00"

MyInt.format( "f3", null );
// Returns the string "12345.000"
```

Select the number of zeros with the integral value to the immediate right of the precision specifier; the default is two zeros.

Format specifiers will greatly help you when formatting output for tables.

"G" General Specifier

The "G" format specifier can switch-hit, converting a number into either fixed point "F" or scientific format "E."

```
int MyInt = 12345;

MyInt.format( "g", null );
// Returns the string "12345"

MyInt.format( "g3", null );
// Returns the exponential string "123e4"
```

This is another specifier that will allow you to limit the size of large numbers. When a number reaches a certain size, the specifier allows it to be converted to scientific notation.

"N" Number Specifier

The "N" format specifier converts a number to the form "[-]n,nnn,nnn.nn" with a decimal placed at the far right of the numeric value, followed by the number of zeros specified by the format specifier; the default is two decimal place precision.

```
int MyInt = 12345;

MyInt.format( "n", null );
// Returns the string "12,345.00"

MyInt.format( "n3", null );
// Returns the string "12,345.000"
```

This is a general purpose specifier that allows you to set both precision and decimal place precision.

"X" Hexadecimal Specifier

Most programmers are familiar with seeing memory dumps displayed in hexadecimal format. The "X" format specifier converts a number to hexadecimal The precision specifier determines the minimum number of digits returned.

```
int MyInt = 12345;

MyInt.format( "x", null );
// Returns the hexadecimal string "3039"

MyInt.format( "x3", null );
// Returns the hexadecimal string "3039"
```

Now you can set your output to hexadecimal and specify the precision of the answer. Integers only, please!

Picture Format Specifiers

Use picture format strings to create custom string output. Picture format strings contain a number of format characters that fine-tune the output of `format()`. Picture number format definitions are described using placeholder strings that identify the minimum and maximum number of digits used, the placement or appearance of the negative sign, and the appearance of any other literals within the numeric value (see Table 10–8).

Table 10–8   Picture Format Specifiers

Format Specifier	Symbol Displayed	Interpretation
0	Use zero placeholders	Will display a non-significant zero when a numeric value has fewer digits than there are zeros in the format.
#	Use digit placeholders	Substitutes the "#" symbol with significant digits only.
.	Displays a decimal point	Outputs the "." character.
,	Group separator	
multiplier	Separates number groups; for example, "1,000".	
%	Percent notation	Outputs the "%" character.
E+0		
E-0		
e+0		
e-0	Exponent notation	Displays exponential notation.
\	Literal character	Used in formatting sequences like "\n", "\t", etc.
"ABC" or 'ABC'	Literal string	Outputs a string within quotes or apostrophes.
;	Section separator	Defines multiple output formats depending on whether the numeric value is positive, negative, or zero.

The following statements demonstrate several of the more popular picture format specifiers in use:

```
Double MyDouble = 12.345;

MyDouble. Format( "000.##", null );
// returns the string "012.35"

Double MyDouble = 5.14129
Int32  MyInt = 42

MyDouble.Format( "0###.##", null )
//Results in "0005.14"

MyDouble.Format( "%#.##", null )
//Results in "%514.13"

MyInt.Format( "My Number = #", null )
//Results in "My Number = 42"

MyInt.Format( "My Number \n= #", null )
//Results in "My Number
//             = 42"
```

The picture format has three forms. If only one picture format is defined, all numbers will be formatted as specified in that section. If two picture formats are defined, the first section will be applied to positive and zero values while the second section will be applied to negative numbers. When there are three picture formats, the first applies to positive values, the second applies to negative values, and the third applies to all zero values, as demonstrated in the following examples:

```
int MyPosInt = 42, MyNegInt = -42, MyZeroInt = 0;

MyPosInt.Format( "Positive Number = #;
                  Negative Number = #;
                  Zero Value = #", null )

//Results in "Positive Number = 42"

MyNegInt.Format( "Positive Number = #;
                  Negative Number = #;
                  Zero Value = #", null )

//Results in "Negative Number =  -42"

MyZeroInt.Format( "Positive Number = #;
                   Negative Number = #;
                   Zero Value = #", null )

//Results in "Zero Value = 0"
```

Summary

In this chapter you learned how to do keyboard and external file input, and console and external file output, along with how to output directly to a printer (in a Windows-based, Intel-architecture environment). You also learned that C# is plagued with its own unique set of dos and don'ts when it comes to data throughput! Chapter 11 ramps up once again to detail some of C#'s more complex language features with its discussions of type conversions, comparison operators, pointers, events, and read-only collision.

Advanced C# Programming Considerations

In this last procedure-oriented discussion of C# funda-
mentals you will explore those features of C# that often become pivotal underpinnings to
robust C# Windows applications. The chapter can be broken down into two logical components: those features of C# that enable an algorithm to change, query, and decide an object's
type, and those features of C# that process events.

Type Conversions

C#'s type conversion keywords, `implicit` and `explicit`, are extensions to type casting.
They allow you to define a set of operations detailing how one user-defined type may be
changed to some other type. The only difference between the two keywords involves how
syntactically obvious you want this conversion process to appear in your source code.
Implied type conversions are behind-the-scenes automated conversions, while explicit conversions lead to more self-documenting source code.

`implicit` Keyword

Use the `implicit` keyword to define an implied (behind-the-scenes, automated) user-
defined type conversion operator. The following code segment demonstrates the straightforward syntax for a conversion from a `UDT` (user-defined type) to `int`:

```
class UDT
{
    public static implicit operator int(UDT udt)
    {
```

```
       // code to convert from UDT to int
   }
}
```

The advantage of implicit conversion operators is that they are *not* invoked in the foreground, as are casts, thereby streamlining code layout.

```
UDT udt;
int iValue = udt; // implicitly call UDT's UDT-to-int conversion
                  // operator
```

This improved readability, however, can predispose an algorithm's logic to unexpected results as the compiler faithfully generates the code truncating, permuting, or altering a variable's internal representation.

explicit Keyword

With the complexity of today's programming environment, and the repetitively unfamiliar territory presented by each new programming language, using automated and hidden language features, such as implied type conversions, is unwise. Today's programmer no sooner acquires a degree of finesse in one programming language, only to find out that those skills are now old hat!

Explicit casts, while similar in raw horsepower to implied casts, at least leave a documentation trail showing how a variable was permuted. The following program, explicit.cs, contrasts the two forms. See which you would rather "desk-check" in a misfiring algorithm. The implicit conversion casts an int into a UDT type, while the explicit conversion changes an integer into a string:

```
struct UDT
{
  public UDT(int i)
  {
    this.iValue = i;
  }
  static public implicit operator UDT(int i)
  {
    return new UDT(i);
  }
  static public explicit operator string(UDT i)
  {
    switch(i.iValue)
    {
      case 0: return "zero ";
      case 1: return "one   ";
      case 2: return "two   ";
      case 3: return "three";
```

```
      case 4: return "four ";
      case 5: return "five ";
      case 6: return "six  ";
      case 7: return "seven";
      case 8: return "eight";
      case 9: return "nine ";
      default:return "unrecognized digit";
    }
  }
```

The `Main()` method creates a UDT variable called `udt` and then implicitly casts the integer value 9 to a UDT instance.

```
UDT udt;
udt = 9;
```

Since `WriteLine()` is not overloaded to understand *how* to output UDT types, the first output statement fails. However, the second `WriteLine()` is successful because of the `explicit` cast of `udt` to `string` easily deciphered in the statement itself.

```
Console.WriteLine(udt);          // outputs "UDT" incorrectly
Console.WriteLine((string)udt);  // explicit cast to string
```

This syntactically visual permutation is often the key to a novice programmer's debugging starting point.

The complete algorithm follows:

```
using System;

struct UDT
{
  public UDT(int i)
  {
    this.iValue = i;
  }
  static public implicit operator UDT(int i)
  {
    return new UDT(i);
  }
  static public explicit operator string(UDT i)
  {
    switch(i.iValue)
    {
      case 0: return "zero ";
      case 1: return "one  ";
      case 2: return "two  ";
      case 3: return "three";
```

```
            case 4: return "four ";
            case 5: return "five ";
            case 6: return "six  ";
            case 7: return "seven";
            case 8: return "eight";
            case 9: return "nine ";
            default:return "unrecognized digit";
        }
    }

    int iValue;
}

public class Class1
{
    public static int Main(string[] args)
    {
        // explicit.cs
        // A C# application demonstrating explicit casting.
        // Copyright (c) Chris H. Pappas and William H. Murray, 2001
        //

        UDT udt;

        udt = 9;

        Console.WriteLine(udt);            // outputs "UDT" incorrectly
        Console.WriteLine((string)udt); // explicit cast to string

        return 0;
    }
}
```

This next example program, implicit.cs, rewrites the explicit conversion documented in the previous algorithm. First, notice how simple it is, syntactically, to change an explicit definition into an implicit one by a quick change of keywords.

```
static public explicit operator string(UDT i)
static public implicit operator string(UDT i)
```

Notice, too, how hidden the use of the rewritten method becomes:

```
Console.WriteLine((string)udt); // explicit cast to string
Console.WriteLine(udt);          // implicit cast to string
```

So which form should you use? The answer is based on your degree of programming experience, your target audience, the anticipated longevity of the algorithm, if there will be a life cycle to the code solution, how programmer-friendly do you want your source code, and/or how "cool" do you want to look in your code. If you code by the rule: "Always write code for *another* programmer to understand," then your answer will be explicit!

The complete implicit.cs program follows:

```
using System;

struct UDT
{
  public UDT(int i)
  {
    this.iValue = i;
  }
  static public implicit operator UDT(int i)
  {
    return new UDT(i);
  }
  static public implicit operator string(UDT i)
  {
    switch(i.iValue)
    {
      case 0: return "zero ";
      case 1: return "one  ";
      case 2: return "two  ";
      case 3: return "three";
      case 4: return "four ";
      case 5: return "five ";
      case 6: return "six  ";
      case 7: return "seven";
      case 8: return "eight";
      case 9: return "nine ";
      default:return "unrecognized digit";
    }
  }

  int iValue;
}

public class Class1
{
  public static int Main(string[] args)
  {
    // implicit.cs
    // A C# application demonstrating implicit casting.
    // Copyright (c) Chris H. Pappas and William H. Murray, 2001
    //
```

```
UDT udt;

udt = 9;

Console.WriteLine(udt); // implicit cast to string

return 0;
    }
}
```

operator

C# uses a similar mechanism for allowing a programmer to add meaning to any standard operator, to C++, called operator overloading. Use the `operator` keyword to overload a class or struct operator. The syntax for `operator` overloading takes on one of the four following styles:

```
public static returnType operator unary-operator

    ( operandType operand )
public static returnType operator binary-operator

    ( operandType operand, operandType2 operand2)

public static implicit operator returnType

    ( sourceType operand )
public static explicit operator returnType

    ( sourceType operand )
```

C# allows you to overload the following unary operators:

```
+    -    !    ~    ++    -    true    false
```

and binary operators:

```
One of: +  -  *  /  %  &  |  ^  <<  >>  ==  !=  >  <  >=  <=
```

Use the first two syntax styles to declare user-defined operators that overload built-in operators. At least one of `operandTypes` must be the type of which the operator is a member. This prevents redefining standard operators such as addition for integral types.

The last two syntax styles define conversion operators. Either the `sourceType` or the `returnType` must be the owning type. The conversion operator can only convert from its owning type to some other type, or from some other type to its owning type, and operators can only take `value` parameters, not `ref` or `out` parameters.

The following algorithm, `operator.cs`, defines an overloaded (+) operator designed to add degrees, minutes, and seconds. The program begins by defining the class `angle_value` and two overloaded constructors. Notice that the second constructor uses the `Substring()` method to go into the instance data, separating out the degrees, minutes, and seconds. `Substring()` has two formal integral arguments—defining the string offset address to begin the substring operation, and how many consecutive characters to grab.

```
class angle_value
{
   int degrees, minutes, seconds;

   public angle_value() {degrees=0; minutes=0; seconds=0;}
   public angle_value(string angle_sum)
   {
     degrees=int.Parse(angle_sum.Substring(0,2));
     minutes=int.Parse(angle_sum.Substring(4,2));
     seconds=int.Parse(angle_sum.Substring(8,2));
   }
```

The overloaded addition operator +'s definition follows the two constructors. Except for the `operator` keyword, the subroutine resembles a simple method body:

```
   public static angle_value operator +(angle_value ang1,
                                        angle_value ang2)
   {
     angle_value ang = new angle_value();
     ang.seconds=(ang1.seconds+ang2.seconds)%60;
     ang.minutes=((ang1.seconds+ang2.seconds)/60+
                    ang1.minutes+ang2.minutes)%60;
     ang.degrees=((ang1.seconds+ang2.seconds)/60+
                    ang1.minutes+ang2.minutes)/60;
     ang.degrees+=ang1.degrees+ang2.degrees;
     totaldegrees=ang.degrees;
     totalminutes=ang.minutes;
     totalseconds=ang.seconds;
     return ang;
   }
}
```

The `Main()` method instantiates four `angle_value` instances `str1` to `str4` with real values:

```
string str1 = "37d 15m 56s";
angle_value angle1 = new angle_value(str1);

string str2 = "10d 44m 44s";
angle_value angle2 = new angle_value(str2);
```

```
string str3 = "75d 17m 59s";
angle_value angle3 = new angle_value(str3);

string str4 = "13d 32m 54s";
angle_value angle4 = new angle_value(str4);
```

followed by a default-initialized instance sum_of_angles which will be used to store the accumulated totals:

```
angle_value sum_of_angles = new angle_value();
```

It is the next statement in Main() that invokes the overloaded addition operator +, that now understands what to do when there is an instance of class angle_value as its two source operand types:

```
sum_of_angles = angle1 + angle2 + angle3 + angle4;
```

The output from the program looks like:

```
The sum of the angles is 136d 51m 33s
```

The complete algorithm follows:

```
using System;
public class Class1
{
   static int totaldegrees, totalminutes, totalseconds;

   class angle_value
   {
     int degrees, minutes, seconds;

     public angle_value() {degrees=0; minutes=0; seconds=0;}
     public angle_value(string angle_sum)
     {
       degrees=int.Parse(angle_sum.Substring(0,2));
       minutes=int.Parse(angle_sum.Substring(4,2));
       seconds=int.Parse(angle_sum.Substring(8,2));
     }

     public static angle_value operator +(angle_value ang1,

                                          angle_value ang2)
     {
       angle_value ang = new angle_value();
       ang.seconds=(ang1.seconds+ang2.seconds)%60;
       ang.minutes=((ang1.seconds+ang2.seconds)/60+
                    ang1.minutes+ang2.minutes)%60;
```

```csharp
      ang.degrees=((ang1.seconds+ang2.seconds)/60+
                    ang1.minutes+ang2.minutes)/60;
      ang.degrees+=ang1.degrees+ang2.degrees;
      totaldegrees=ang.degrees;
      totalminutes=ang.minutes;
      totalseconds=ang.seconds;
      return ang;
    }
}

public static int Main()
{
   // operator.cs
   // A C# application demonstrating how to overload
   // a class operator using the C# operator keyword.
   // Copyright (c) Chris H. Pappas and William H. Murray, 2001
   //

   string str1 = "37d 15m 56s";
   angle_value angle1 = new angle_value(str1);

   string str2 = "10d 44m 44s";
   angle_value angle2 = new angle_value(str2);

   string str3 = "75d 17m 59s";
   angle_value angle3 = new angle_value(str3);

   string str4 = "13d 32m 54s";
   angle_value angle4 = new angle_value(str4);

   angle_value sum_of_angles = new angle_value();

   sum_of_angles = angle1 + angle2 + angle3 + angle4;
   Console.WriteLine("The sum of the angles is" +

                     " {0}d {1}m {2}s",

                     totaldegrees, totalminutes,

                     totalseconds);

   return 0;
  }
}
```

`typeof()` Keyword

Use the `typeof()` operator to find out the `System.Type` object for a type. The `typeof()` operator cannot be overloaded. To find out the runtime type of an object, use the method `GetType()`. The following program, `TypeOf.cs`, illustrates the syntax and logical use for `typeof()`.

The program begins by including a new `using` statement:

```
using System;
using System.Reflection;
```

The `System.Reflection` namespace defines classes and interfaces that provide a managed view of loaded types, methods, and fields, which `TypeOf.cs` defines to demonstrate how the namespace operates:

```
public class TypeOf
{
    public int iValue;
    public char cValue;
    public double dValue;

    public int int32Method()
    {
      return 0;
    }

    public void voidMethod()
    {
    }
```

Next, `Main()` defines two `Types` and one `TypeOf` instances. `System.Type` is the root of all reflection operations and the `Object` that represents a type inside the system. `Type` is an abstract base class that allows multiple implementations. The system will always provide the descendant `__RuntimeType`. In reflection, `__RuntimeXXX` classes are created only once per object in the system allowing you to test for equality.

```
Type sampleType1 = typeof(TypeOf);
TypeOf sampleType2 = new TypeOf();
Type sampleType3 = sampleType2.GetType();
```

`Main()` then invokes the `GetMembers()` method, storing its results in the member-Info array. `GetMembers()` returns the members: properties, methods, fields, and events of the specified `Type` which in this case is `sampleType1`:

```
MemberInfo[] memberInfo = sampleType1.GetMembers();
Console.WriteLine("\"MemberInfo[]\"");
foreach (MemberInfo xtemp2 in memberInfo)
```

```
{
   Console.WriteLine("\t\t\t{0}",xtemp2.ToString());
}
```

After displaying the results of the GetMembers() method call in the foreach loop, Main() then invokes the GetMethods() subroutine:

```
MethodInfo[] methodInfo = sampleType1.GetMethods();
Console.WriteLine("\"MethodInfo[]\"");
foreach (MethodInfo xtemp in methodInfo)
{
   Console.WriteLine("\t\t\t{0}",xtemp.ToString());
}
```

The subroutine GetMethods() returns the methods of the specified Type and again is applied to the sampleType1 instance. The output from the program looks like:

```
"MemberInfo[]"
                      Int32 iValue
                      Char cValue
                      Double dValue
                      Int32 GetHashCode()
                      Boolean Equals(System.Object)
                      System.String ToString()
                      Int32 int32Method()
                      Void voidMethod()
                      Int32 Main()
                      System.Type GetType()
                      Void .ctor()

"MethodInfo[]"
                      Int32 GetHashCode()
                      Boolean Equals(System.Object)
                      System.String ToString()
                      Int32 int32Method()
                      Void voidMethod()
                      Int32 Main()
                      System.Type GetType()
```

The complete algorithm follows:

```
using System;
using System.Reflection;

public class TypeOf
{
   public int iValue;
   public char cValue;
```

```
public double dValue;

public int int32Method()
{
  return 0;
}

public void voidMethod()
{
}

public static int Main()
{
  // TypeOf.cs
  // A C# application demonstrating the use of TypeOf.
  // Copyright (c) Chris H. Pappas and William H. Murray, 2001
  //

  Type sampleType1 = typeof(TypeOf);
  TypeOf sampleType2 = new TypeOf();
  Type sampleType3 = sampleType2.GetType();

  MemberInfo[] memberInfo = sampleType1.GetMembers();
  Console.WriteLine("\"MemberInfo[]\"");
  foreach (MemberInfo xtemp2 in memberInfo)
  {
    Console.WriteLine("\t\t\t{0}",xtemp2.ToString());
  }

  Console.WriteLine();

  MethodInfo[] methodInfo = sampleType1.GetMethods();
  Console.WriteLine("\"MethodInfo[]\"");
  foreach (MethodInfo xtemp in methodInfo)
  {
    Console.WriteLine("\t\t\t{0}",xtemp.ToString());
  }

  return 0;
  }
}
```

is Keyword

C# includes the is keyword allowing you to check the runtime type of an object to see if it is identical to some specified type. An is expression evaluates to true when an expression is *not* null and can be cast to the specified type. A compile-time warning will be issued if the comparison is known to always be true or always be false. The is operator cannot be overloaded.

The following program, is.cs, illustrates the use of is by defining three classes: is1, is2, and isClass:

```
class is1
{
}

class is2
{
}
```

The isClass definition includes an isMethod() to return the results of the is comparisons:

```
public class isClass
{
    public static int isMethod (object objectParameterType)
    {
      if (objectParameterType is is1)
         return 1;
       else if (objectParameterType is is2)
           return 2;
         else return 0;
    }
```

The results of the is comparison are displayed via the isClass.printAnswer() method:

```
public static void printAnswer(string sInstance, int iCode)
{
  Console.Write("{0} is ",sInstance);
  switch(iCode)
  {
    case 1: Console.WriteLine(" \"is1\"");
            break;
    case 2: Console.WriteLine(" \"is2\"");
            break;
    case 0: Console.WriteLine("neither \"is1\" or \"is2\"");
            break;
  }
}
```

The Main() method instantiates is1 and is2 with is1_Instance and is2_Instance, respectively:

```
is1 is1_Instance = new is1();
is2 is2_Instance = new is2();
```

then goes on to invoke the isClass.printAnswer() method displaying the returned results of the nested call to isClass.isMethod():

```
printAnswer("is1_Instance",isMethod(is1_Instance));
printAnswer("is2_Instance",isMethod (is2_Instance));
printAnswer("Literal String",isMethod ("Literal String"));
```

Notice that the last call to printAnswer() uses a *"Literal String,"* demonstrating the ability of is to detect the incompatability.

The output from the program looks like:

```
is1_Instance is  "is1"
is2_Instance is  "is2"
Literal String is neither "is1" or "is2"
```

The complete algorithm follows:

```
using System;
class is1
{
}

class is2
{
}

public class isClass
{
    public static int isMethod (object objectParameterType)
    {
      if (objectParameterType is is1)
         return 1;
       else if (objectParameterType is is2)
           return 2;
         else return 0;
    }

    public static void printAnswer(string sInstance,
                                    int iCode)
    {
      Console.Write("{0} is ",sInstance);
      switch(iCode)
      {
        case 1: Console.WriteLine(" \"is1\"");
                break;
```

```
        case 2: Console.WriteLine(" \"is2\"");
                break;
        case 0: Console.WriteLine("neither \"is1\" or
                                  \"is2\"");
                break;
    }
}

public static int Main()
{
  // is.cs
  // A C# application demonstrating the is keyword
  // to check compatibility of objects.
  // Copyright (c) Chris H. Pappas and William H. Murray, 2001
  //

    is1 is1_Instance = new is1();
    is2 is2_Instance = new is2();

    printAnswer("is1_Instance",isMethod(is1_Instance));
    printAnswer("is2_Instance",isMethod (is2_Instance));
    printAnswer("Literal String",isMethod ("Literal String"));

    return 0;
  }
}
```

this Keyword

C#, like C++, uses the `this` keyword to select the current instance for which a method is called. You can use the `this` keyword to access members from within constructors and instance methods, but `this` may *not* be used in `static` member functions which do not have a `this` reference pointer. The following program, `this.cs`, illustrates just one of the many uses for `this`.

The program begins by defining the class `setvalue`:

```
public class setvalue
{
  private int x, y;
```

It is `setvalue`'s constructor that uses the `this` pointer to know which instance the constructor is being invoked upon and to separate out the name collisions between the constructor's dummy arguments x and y from the formal class' `private` data members x and y:

```
     public setvalue(int x, int y)
     {
       this.x = x;
       this.y = y;
     }
}
```

The Main() method instantiates two setvalue instances svInstance1 and svInstance2.

```
setvalue svInstance1 = new setvalue(10,20);
setvalue svInstance2 = new setvalue(30,40);
```

The simplest concept to remember when trying to figure out why the this pointer reference is necessary is that while class instances can *share* a class' method bodies, each instance gets its own member data, as seen in Figure 11–1.

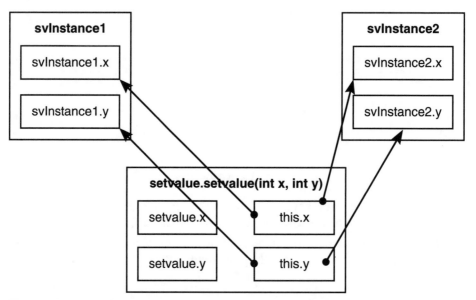

Figure 11–1   Instance member data versus shared class methods.

The complete program follows:

```
using System;
public class Class1
{
  public class setvalue
  {
    private int x, y;
```

```
    public setvalue(int x, int y)
    {
      this.x = x;
      this.y = y;
    }
}
public static int Main(string[] args)
{
  // this.cs
  // A C# application demonstrating the this pointer.
  // Copyright (c) Chris H. Pappas and William H. Murray, 2001
  //

  setvalue svInstance1 = new setvalue(10,20);
  setvalue svInstance2 = new setvalue(30,40);

  return 0;
  }
}
```

Note that when you execute this program, you will not see any output on the command line screen.

The this keyword is powerful and easy to incorporate into your program code.

event Keyword

Use the event and delegate keywords simultaneously. The event keyword specifies an automatically invoked delegate having one or more associated methods designed to handle the event when your code indicates that the event has occurred, as seen in the event.cs algorithm that follows.

The program begins by defining the delegateFunction() using the delegate keyword. A delegate is a reference type that specifies a static or instance method with a specific signature, similar to C++'s function pointers type:

```
public delegate void delegateFunction();
```

The event is defined within the class Class:

```
public class Class
{
  public event delegateFunction Event;
```

The syntax requires the use of the keyword event along with a delegate definition, in this case delegateFunction(). The FlagEvent() method is included here as a piece of test code that will actually throw the Event():

```
public void FlagEvent()
{
  if (Event != null)
      Event();
}
}
```

The `TestClass` contains the definition for the method `EventHandler()` that will be passed as an argument to the delegate `delegateFunction()`:

```
public class TestClass
{
  static void EventHandler()
  {
    Console.Write("Processing Event");
  }
```

The `Main()` method instantiates a `Class` instance, `ClassInstance`, and registers the `EventHandler()` delegate function, giving the `ClassInstance.Event` a valid pointer reference so that when `FlagEvent()` is invoked, `Event` is `!= null`.

```
Class ClassInstance = new Class();

ClassInstance.Event += new delegateFunction(EventHandler);
ClassInstance.FlagEvent();

return 0;
  }
}
```

The output from the program looks like:

```
Processing Event
```

showing that the event was indeed thrown and processed. The complete algorithm follows:

```
using System;
public delegate void delegateFunction();

public class Class
{
  public event delegateFunction Event;

  public void FlagEvent()
  {
    if (Event != null)
        Event();
  }
```

```
}

public class TestClass
{
  static void EventHandler()
  {
    Console.Write("Processing Event");
  }

  static public int Main ()
  {
    // event.cs
    // A C# application detailing how to have
    // your own class flag an event.
    // Copyright (c) Chris H. Pappas and William H. Murray, 2001
    //

    Class ClassInterface = new Class();

    ClassInterface.Event += new delegateFunction(EventHandler);
    ClassInterface.FlagEvent();

    return 0;
  }
}
```

Whenever any algorithm wants to store multiple values of the same type, a programmer naturally chooses an array container. The same holds true for any algorithm desiring to track multiple events. Hash tables are ideal for storing event instances, especially when there are a very large number of events but few actually implemented. The objects used as keys in a Hashtable are the events, as seen in the following program hashTable.cs.

The program begins by including System.Collections, providing access to the Hashtable definitions. The algorithm next defines five delegate reference function pointers, along with individual events for each delegate type. Notice that DelegateE(), has *two* associated events, EventE() and EventF():

```
using System;
using System.Collections;

public delegate void DelegateA();
public delegate void DelegateB(int iValue);
public delegate void DelegateC(double dValue);
public delegate void DelegateD(string sValue);
public delegate void DelegateE(int iValue, object Object);
```

```
public class Class
{
  public class EventProperties
  {
      public Hashtable hashedEvents = new Hashtable();

      public event DelegateA EventA
      {
        get
        {
          return (DelegateA) hashedEvents["EventA"];
        }
        set
        {
          hashedEvents["EventA"] = value;
        }
      }

      public event DelegateB EventB
      {
        get
        {
          return (DelegateB) hashedEvents["EventB"];
        }
        set
        {
          hashedEvents["EventB"] = value;
        }
      }

      public event DelegateC EventC
      {
        get
        {
          return (DelegateC) hashedEvents["EventC"];
        }
        set
        {
          hashedEvents["EventC"] = value;
        }
      }

      public event DelegateD EventD
      {
        get
        {
          return (DelegateD) hashedEvents["EventD"];
```

```
        }
        set
        {
           hashedEvents["EventD"] = value;
        }
     }

     public event DelegateE EventE
     {
       get
       {
         return (DelegateE) hashedEvents["EventE"];
       }
       set
       {
         hashedEvents["EventE"] = value;
       }
     }

     public event DelegateE EventF
     {
       get
       {
         return (DelegateE) hashedEvents["EventF"];
       }
       set
       {
         hashedEvents["EventF"] = value;
       }
     }

   public static int Main(string[] args)
   {
     // hashTable.cs
     // A C# application using a Hashtable container
     // to store events.
     // Copyright (c) Chris H. Pappas and William H. Murray, 2001
     //

     EventProperties EP = new EventProperties();

     return 0;
   }
 }
}
```

All that is left is for the algorithm to generate the necessary code conditions for throwing the registered events.

The most sophisticated syntax involving events revolves around the implementation of two interfaces sharing an event by the same name; this is the event `Event` in the following program. Syntactically, this requires the use of an `explicit` event property implementation. The following algorithm, `multipleIntfEvnts.cs`, illustrates the syntax.

The program begins, in what is now standard `event/delegate` fare, with the prerequisite `delegate` reference pointer declarations.

```
using System;
public delegate void DelegateA();
public delegate int DelegateB(string s);

public class Class
{
  public interface InterfaceA
  {
    event DelegateA Event;
  }

  public interface InterfaceB
  {
    event DelegateB Event;
  }

  public class explicitEvents: InterfaceA, InterfaceB
  {
    // standard implementation
    public event DelegateA Event;
    // mem. for InterfaceB.MyEvent
    private DelegateB DelegateBEventCapture;
    // explicit implementation
    event DelegateB InterfaceB.Event
    {
      get
      {
        return DelegateBEventCapture;
      }
      set
      {
        DelegateBEventCapture = value;
      }
    }

    private void ThrowEvent()
    {
```

```
        if( Event != null )
            Event();
        if( DelegateBEventCapture != null )
            DelegateBEventCapture("DelegateB Event Processing");
    }
  }

  public static int Main(string[] args)
  {
    // multipleIntfEvnts.cs
    // A C# application demonstrating shared events
    // across multiple interfaces.
    // Copyright (c) Chris H. Pappas and William H. Murray, 2001
    //

    return 0;
  }
}
```

The method ThrowEvent() has been modified to detect the throw to respective Event() types by including the second if() statement.

readonly Keyword

The readonly keyword is a modifier that you can use on fields. When a field declaration includes a readonly modifier, assignments to the fields introduced by the declaration can only occur as part of the declaration or in a constructor in the same class.

The program readOnly.cs begins by defining one integer nonReadonly_iValue and two readonly integer data members. Notice that only the Initialized_Readonly _iValue is explicitly initialized:

```
public int nonReadonly_iValue;
// Initialize a readonly field
public readonly int Initialized_Readonly_iValue = 2;
public readonly int Constructor_Initialized_Readonly_iValue;
```

The overloaded constructor ReadOnlyClassMembers() is responsible for either assigning Constructor_Initialized_Readonly_iValue to 4, or using all three instance supplied values iValue1, iValue2, and iValue3:

```
public ReadOnlyClassMembers()
  {
    // Initialize a readonly instance field
    Constructor_Initialized_Readonly_iValue = 4;
  }
```

```
public ReadOnlyClassMembers(int iValue1, int iValue2, int iValue3)
{
  nonReadonly_iValue = iValue1;
  Initialized_Readonly_iValue = iValue2;
  Constructor_Initialized_Readonly_iValue = iValue3;
  }
}
```

Main() is responsible for instantiating two instances, ROCM1 and ROCM2, to test the overloaded constructors and demonstrate how readonly works:

```
ReadOnlyClassMembers ROCM1 = new ReadOnlyClassMembers();
ReadOnlyClassMembers ROCM2 = new ReadOnlyClassMembers(1,7,9);

ROCM1.nonReadonly_iValue = 11;
Console.WriteLine("ROCM1: nonReadonly_iValue
= {0}",
  ROCM1.nonReadonly_iValue);
Console.WriteLine("        Initialized_Readonly_iValue
= {0}",
  ROCM1.Initialized_Readonly_iValue);
Console.WriteLine("        Constructor_Initialized_Readonly_iValue
= {0}",
  ROCM1.Constructor_Initialized_Readonly_iValue);

Console.WriteLine("ROCM2: nonReadonly_iValue
= {0}",
  ROCM2.nonReadonly_iValue);
Console.WriteLine("        Initialized_Readonly_iValue
= {0}",
  ROCM2.Initialized_Readonly_iValue);
Console.WriteLine("        Constructor_Initialized_Readonly_iValue
= {0}",
  ROCM2.Constructor_Initialized_Readonly_iValue);

  ROCM1.nonReadonly_iValue = 13;
  // ROCM1.Initialized_Readonly_iValue = 13;
  // ROCM1.Constructor_Initialized_Readonly_iValue = 13;
```

Before discussing the algorithm, take a look at its output. There's an embedded key to understanding the output values—all even integer values were supplied by the instance data, and all odd values were defined by the class itself:

```
ROCM1: nonReadonly_iValue                        = 11
       Initialized_Readonly_iValue               = 2
       Constructor_Initialized_Readonly_iValue = 4
```

```
ROCM2: nonReadonly_iValue                     = 1
       Initialized_Readonly_iValue            = 7
       Constructor_Initialized_Readonly_iValue = 9
```

It is actually the final three Main() statements that demonstrate the restrictive features of readonly members. While it is legal to change ROCM1.nonReadonly_iValue to 13, the two data members marked readonly are *not* allowed to appear as legal lValues. Unlike const marked variables, which must be initialized when declared, notice that readonly data members *may* be assigned values *after* their declaration by the class' constructor. These are also the only contexts in which it is valid to pass a readonly data member as an out or ref parameter.

The complete algorithm follows:

```
using System;
public class Class1
{
  class ReadOnlyClassMembers
  {
    public int nonReadonly_iValue;
    // Initialize a readonly field
    public readonly int Initialized_Readonly_iValue = 2;
    public readonly int Constructor_Initialized_Readonly_iValue;

    public ReadOnlyClassMembers()
    {
      // Initialize a readonly field
      Constructor_Initialized_Readonly_iValue = 4;
    }

    public ReadOnlyClassMembers(int iValue1, int iValue2,
                                int iValue3)
    {
      nonReadonly_iValue = iValue1;
      Initialized_Readonly_iValue = iValue2;
      Constructor_Initialized_Readonly_iValue = iValue3;
    }
  }

  public static int Main(string[] args)
  {
    // readOnly.cs
    // A C# application demonstrating the readonly modifier.
    // All even integral values are internal
    // to the class initialization.
    // All odd values are supplied via main().
    // Copyright (c) Chris H. Pappas and William H. Murray, 2001
    //
```

```
        ReadOnlyClassMembers ROCM1 = new ReadOnlyClassMembers();
        ReadOnlyClassMembers ROCM2 = new ReadOnlyClassMembers(1,7,9);

        ROCM1.nonReadonly_iValue = 11;
        Console.WriteLine("ROCM1: nonReadonly_iValue" +
                          "                  = {0}",
                          ROCM1.nonReadonly_iValue);
        Console.WriteLine("        " +
                          "Initialized_Readonly_iValue" +
                          "              = {0}",
                          ROCM1.Initialized_Readonly_iValue);
        Console.WriteLine("        " +
                          "Constructor_Initialized_Readonly_iValue = {0}",

ROCM1.Constructor_Initialized_Readonly_iValue);

        Console.WriteLine("ROCM2: nonReadonly_iValue" +
                          "                  = {0}",
                          ROCM2.nonReadonly_iValue);
        Console.WriteLine("        " +
                          "Initialized_Readonly_iValue" +
                          "              = {0}",
                          ROCM2.Initialized_Readonly_iValue);
        Console.WriteLine("        " +
                          "Constructor_Initialized_Readonly_iValue = {0}",

ROCM2.Constructor_Initialized_Readonly_iValue);

        return 0;
    }
}
```

Summary

In this last procedure-oriented discussion of C# fundamentals, you explored those features of C# that often become pivotal underpinnings to robust C# Windows applications; those features that enable an algorithm to change, query, and decide an object's type, and those features that process events.

With Chapters 1 through 11 under your belt, with knowledge of C#'s data types, logic control statements, and unique language features, you are ready to write a C# Windows application. All of the material up to this point has given you the tools for solving a problem in the C# language. The next chapter demonstrates just how easy it is to use Visual Studio.NET to fuse that horsepower with a Windows look!

C# and Windows—Project Design Fundamentals

Microsoft's success with the Windows ME and 2000 operating systems has placed more and more demand on programmers to design applications for these graphics environments. Microsoft designed C# to make this type of Windows application development an easy process. With the latest release of Visual Studio NET, programmers can use this exciting new language to develop 32-bit object-oriented applications for both Windows ME and 2000.

Now, instead of the steep learning curve encountered by C or C++ programmers working with the Microsoft Foundation Library, C# offers the programmer a toolkit that allows quick construction of very advanced applications—something the Visual Basic programmer has had for years.

In this chapter we will first examine the evolution of the graphical design environment. Then we'll examine the elements of good C# Windows application design. You'll learn basic definitions for forms and controls and how these elements play a role in developing C# projects for Windows.

A Short While Ago (or so it seems)

Applications design has changed drastically over the last few years as a result of user demand and dramatic hardware improvements. The first challenge was to be able to run more than one program at a time. The earliest solution for running multiple programs was a new breed of software involving DOS enhancers. Products like Quarterdeck's DESQVIEW and Microsoft's first version of Windows permitted several applications to be initialized and swapped to and from disks as needed. The problems with these environments, however, were that they would frequently lock up and crash the system. This major inconvenience often led to the loss of critical data.

DOS enhancers were obviously not the answer, but it would take both a hardware and software solution to solve the problem. The solution started to evolve when Intel designed a whole new family of microprocessors designed specifically for multitasking environments (80386, 80486, and eventually the Pentium family). Now, only a software solution was needed.

Microsoft's Windows seemed to fit the solution to the software problem. The advantage of Microsoft Windows was that it presented both the user and the programmer with a common interface. The user got a graphical point-and-click environment that was the same across all applications. Programmers got a predefined set of tools, called the Microsoft Windows Software Development Kit (SDK), that enabled them to create this common look. Windows also freed the programmer from having to worry about the end-user's unique hardware configurations, including printers, scanners, video cards, zip disks, USB ports, and so on.

There was just one tiny problem—the Microsoft SDK had over 600 new functions to master along with the overlaid concept of event-driven programming. This was quite a problem for the traditional DOS command-line programmer. Not only did these programmers have to master the philosophy of event-driven programming and the 600 functions, but all this was written in C. Most programmers at this time were programming in Pascal, assembly language, or BASIC. Not only did the programmer have to master the Windows SDK, but they also had to learn the new C programming language. Something needed to be done to give the average programmer easy access to Windows.

Visual Basic was the first design language that allowed the programmer to concentrate on the programming task while designing their Windows forms from a group of predefined controls. The success of Visual Basic, coupled with the power of the C/C++ programming language, has led to the development of the C# language and programming environment for Windows.

C#, when coupled with the Visual Studio NET design tools for Windows, makes developing a graphical Windows application as easy as possible. C# and Visual Studio automatically take care of the more tedious tasks of creating an application's graphical look. The programmer is free to concentrate more on an application's features rather than how to style it for Windows. All of this is accomplished by programming in the powerful object-oriented C# language.

Some C/C++ programmers will no doubt turn their nose up at the C# language for developing Windows applications. They prefer object-oriented environments that use the Microsoft Foundation Class library (MFC). Fine! Let them write their MFC applications, because you'll be developing robust Windows applications that contain all of the features of their MFC applications in 1/20 of the time. That's a promise!

Why C# is Ideal for Windows Projects

C# will probably be the most addicting Windows application development environment you will ever use! C# coupled with the Visual Studio NET comes with a complete set of graphical tools and high-level language constructs that make it easy and quick to go from an idea to a full-fledged running application.

You will find this new environment not only easy to use, but also fun to use. You will quickly be inventing and experimenting with new project designs. And, almost as quickly as you conjure up these ideas, you can implement them. You will also find C#'s feedback and online debugging tools invaluable when developing new applications.

Each C# Windows project you design will follow three basic steps. Note that no code is written for the first two steps:

- Drag-and-Drop the objects that will make up the user interface.
- Set the properties for each object, when necessary, to change its appearance and behavior.
- Attach C# program code to each object when necessary.

C# and Windows Applications

There are really only two major prerequisites to using C#. First, you need to be comfortable in the Windows ME and 2000 environments. This means that you must be comfortable with how to use a mouse, the selection of menus and menu features, use of dialog boxes, etc. Second, you need to understand certain computer language operations, such as those discussed in the first eleven chapters of this book. For example, you should understand `for` and `while` loops and how to define constants, variables, and create classes in C#.

Events

All Windows applications (Windows ME and Windows 2000) have a common graphical user interface called the GUI. Multiple Windows applications all share the same hardware, computer, monitors, printers, etc. Because of their concurrent nature, it is no longer possible for a single program to first begin, execute, and terminate before the next application is loaded and run. Windows, therefore, requires that all applications respond to everchanging and unpredictable occurrences.

This is the world of event-driven programming. Instead of writing a program that executes from top to bottom, you design an application that responds to events. These events, such as a key press, can be generated by the user. Windows, itself, generates other events. For example, when two applications want access to one modem at the same time, Windows has to decide which one uses the modem and which one waits. When the privileged application is finished communicating, Windows tells the idle application to get started.

While the idle application is waiting for an event, it remains in the environment. The user can run other applications, perform data entry, open, close or resize windows, or customize system settings. But the idle application's code is always present and ready to be activated when the user returns to the program.

Visual Studio.NET Tools

The Visual Studio, when used with the C# language for developing Windows applications, is complete with all the design tools necessary to efficiently create, debug, and test applications that will take full advantage of Microsoft Windows' capabilities. C#, when used in this environment, includes the following features or provides support for their implementation:

- A color palette for defining the colors of the user interface, including forms and controls
- A Menu Designer for creating a hierarchical menu bar with accelerator keys, keyboard access keys, and grayed or checked menu items
- A property pane that makes it easy to edit the initial properties of each object (form or control) without writing code
- A quick double-click on any object and Visual Studio automatically adds the event handler for that item
- An entire toolbox of objects for point, click, and drag creation of user interfaces
- Access to the complete C/C++ math libraries
- A currency data type for use in financial calculations
- Online debugging and interpreting of each statement as it is being written
- Predefined command objects that allow you to create Button, CheckBox, Label, TextBox, ListBox, ComboBox, and other controls; additionally, it is easy to add horizontal and vertical scroll bars and menus
- Development of (OCX) Custom Controls
- Ability to use Common Dialog Boxes, such as Color, Font and Print

While this list is impressive to the experienced Windows programmer, it is by no means exhaustive. C# is capable of so much as you have already learned.

Standard Controls

For the purposes of C#, a standard control is a graphical object that is placed on a form. A Button or TextBox control is an example of a standard control. Every control has its own set of recognized properties and events. All C# interfaces are designed using a combination of these controls and their related events.

The following list summarizes the most frequently used controls from all of the controls that appear in the C# Visual Studio Toolbox. The Toolbox is generally found in the leftmost pane on your Visual Studio screen. If the Toolbox is not visible, use the View ➤ Toolbox menu sequence or type Ctrl+Alt+X to bring the Toolbox to the screen. Figure 12–1 shows the C# Toolbox in the Visual Studio.

You can scroll this entire Toolbox to view all of the controls. Additional information on any particular control in the Toolbox can be found by dragging the control to an open form, finding its name in the Properties pane, and using the Help facility. The Property pane is also visible in the right pane of Figure 12–1.

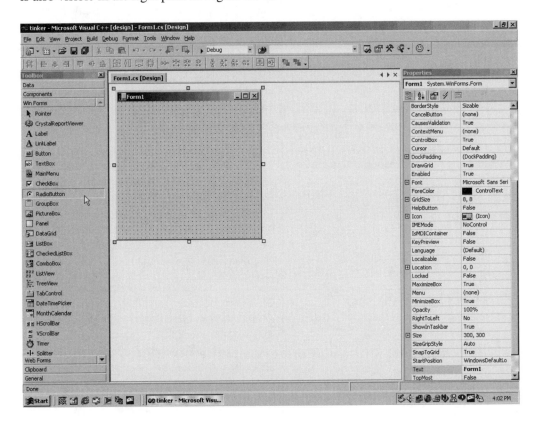

Figure 12–1   The Visual Studio's C# Toolbox.

Table 12–1 lists the most popular controls in the Toolbox along with a brief description and use.

Table 12–1   Frequently Used Controls and Descriptions

Control's Function	Control's Name	Description
button	Button	The Button control appears iconically as two letters "ab." Button controls are used to execute an instruction sequence when the user activates them. Sometimes these controls are called push buttons. Button controls graphically depress when they are selected by the user. The Button control is usually activated by its associated `command_Click ()` event. Two properties that are unique to Button controls are Default and Cancel. These are used to create the frequently seen OK and Cancel buttons that respond to the ENTER and ESC keys, respectively.
calendar	MonthCalendar	The MonthCalendar control icon is a small calendar. The MonthCalendar control initially displays a small calendar of the current month. The calendar is scrollable, forward and backward, to other months. A particular date can be selected by clicking on the date in the calendar. This data can then be retrieved by the program.
check box	CheckBox	CheckBox controls provide the user with a yes/no, include/exclude option. When the option is selected, the check box control will display a check symbol. An unselected item has a clear check box. Multiple boxes can be checked.
combo box	ComboBox	ComboBox controls combine the features of TextBox and ListBox controls. The Style property of a ComboBox control allows you to select anyone of three styles: drop-down ComboBox (Style = 0), simple - list always displayed (Style = 1), and drop-down list box (Style = 2).

Table 12–1 Frequently Used Controls and Descriptions *(Continued)*

Control's Function	Control's Name	Description
common dialog	OpenFileDialog, SaveFileDialog, FontDialog, ColorDialog, PrintDialog, PrintPreviewDialog	These common dialog controls are used to bring into a C# application a predefined dialog box. The purpose of predefining these frequently used dialog boxes is to ensure a common look, feel, and functionality across all Windows applications. Additionally, since they are predefined, a large amount of design time is saved with their use.
date/time	DateTimePicker	The DateTimePicker control icon is a small text box placed over a calendar. The DateTimePicker control is used to display the current date, or another scrollable date, and allow the user to use that date and program data.
group	GroupBox	The GroupBox icon is a small rectangular shape with two letters at the top. GroupBox controls are used to group other controls together on a form. These group controls are related in their purpose.
label	Label	The Label control uses a large looking "A" icon. Label controls are used to display text labels. Label controls frequently used for labeling other controls that do not have their own caption property. Label controls can, however, be changed by program code.
list box	ListBox	ListBox controls display a list of items from which the user can select one. A ListBox control is defined as a string array. You can access the List array using the ListIndex. The ListCount property returns the number of rows in the array. ComboBox controls and all the file-system controls use similar properties.
menu	MainMenu	The MainMenu icon is a small iconic menu with menu items. The MainMenu control adds a menu bar to the form. From this menu bar, menus and also menu items can be entered.

Table 12–1 Frequently Used Controls and Descriptions *(Continued)*

Control's Function	Control's Name	Description
picture	PictureBox	The PictureBox icon is a small picture. The PictureBox control is used for adding pictures or other bitmapped resources to a form.
pointer	Pointer	The Pointer resembles a mouse pointer and is used to select, move, or resize any control in the Toolbox.
progress	ProgressBar	The ProgressBar icon is a small rectangle with several small rectangles used to represent progress across the bar. The ProgressBar control is used to indicate progress, to the user, of time-consuming operations. These can include timer events, file up and downloads, and so on.
radio button	RadioButton	The radio button icon is a small circle enclosed ".". The radio button control is used to allow a user to make a single selection from a group of selections.
scrollbars	HScrollbar and VScrollBar	Horizontal and vertical scroll bar controls give the user a graphical means of moving through lists or selecting data ranges.
text box	TextBox Control	A TextBox control is used to display text generated by the application or to receive input from the user. TextBox controls can be made multiline capable by turning on the control's MultiLine property. When in multiline mode, TextBox controls can take advantage of automatic word wrapping. The most important property of a TextBox control is the Text property, which returns the box's contents in string form.
timer	Timer	Timer controls are used to activate a specific event at periodic intervals. Using the Interval property (specified in milliseconds), Timer controls can be used to create alarms, run procedures in the background, or coordinate other time-related events.

The controls listed in Table 12–1 are by no means the only controls used by C# for Windows; however, they are the controls used most frequently by programmers.

Control Properties

Once the form for the C# project has been designed using the various control objects, described in the previous section, you can alter their behavior and appearance. Figure 12–2 shows a Properties pane for a TextBox control. The Properties pane gives you direct access to these control enhancers.

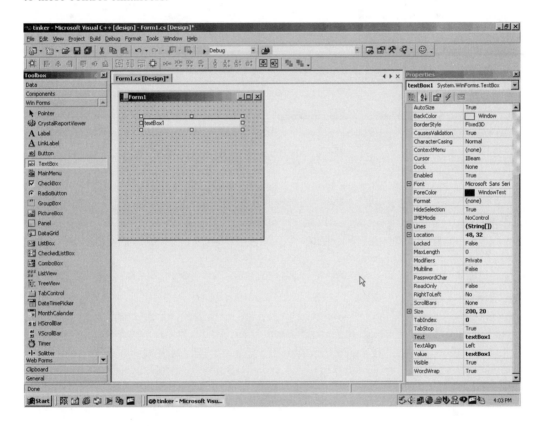

Figure 12–2   The Properties pane for a TextBox control.

Every object you place in a form has an associated set of characteristics called *properties*. The most common set of properties defines an object's size, screen location, and color. Each time you place an object on a form, the Visual Studio will assigns the appropriate properties to it and initializes them to a set of predefined values. The Properties pane contains a list of properties appropriate to the selected object and allows you to change their

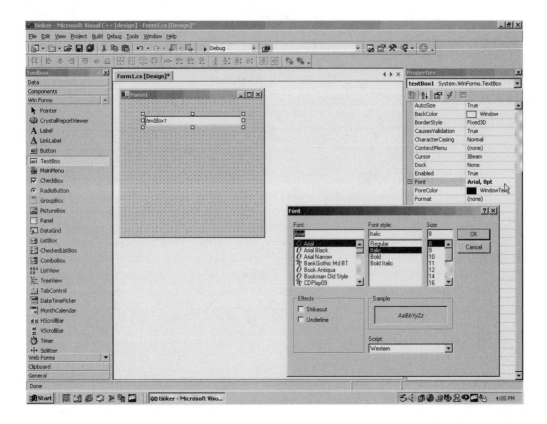

Figure 12–3   Changing the font style in the Properties pane for the TextBox control.

values. For example, Figure 12–3 shows what happens when you change the type of font, and Figure 12–4 shows what happens when you change the font size in the TextBox control.

Each time a control is added to a form, the Visual Studio will automatically name and sequentially number it. For example, if you use two Button controls, the Visual Studio will label and number them button1 and button2.

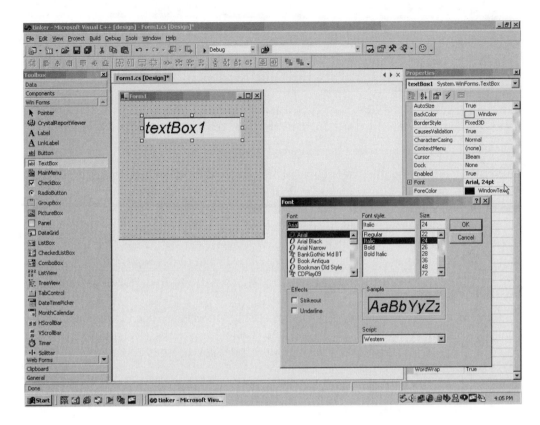

Figure 12–4   Changing the font size in the Properties pane for the TextBox control.

Changing Default Control Properties

To gain experience with control properties, open a C# project with the Visual Studio. Name this project Tinker. With Form1 in the design pane, move the mouse to the Toolbox and place the pointer over a TextBox control. The TextBox control uses the icon with a lower-case "ab" in it. Now double-click the left mouse button and a copy of the control will automatically be transferred to Form1. Make sure the Property pane is visible in the Window by using the View ➤ Properties or by pressing the F4 key.

The newly installed TextBox control can be sized by grabbing its edges with the mouse. It can also be repositioned anywhere on the form. As you size or move the TextBox control, notice that certain numbers change in the Properties box for Text1.

Now, from the Properties pane, use the mouse to select the Font property and click on it. The Properties box transfers the default font size of 8 to the edit window. Click on the edit window and you'll be able to type in a replacement font size. When you hit the return key, the control's text size changes immediately.

Did you notice any problem? Depending on the size font you chose, the control may not be wide enough to contain all the larger text. No problem. Simply click on the control and resize it! You may have asked for a 24 point font and only got an 18 point font. Windows will give you the closest size available that matches your request.

Quickly Changing Properties for Several Controls

Applications quickly become more complex with numerous controls on a form. It is possible, for example, that a form contains 20 TextBox controls. Changing the properties of each one of them could become very time-consuming and error-prone. Rather than selecting each control with the mouse then changing the property in the Properties box, simply scroll down the list of controls from within the Properties pane using the list box. The list box is at the top of the Properties pane. Once you have selected an object's property for one control, for example, the Font property, the selected property remains highlighted as you move from one control to another.

If you want all the controls on your form to have the same property, for example, the Font property, select one of the controls and the new font size. Now select the other controls in order. The selected property will be highlighted in the properties edit window for each object, waiting for you to type in the new setting.

Object Names and Labels

Each time a new control is added to a form, Visual Studio automatically labels and numbers it for you. One of the properties that you can change for any control is its name (name). The name determines how the control will be referred to throughout your application. A control's name is not the same as its label (or Text).

Click on the TextBox control you created earlier and go back to the Properties pane. Slide down the list until you see (name). Now click on it. Notice that the edit box now displays TextBox1. Change the entry by clicking on the settings box and typing the word OPEN. Notice that the control's label didn't change, that is, the text within the control, just the name of the control. To change the control's text you need to select the control, click on the Text property, and immediately type the new label. Try changing the TextBox control's text from TextBox1 to OPEN.

Event Handlers

Forms and controls not only have a predefined set of properties, but a set of events that they will respond to. Typically, these events are generated by the user, for example, a mouse click, but they can also be generated by the program or system itself. Whenever you want an object to respond to an event, put the instructions in an *event handler*. Event handlers are simply methods added to your project. Figure 12–5 shows a list of events that a RadioButton control can respond to.

The various events for a control are viewed in the Properties pane by clicking on the lightning bolt icon. This brings up the list of events for that control.

When viewing the events for the RadioButton1 control, select the DoubleClick event in the Properties pane by double-left clicking the mouse on the event name. This will add the event to the project. You can view this code by switching to the code view (press F7).

Because of this close association, event handlers (methods) are said to be attached to controls and forms.

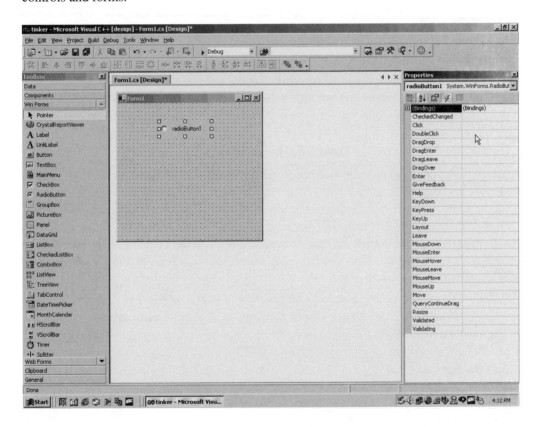

Figure 12–5   Events that a RadioButton control can respond to.

Using Code to Change Properties

You have already learned how to change a control's properties while in the design phase of the project. It is also possible to change many properties while the application is executing. For example, add a Button control to an empty form. By default, the name for this control is button1. This is also the text that will be printed as the control's default label.

Now, view the list of events for the Button control in the Properties pane. Double-left click the mouse on the Click event to add this event handler to the project's code.

Add the line of code shown next in a bold font to the event handler code.

```
protected void button1_Click(object sender, System.EventArgs e)
{
    button1.Text = "The party's over!";
}
```

The syntax for changing an object's property using code is to use the object's name, followed by a period, then the property name. On the right side of the assignment operator put a legal substitute. When you test this program and click on the button, the label will change from the default "button1" to "The party's over!"

User Interface Designs

The user interface is the most important component of any C# Windows application. To put it crudely, it is the user interface that is stuck in the user's face as they use your application. If the interface is well designed, your application will be easy, almost intuitive, to use. Design the interface poorly, and users will start looking elsewhere for an easier to use product. It doesn't matter how slick the code is under the hood, if the visual appearance and ease of use isn't there, the product will be a flop. America Online (AOL) is a success story directly related to its user interface.

In the following sections, we'll look at the forms and controls we already discussed in the previous sections, but with any eye to good layout design. We'll examine several controls and make suggestions for their placement.

Good Design

A well designed software package almost anticipates your every move. Consider Visual Studio.NET itself. Here is software designed to be used!

You have probably also used software that was advertised as easy to use, only to find it impossible to cope with. We've thrown away word processors, communications software, and video software for this very reason—we're sure you have too.

This software had one fatal flaw: its visual appearance. The product gave you no hint of what you were suppose to do next. Cryptic commands, unclear instructions, and poorly written manuals make products a nightmare to use.

There are a couple of reasons for poorly designed products:

- The simplest yet most common reason for a design failure is one that we've all experienced—the deadline. How often have you said, "I could have… if only I had more time!"

- Another reason involves the graphical interface. Once programmers leave the command-line prompt for the graphics interface, they have two programming chores: design the graphical interface and design the code to go with it. It can take the average programmer a considerable amount of time to learn a comprehensive palette of graphics subroutines. Then, the programmer must typically learn how to write the code necessary for the end-user's unique hardware configuration.

The sad truth is that good programmers can master all of this only to come up with a cluttered and confusing user interface. What happened? The average intelligent, well-trained programmer is not a commercial artist. To design good interfaces, you need to understand the elements of a good graphical design.

Using the Grid

During the design of a project's interface, the needed control objects are selected from the Toolbox and placed on a form. If you looked closely at the default forms, shown in both Chapter 1 and 2, you probably noticed a background composed of dots. These dots form a user-definable grid. By using this grid, you can visually align the controls as they are placed on the form.

By changing the Grid Width and Grid Height parameters using the GridSize property, you can vary the distance between the dots. Larger values space the dots farther apart; smaller values do just the opposite. The SnapToGrid property selects the grid's auto-alignment mode. If this parameter is true, each time a new control is placed on the form it will automatically jump to the nearest row/column marked by the grid.

Auto-alignment can be a help or a hindrance depending on the types and sizes of your controls. Whenever you want to place a control between grid marks you have two options: You can turn auto-alignment off, or change the width and height settings for the grid dots. Turning auto-alignment off leaves the grid displayed so that you can still orient yourself on the form. However, for critical applications, it's probably better to narrow the grid's dot settings so that each control lines up to the pixel.

Control Fundamentals

Start this section using a clean form in the design pane. The project name, for this example, in not significant.

Choosing A Control

Controls can be selected from the Toolbox by using a single- or double-mouse click. Here is how the *single-click* technique works:

- Place the mouse pointer over any control and click once.
- Move the mouse pointer to the form.
- The mouse pointer will change into a crosshair.
- Move the crosshair to where you want the upper-left corner of your control to begin.
- Press and hold the left mouse button.
- Drag the crosshair to the lower-right corner of where you want the control to end.
- Release the mouse button.

While the single-click technique is easy to use, you might prefer the double-click technique. When you use the double-click technique you need to know ahead of time how many and what types of controls are needed. Here is how the *double-click* technique works:

- Place the mouse pointer over the selected control and press the left button twice.
- The control will automatically appear in the center of the form.
- Repeat the first two steps as needed.
- Each time you select a new control it will automatically appear in the center of the form overlaying any previously created controls.
- Move to the center of the form after you have selected all of the controls needed.
- Starting with the form's top control, move and size the control to the desired location.
- Each control in turn will be displayed in reverse order from the way they were selected, similar to removing cards off the top of a deck.

While the double-click approach can save time by eliminating the back-and-forth movement of the mouse pointer between the Toolbox and the form, it is usually confusing to the novice user. We suggest using the single-click technique. If you are a perfectionist, beware: randomly picking this and that control without thought to order will also lead to a random initialization of controls in the project's C# code. We just thought we'd mention that fact—some programmers like to see all of the button controls in line, followed by all radio button controls and so on.

Controls: Moving and Resizing

After a control has been placed on a form it can be moved and sized by using the mouse pointer. Figure 12–6 shows a default size TextBox control that was placed on the form using the double-click technique.

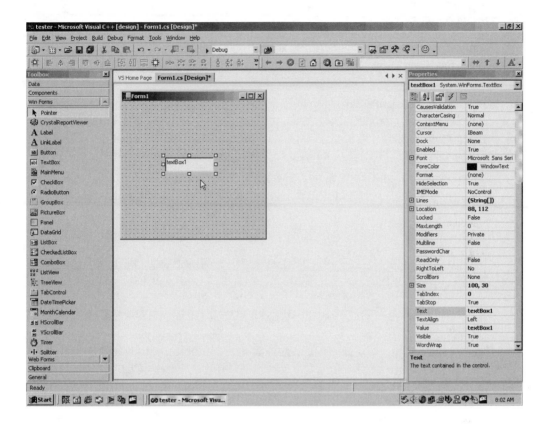

Figure 12–6   TextBox control shown in the default size.

Recall that the TextBox control is the one with the "ab" in the icon. Now, notice that the frame of the control has a dark border with eight strategically placed "handles."

The simplest action you can take with a control is to move it. By placing the mouse over the center of the control and holding down the left mouse button, you can move the control to a new location on the form.

Resizing a control is just about as easy. The handles in the center of each horizontal frame edge are used to change the height of each control. The handles in the center of each vertical frame edge are used to change a control's width. Handles on the diagonal corners are used to simultaneously change a control's height and width. At this point you should stop and practice both moving and resizing the TextBox control.

The Tiny Control

Windows almost demands that users adapt to the point-and-click graphical interface. There are a few complaints, however. These complaints are the result of a poor interface design rather than an inherent weakness in Windows.

One area that demands designer attention has to do with the ease in activating a program's control options. Complaints arise when control options are too small, too hard to hit, or congest the screen. How much fun can it be for a user to aim their rollerball mouse at a 1/4" square button labeled EXIT while holding their laptop on a commuter plane?

The good design solution is obvious! Make your controls big enough to be easily activated and place controls in an uncluttered manner on the form. No tiny controls.

Deleting a Control

If, for some reason, you decide that you do not want a particular control on a form once the control has been placed, the control can easily be deleted. There are two ways to delete a control. The first technique to delete a control involves selecting the control by clicking the mouse on it. Once the focus is on the control, press the Del key or choose the Edit ➤ Delete menu option.

The second technique is also useful for deleting multiple controls at the same time. Here, the only difference needed to delete several controls is that the Ctrl key is held down as each unwanted object is selected. To remove the group of unwanted controls, press either Del or use the Edit ➤ Delete menu sequence.

Duplicating Controls

When it is necessary to duplicate a control's design across forms or even across applications, the Visual Studio NET is designed to make this a simple process. First, the control to be duplicated is selected by left-clicking the mouse on the control in the Toolbox. Next, move the first copy of the control to the form. Now, right-click the mouse on the control and use the Copy menu item to make a copy of the control. Move the mouse cursor on the form and right-click again, but this time select the Paste menu item. A copy of the original control will be duplicated over the original control. Now just click and drag the new copy to the desired location on the form.

A Sales Tax Calculator

When constructing C# Windows applications, one of the most addicting features of the Visual Studio NET is the ease with which you can create the application's visual interface. Figure 12–7 shows a simple Sales Tax Calculator design that can be completed in less than a few minutes.

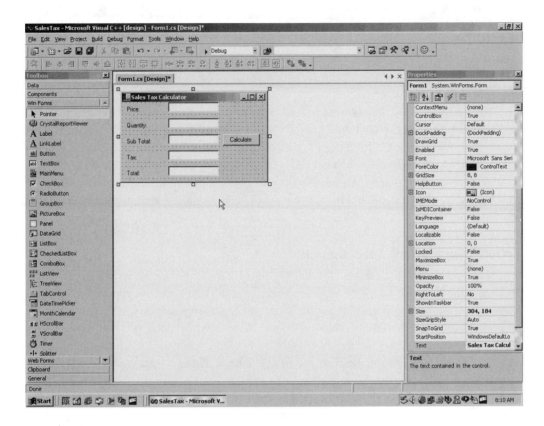

Figure 12–7   The design of a Sales Tax Calculator.

In the next sections you'll learn how to design this form step-by-step and then implement the code to make the project functional. The Sales Tax Calculator design uses only three types of controls: one Button, five Label, and five TextBox controls. The first two TextBox controls are used to input an item's price and quantity sold. The last three TextBox controls are used to display a subtotal, tax for the item(s), and a total. Each of the five Label controls is used to clearly identify what each TextBox control contains. The Button control signals the calculator to generate and display the final results. As you view Figure 12–7, notice that the size of the calculator's display has been designed to be smaller than the default form size.

Sizing a Form

To begin developing the calculator's interface, create a new C# Windows project named SalesTax. Size the default form to approximately the size shown earlier in Figure 12–7.

It seems that no matter what project you are developing, the application has a unique interface size. As an example, consider an event timer or calculator. An event timer could be used to simply flash an entire screen with the message: "Meeting on Tuesday at 1:00 PM." The Sales Tax Calculator was designed with a small window size since there were only a few controls on its form.

It is recommended that a form be sized before placing controls. This is important since the Visual Studio design pane treats a control's user-defined dimensions as an unchangeable parameter. Thus, resizing a form does not automatically adjust the form's contents. When a form is resized, the controls will have to be repositioned, manually, one at a time.

To size a form, place the mouse pointer over the appropriate form border and wait until the image changes to a bidirectional arrow. Click the mouse and pull the border to its new location.

Selecting and Placing Label Controls

The first control to be placed is a Label control. This is the control with a large "A" for an icon in the Toolbox. Click the mouse pointer over the label control icon in the Toolbox. Now, move the mouse pointer onto the form placing the crosshair where you want the upper-left corner of the label control to begin. Next, hold the mouse button down while dragging the mouse to the lower-right edge of the displayed rectangle until you have created and sized the Label control. Release the mouse button. Design your control so that your form now looks like Figure 12–8.

The next four Label controls needed by the calculator are going to be designed using the double-click method. Move the mouse pointer back to the Toolbox and double-click on the Label icon four times. Notice that each time you select the control it automatically appears labeled (Label2..Label5) in the center of the form. When you are finished, Label5 will be the form's bottom-most control. Now, simply move and size each control to the correct position, shown earlier in Figure 12–7.

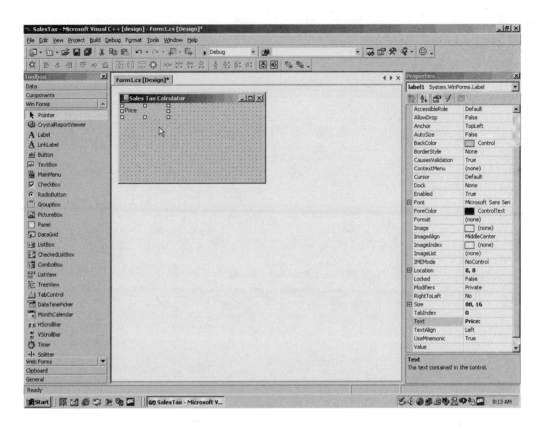

Figure 12–8   The first Label control is placed on a form.

Selecting and Placing TextBox Controls

The process for selecting a TextBox control (the control that uses the "ab" for an icon), or any other control in the Toolbox, is the same as the process used to place Label controls. Finish the Sales Tax Calculator by placing the remaining controls. Its final appearance should resemble Figure 12–7, shown earlier. You will need to add five TextBox controls and one Button control to complete the form.

Adding Code to the Sales Tax Calculator

In order to gain experience attaching code to controls, let's make another pass at the Sales Tax Calculator. The previous section left this example designed but not functional.

We'll add some default values to three of the TextBox controls so that the user will have an idea of how to enter data. To do this, modify the Text properties of the three TextBox controls to reflect the values shown in Figure 12–9.

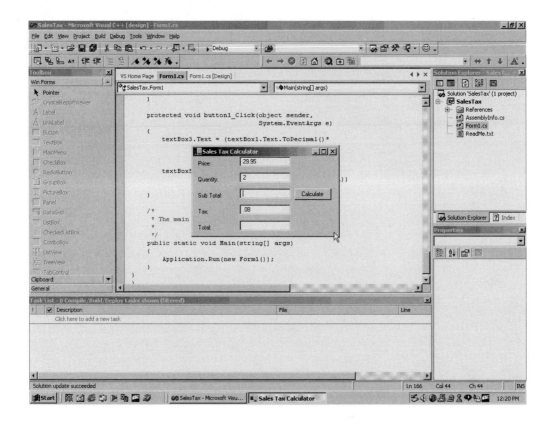

Figure 12–9   Three TextBox controls are modified to reflect initial values.

Next, add a `button_Click` event to the Button control shown on the form. To this event, add the following code:

```
private void button1_Click(object sender,
                           System.EventArgs e)
{
    textBox3.Text = (decimal.Parse(textBox1.Text) *
                     decimal.Parse(textBox2.Text)).
                     ToString();

    textBox5.Text = (decimal.Parse(label6.Text) *
                     (decimal.Parse(textBox4.Text) + 1)).
                     ToString();
}
```

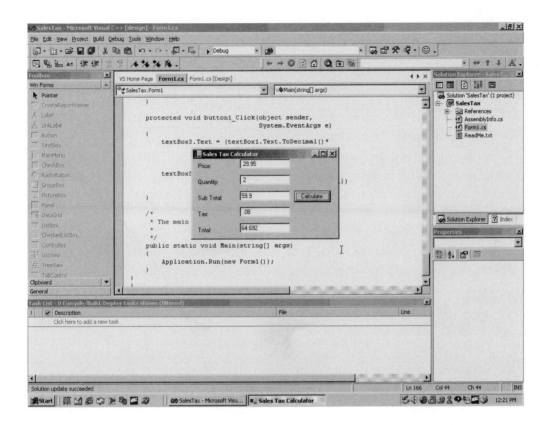

Figure 12–10   The Sales Tax Calculator calculates the tax for the default values.

The `textBox3.Text` property reflects the text that will be displayed in the Sub Total TextBox control on the form. To calculate this value, the text from the Price and Quantity TextBox controls are converted to a decimal number, multiplied together, then converted back to a string. Decimal conversions are achieved by using the `decimal.Parse()` method while conversions to a string are accomplished with the `ToString()` method.

The value displayed in the Total TextBox control is calculated in a similar manner. Figure 12–10 shows the calculated values for the default values provided.

You might want to experiment with other values as soon as you compile this project.

Selecting the Right Control for the Job

Selecting the right control for the job is always important. In the previous section, you saw a functional Sales Tax Calculator project that worked very well.

We would like to suggest that the selection of the TextBox controls for the Sub Total and Total values was an inappropriate control selection! While the TextBox controls work correctly, they are not the correct control for the intensions of this application.

TextBox controls allow user input as well as displaying output. However, in this application, user input is not allowed on the Sub Total or Total locations. Go back to the previous application and try it. You can run the application and enter all the values in these two Text-Box controls you desire, but nothing will happen!

Herein lies the problem, a user may think the application is not operating properly or could become confused at the non-working options. It would be better to replace these controls with a control that will only display results. Ah, the Label control would work just fine here. A Label control can change its Text property to reflect calculated results, but a Label control never implies input capabilities as a TextBox control does.

Figure 12–11 shows the Sales Tax Calculator modified with two Label controls replacing two TextBox controls.

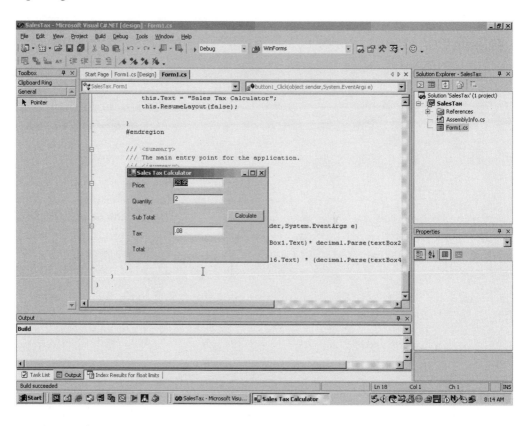

Figure 12–11   Two Label controls replace the troublesome TextBox controls.

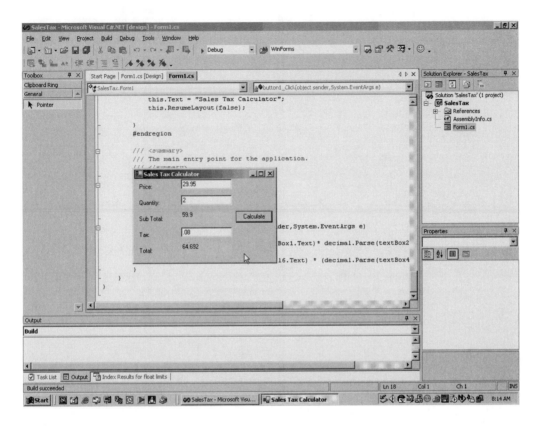

Figure 12–12   Label controls are used to present calculated results to the user.

The background color can be changed in these two Label controls to highlight their special function in reporting calculated results. Figure 12–12 shows the output from the newly modified project.

In the next section we'll take a quick look at the code used to implement this C# Windows project.

Examining the Project Code

The code for the SalesTax project is shown in the following listing. The code set in a bold font is code we added to the original form and controls.

```
using System;
using System.Drawing;
using System.Collections;
using System.ComponentModel;
using System.Windows.Forms;
```

```csharp
using System.Data;

namespace SalesTax
{
    /// <summary>
    /// Summary description for Form1.
    /// </summary>
    public class Form1 : System.Windows.Forms.Form
    {
        /// <summary>
        /// Required designer variable.
        /// </summary>
        private System.ComponentModel.Container components =
            null;
        private System.Windows.Forms.Button button1;
        private System.Windows.Forms.TextBox textBox4;
        private System.Windows.Forms.TextBox textBox2;
        private System.Windows.Forms.TextBox textBox1;
        private System.Windows.Forms.Label label7;
        private System.Windows.Forms.Label label6;
        private System.Windows.Forms.Label label5;
        private System.Windows.Forms.Label label4;
        private System.Windows.Forms.Label label3;
        private System.Windows.Forms.Label label2;
        private System.Windows.Forms.Label label1;

        public Form1()
        {
            //
            // Required for Windows Form Designer support
            //
            InitializeComponent();

            //
            // TODO: Add any constructor code after
            // InitializeComponent call
            //
        }

        /// <summary>
        /// Clean up any resources being used.
        /// </summary>
        protected override void Dispose( bool disposing )
        {
            if( disposing )
            {
                if (components != null)
```

```
        {
            components.Dispose();
        }
    }
    base.Dispose( disposing );
}

#region Windows Form Designer generated code
/// <summary>
/// Required method for Designer support - do
/// not modify the contents of this method
/// with the code editor.
/// </summary>
private void InitializeComponent()
{
    this.textBox1 = new System.Windows.Forms.TextBox();
    this.textBox2 = new System.Windows.Forms.TextBox();
    this.textBox4 = new System.Windows.Forms.TextBox();
    this.label1 = new System.Windows.Forms.Label();
    this.label2 = new System.Windows.Forms.Label();
    this.label3 = new System.Windows.Forms.Label();
    this.label4 = new System.Windows.Forms.Label();
    this.label5 = new System.Windows.Forms.Label();
    this.label6 = new System.Windows.Forms.Label();
    this.label7 = new System.Windows.Forms.Label();
    this.button1 = new System.Windows.Forms.Button();
    this.SuspendLayout();
    //
    // textBox2
    //
    this.textBox2.Location = new System.Drawing.
                                    Point(96, 32);
    this.textBox2.Name = "textBox2";
    this.textBox2.Size = new System.Drawing.
                                    Size(104, 20);
    this.textBox2.TabIndex = 6;
    this.textBox2.Text = "2";
    //
    // textBox1
    //
    this.textBox1.Location = new System.Drawing.
                                    Point(96, 0);
    this.textBox1.Name = "textBox1";
    this.textBox1.Size = new System.Drawing.
                                    Size(104, 20);
    this.textBox1.TabIndex = 5;
    this.textBox1.Text = "29.95";
```

```csharp
//
// textBox4
//
this.textBox4.Location = new System.Drawing.
                                Point(96, 96);
this.textBox4.Name = "textBox4";
this.textBox4.Size = new System.Drawing.
                                Size(104, 20);
this.textBox4.TabIndex = 8;
this.textBox4.Text = ".08";
//
// label1
//
this.label1.Location = new System.Drawing.
                                Point(8, 8);
this.label1.Name = "label1";
this.label1.Size = new System.Drawing.
                                Size(88, 16);
this.label1.TabIndex = 0;
this.label1.Text = "Price:";
//
// label2
//
this.label2.Location = new System.Drawing.
                                Point(8, 40);
this.label2.Name = "label2";
this.label2.Size = new System.Drawing.
                                Size(88, 16);
this.label2.TabIndex = 1;
this.label2.Text = "Quantity:";
//
// label3
//
this.label3.Location = new System.Drawing.
                                Point(8, 72);
this.label3.Name = "label3";
this.label3.Size = new System.Drawing.
                                Size(88, 16);
this.label3.TabIndex = 2;
this.label3.Text = "Sub Total:";
//
// label4
//
this.label4.Location = new System.Drawing.
                                Point(8, 104);
this.label4.Name = "label4";
this.label4.Size = new System.Drawing.
```

```
                              Size(88, 16);
this.label4.TabIndex = 3;
this.label4.Text = "Tax:";
//
// label5
//
this.label5.Location = new System.Drawing.
                              Point(8, 136);
this.label5.Name = "label5";
this.label5.Size = new System.Drawing.
                              Size(88, 16);
this.label5.TabIndex = 4;
this.label5.Text = "Total:";
//
// label6
//
this.label6.BackColor = System.Drawing.Color.
                              PowderBlue;
this.label6.Location = new System.Drawing.
                              Point(96, 64);
this.label6.Name = "label6";
this.label6.Size = new System.Drawing.
                              Size(104, 24);
this.label6.TabIndex = 11;
//
// label7
//
this.label7.BackColor = System.Drawing.Color.
                              PowderBlue;
this.label7.Location = new System.Drawing.
                              Point(96, 128);
this.label7.Name = "label7";
this.label7.Size = new System.Drawing.
                              Size(104, 24);
this.label7.TabIndex = 12;
//
// button1
//
this.button1.Location = new System.Drawing.
                              Point(208, 64);
this.button1.Name = "button1";
this.button1.TabIndex = 10;
this.button1.Text = "Calculate";
this.button1.Click += new System.EventHandler
                              (this.button1_Click);
//
// Form1
```

```csharp
            //
            this.AutoScaleBaseSize = new System.Drawing.
                                    Size(5, 13);
            this.ClientSize = new System.Drawing.
                                    Size(288, 165);
            this.Controls.AddRange
                (new System.Windows.Forms.
                Control[] {
                            this.button1,
                            this.textBox4,
                            this.textBox2,
                            this.textBox1,
                            this.label7,
                            this.label6,
                            this.label5,
                            this.label4,
                            this.label3,
                            this.label2,
                            this.label1});
        this.Name = "Form1";
        this.Text = "Sales Tax Calculator";
        this.ResumeLayout(false);
    }
    #endregion

    /// <summary>
    /// The main entry point for the application.
    /// </summary>
    [STAThread]
    static void Main()
    {
        Application.Run(new Form1());
    }

    private void button1_Click(object sender,
        System.EventArgs e)
    {
        label6.Text = (decimal.Parse(textBox1.Text)*
                        decimal.Parse(textBox2.Text)).
                        ToString();

        label7.Text = (decimal.Parse(label6.Text) *
                        (decimal.Parse(textBox4.Text) + 1)).
                        ToString();
    }
  }
}
```

We think you'll agree that the modifications were simple enough to make and reduce the overall potential for user error or frustration.

Additional Controls

Before you can become proficient at designing a good interface, you need to gain experience selecting, placing, and sizing other types of controls. In this section you will learn to select other popular controls, learn about any peculiarities in placing them, and uncover their purpose. Remember, while the forms and controls are complete in this section, we have not added code to make these projects functional.

GroupBox Control

GroupBox controls are used to either graphically group logically related controls or to visually subdivide a form. When related controls are to be grouped, it is important to place the GroupBox control on the form first, then overlay the GroupBox control with other selected controls. If this technique is used, every time the GroupBox control is moved, all controls associated with it will move too.

To enable this synchronous movement of a GroupBox control and its associated controls, you should use the single-click approach to place the controls within the GroupBox control. The single-click method allows you to create the control directly within the GroupBox. The double-click method will not work satisfactorily because, by default, it places the control in the center of the form, not within the Frame control!

A proper GroupBox control design will also allow you to properly copy an entire group from one form to another with predictable results. If a control was placed with the double-click method, it will be left out of any duplicated GroupBox controls. Figure 12–13 shows a GroupBox control being used to graphically group five related controls.

You will find that well designed GroupBox control groups simplify the user interface, making the application more intuitive and easier to use.

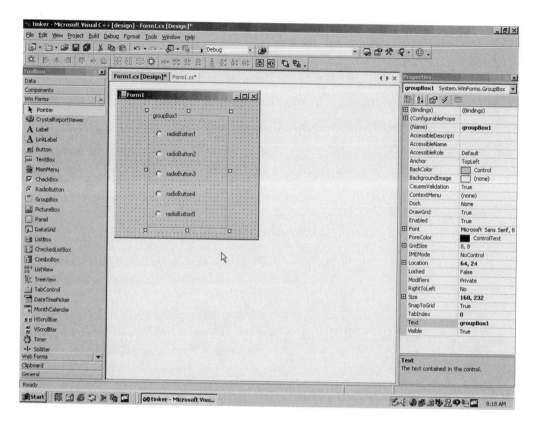

Figure 12–13   A GroupBox control is used to group five related controls on a form.

CheckBox Control

The CheckBox control (a rectangle with a check mark in it) is used to present the user with a list of items that can be individually selected. Figure 12–14 shows an example of how CheckBox controls can be used to obtain a user's boat preferences.

The important characteristic to remember about this type of control is that any, all, or none of the listed items may be selected.

The key to good design when using CheckBox controls is to keep the check options to a minimum and make sure they are logically related.

You may ask, "Why not use a GroupBox control to group those CheckBox controls?" A GroupBox control would usually be a valid choice for a form that has two or three logically related categories of this type of control. GroupBox controls used in this manner prevent conflicts between controls of unrelated CheckBox controls.

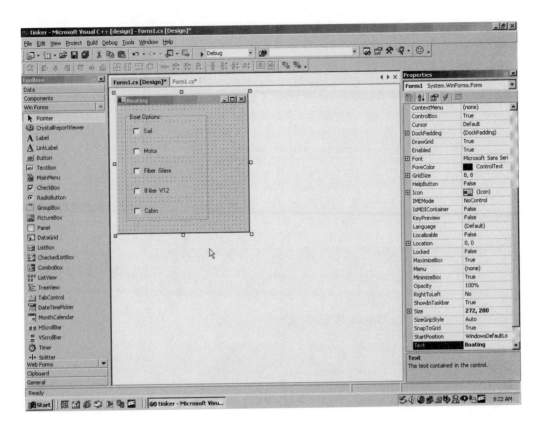

Figure 12–14   Selecting boat preferences with the use of CheckBox controls.

We recommend that anytime a form contains CheckBox controls, those controls should be placed in a GroupBox control. Does a GroupBox control used in this manner hurt the form's design? Most likely not! A well designed form is like a well documented program: there is neither too little information nor too much! Putting a GroupBox control around the CheckBox controls might have added little extra understanding to the overall interface.

RadioButton Control

The RadioButton control (a "bull's eye" icon) allows the user to make one choice in a group. This control is different from a CheckBox control because check boxes allow the user to choose as many items as desired.

A RadioButton control differs from a CheckBox control in one other area: one option must always be selected in the group. The analogy with a car's radio buttons works quite well. A radio always has one station selected and any new selection cancels the previous one. Two or more stations cannot be selected at the same time.

Rules for good design when placing RadioButton controls are the same as for placing CheckBox controls—keep the design simple and logical. Be careful not to use RadioButton controls whenever the application really needs CheckBox controls. Also, the first RadioButton control that is placed in a group will be the one the program chooses as its default (it receives the "focus"). The default can be changed, but you'll have to write a little code to do it. Figure 12–15 shows the proper use and a valid graphical layout for several RadioButton controls.

As with CheckBox controls, our recommendation is to always group related RadioButton controls within a GroupBox control. This will prevent interaction between multiple groups of RadioButton controls and also give your form a neat appearance.

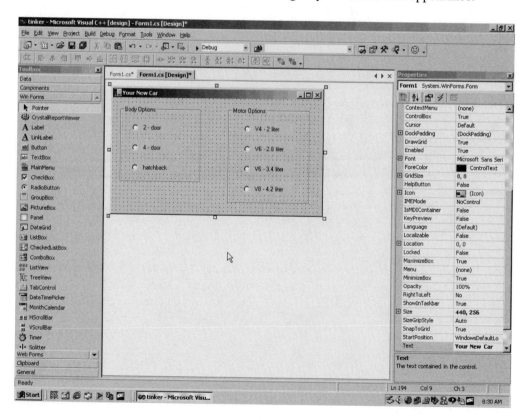

Figure 12–15   Placing RadioButton controls on a form.

ComboBox Control (3 Styles)

A ComboBox control (an icon with several small rectangular areas) combines the characteristics of a TextBox control and a ListBox control. A ComboBox control allows the user to type in a selection or go to the list and pick an item directly.

ComboBox controls have three styles that allow you to tailor the application's interface. Figure 12–16 shows the three styles in order: Simple (default), DropDown, and DropDownList.

Using the Simple style property creates a ComboBox control that has both an edit window and a drop-down list. The DropDown style property is similar to the first with the exception that it simultaneously displays the edit window and the list. The third style property, DropDownList, produces a drop-down list only and has no editing capabilities. With this last style the user must choose one of the listed options.

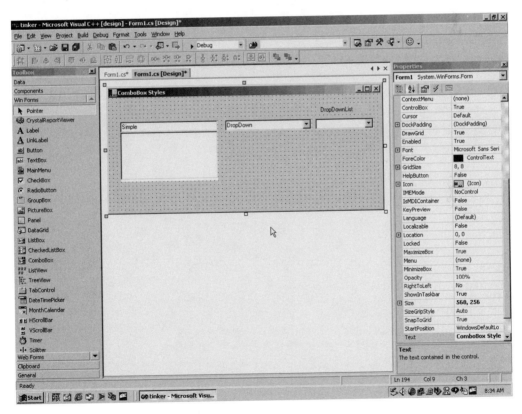

Figure 12–16   ComboBox controls come in three styles.

NOTE

ComboBox controls with a Simple style property can be resized horizontally and vertically. The other two styles will permit you to change their widths only.

There are two considerations to be made when creating a form that uses ComboBox controls. First, the appropriate style ComboBox control must be selected for the particular application. Second, there must be enough room left on the form, or later when the program is running, to display the list. Also, care should be taken when placing the last two ComboBox styles so that at runtime the displayed list will not cover critically important screen output.

ListBox Control

A ListBox control (the icon uses four small rectangles grouped together) displays a catalog of items from which only one can be selected. If the list is longer than the dimensioned ListBox, Visual Studio NET will automatically add a scroll bar. ListBox controls, unlike ComboBox controls, do not expand down the screen when active. This makes placing a ListBox control much simpler since the size you see on the design form is the size displayed at runtime. Figure 12–17 shows the use of a ListBox control.

For reasons of visual design, many developers prefer ListBox controls over ComboBox controls.

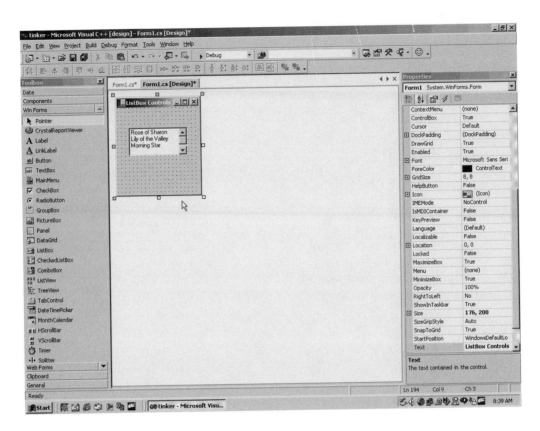

Figure 12–17   Using a ListBox control.

Scroll Bar Controls

Scroll bar controls, VScrollBar controls and HScrollBar controls (an icon with two vertical or horizontal rectangles containing arrows), allow the user to graphically move through a range of items. This range may be physical space, as in word processor pages, or values such as those used to describe colors for rendering a picture. Figure 12–18 shows several ScrollBar controls placed on a form.

Horizontal and vertical scroll bar controls are placed on a form using the same design techniques as other controls. They can be resized both in width and height. They are better substitutes for TextBox controls whenever the input values are unknown by the user. For example, changing control colors with user-defined input requires a knowledge of system color codes. However, a scroll bar allows the user to make these selections without requiring any previous knowledge of valid code settings.

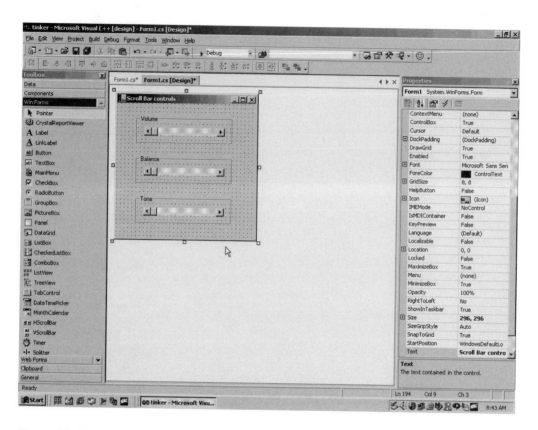

Figure 12–18   Several scroll bar controls placed on a form.

Timer Control

Figure 12–19 shows a Timer control (an icon with a clock face) that was initially placed within the form.

When applications are run, Timer controls are not visible, as are other controls. Timer controls, initially placed on a form, are moved by the Visual Studio to the design area just below the form. Timer controls are used to respond to the timer Interval property which represents the passing of time. They are used to execute code at regular time intervals. In Figure 12–19, notice that the Interval property has been changed to 1000. This value represents 1000 milliseconds, or one second of time.

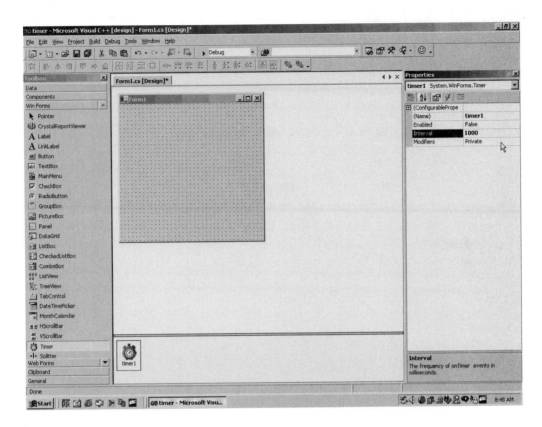

Figure 12–19   A Timer control is placed in a project.

Design Standards

Now that you are familiar with the most popular controls in the C# Toolbox you should experiment with other controls in the Toolbox. Regardless of which controls you select, good design suggests the following rules:

When laying out an application's user interface the most important rule to remember is: Keep it simple.

- Check that controls with runtime drop-down lists do not cover up critical screen output.

- Don't use cluttered forms. If necessary, break the interface down into two or more forms.

- Explain screen output by using labels, meaningful command names, and titled group boxes.

- Good form design should be similar to good subroutine design—it should neither do too much nor too little.
- Properly size and place each control—be consistent.
- Select the correct control for the task.
- Use as few controls as is absolutely necessary.

Following these simple design rules when designing projects will make them more user-friendly and less prone to errors in data entry.

More?

If designing Windows applications with C# has caught your attention, you'll want to get another book in this series, *C# for Windows*. *C# for Windows* is also written by Pappas and Murray and published by Prentice-Hall. The ISBN number is 0130932876 and was published simultaneously with the book you are now reading.

Index

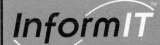

Solutions from experts you know and trust.

Articles | Free Library | eBooks | Expert Q & A | Training | Career Center | Downloads | MyInformIT

Login   Register   About InformIT

Topics

Operating Systems
Web Development
Programming
Networking
Certification
and more...

**Expert
Access**

**Free
Content**

www.informit.com

Free, in-depth articles and supplements

Master the skills you need, when you need them

Choose from industry leading books, ebooks, and training products

Get answers when you need them - from live experts or InformIT's comprehensive library

Achieve industry certification and advance your career

Visit InformIT today
and get great content
from PH
        PTR

Prentice Hall and InformIT are trademarks of Pearson plc /
Copyright © 2000 Pearson

Prentice Hall: Professional Technical Reference

Back Forward Reload Home Search Guide Images Print Security Stop

http://www.phptr.com/

PRENTICE HALL

Professional Technical Reference
Tomorrow's Solutions for Today's Professionals.

Keep Up-to-Date with
PH PTR Online!

We strive to stay on the cutting edge of what's happening in professional computer science and engineering. Here's a bit of what you'll find when you stop by **www.phptr.com**:

@ Special interest areas offering our latest books, book series, software, features of the month, related links and other useful information to help you get the job done.

Deals, deals, deals! Come to our promotions section for the latest bargains offered to you exclusively from our retailers.

$ Need to find a bookstore? Chances are, there's a bookseller near you that carries a broad selection of PTR titles. Locate a Magnet bookstore near you at www.phptr.com.

! What's new at PH PTR? We don't just publish books for the professional community, we're a part of it. Check out our convention schedule, join an author chat, get the latest reviews and press releases on topics of interest to you.

✉ Subscribe today! Join PH PTR's monthly email newsletter!

Want to be kept up-to-date on your area of interest? Choose a targeted category on our website, and we'll keep you informed of the latest PH PTR products, author events, reviews and conferences in your interest area.

Visit our mailroom to subscribe today! **http://www.phptr.com/mail_lists**

www.phptr.com